Malawi

THE BRADT TRAVEL GUIDE

THE BRADT STORY

The first Bradt travel guide was written in 1974 by George and Hilary Bradt on a river barge floating down a tributary of the Amazon. In the 1980s and 1990s the focus shifted away from hiking to broader-based guides to new destinations – usually the first to be published on those places. In the 21st century Bradt continues to publish these ground-breaking guides, along with guides to established holiday destinations, incorporating in-depth information on culture and natural history alongside the nuts and bolts of where to stay and what to see.

Bradt authors support responsible travel, with advice not only on minimum impact but also on how to give something back through local charities. Thus a true synergy is achieved between the traveller and local communities.

* * *

I visited Malawi 27 years ago, in 1976. The political scene has changed (thank goodness!) but the extraordinary natural world of lake and mountain is still the same. The hiking we enjoyed on the Mulanje Plateau rivalled the best in Africa, and the lakes provided the perfect post-hiking relaxation. We also loved the warmth and friendly self-confidence of the people. It is a pleasure to know, through the descriptions of Philip Briggs and Mike Copeland, that in this respect Malawi hasn't changed. You're in for a treat.

Happy travels

Hilary Bradt

Hilary Bradt

19 High Street, Chalfont St Peter, Bucks SL9 9QE, England
Tel: 01753 893444 Fax: 01753 892333
Email: info@bradt-travelguides.com
Web: www.bradt-travelguides.com

Malawi

THE BRADT TRAVEL GUIDE

Third Edition

Philip Briggs

updated by Mike Copeland

Bradt Travel Guides Ltd
The Globe Pequot Press Inc, USA

Third edition published 2003

First published 1996

Bradt Travel Guides Ltd,
19 High Street, Chalfont St Peter, Bucks SL9 9QE, England
www.bradt-travelguides.com
Published in the USA by The Globe Pequot Press Inc, 246 Goose Lane,
PO Box 480, Guilford, Connecticut 06475-0480

British Library Cataloguing in Publication Data
A catalogue record for this book is available from the British Library

ISBN 1 84162 067 X

Photographs
Front cover Fish eagle (Richard du Toit)
Text Ariadne Van Zandbergen

Illustrations Annabel Milne
Maps Steve Munns

Typeset from the author's disc by Wakewing
Printed and bound in Italy by Legoprint SpA, Trento

Authors

Philip Briggs is a travel writer specialising in Africa. Raised in South Africa, where he still lives, Philip first visited East Africa in 1986 and has since spent an average of six months annually exploring the highways and back roads of the continent. His first Bradt Travel Guide, to South Africa, was published in 1991, and he has subsequently written Bradt's guides to Tanzania, Uganda, Ethiopia, Malawi, Mozambique, Ghana, and East and southern Africa, and he recently co-authored the first travel guide to Rwanda. Philip has contributed sections to numerous other books about Africa, he writes a column for independent travellers for the magazine *Travel Africa*, and also contributes regular travel and wildlife features to *Travel Africa*, *Africa Geographic* and *Africa Birds & Birding*.

Mike Copeland regards himself as a traveller who writes, rather than a writer who travels, and who promotes the live-like-a-local way of experiencing other countries and cultures. Born and raised in Cape Town, he has spent his life exploring Africa and, while his knowledge of the continent fills his writings, his love for Africa fills his heart. From his home in the beautiful Cape winelands, Mike travels and writes mainly for travel magazines and this is his first foray into guidebook updating.

Contents

Introduction   XI

PART ONE   **GENERAL INFORMATION**   I
Chapter 1   **Background and History**   3
                 Facts and figures 3, History 4

Chapter 2   **The Natural World**   23
                 Geography 23, Climate 23, Vegetation 24, Conservation
                 areas 25, Wildlife 27

Chapter 3   **Planning and Preparations**   37
                 When to visit 37, Getting to Malawi 37, Red tape 46,
                 Money matters 47, What to take 49, Planning an itinerary
                 55

Chapter 4   **Travelling in Malawi**   59
                 Tourist information 59, Public holidays 59, Money 59,
                 Getting around 61, Accommodation 66, Eating and
                 drinking 67, Bargaining and overcharging 69, Hassles 70,
                 Curios 74, Media and communications 75, Electricity 76,
                 Communicating with Malawians 76

Chapter 5   **Health**   81
                 Preparations 81, Major hazards 87, Common medical
                 problems 87, Further reading 97

PART TWO   **THE GUIDE**   99
Chapter 6   **Blantyre**   101
                 Orientation 101, Climate 102, Getting there and away 102,
                 Where to stay 103, Where to eat 105, Tourist information
                 106, Things to do 109

Chapter 7   **The Shire Valley**   113
                 Climate 114, Getting around 114, Chikwawa 114,
                 Majete Wildlife Reserve 114, Lengwe National Park 115,
                 Nchalo 116, Bangula 116, Mwabvi Wildlife Reserve 117,
                 Elephant Marsh 117, Backroads north of Elephant
                 Marsh 119

Chapter 8 **Thyolo and Mulanje** 121
Climate 121, Getting around 121, Thyolo 122, Thyolo
Forest Reserve 122, Mulanje 123, Mulanje Massif 125,
Phalombe and Migowi 130

Chapter 9 **Zomba and Surrounds** 131
Climate 131, Getting around 131, Zomba 131, Zomba
Plateau 135, Lake Chilwa 139, Liwonde 141, Liwonde
National Park 143

Chapter 10 **The Lakeshore from Mangochi to Cape Maclear** 149
Climate 149, Getting around 149, Mangochi 150, From
Mangochi to Monkey Bay 152, Monkey Bay 154, Cape
Maclear 154

Chapter 11 **Dedza and Surrounds** 161
Climate 161, Getting around 161, Dedza 162, Chongoni
Forest Reserve 164, Mua-Livulezi Forest Reserve 166,
Nkhoma Mountain 167

Chapter 12 **Lilongwe** 169
Climate 170, Orientation 170, Getting there and away 170,
Getting around 171, Where to stay 171, Where to eat 174,
Tourist information 175, Things to do 179, Short trips
from Lilongwe 179

Chapter 13 **The Lakeshore around Salima** 183
Climate 183, Getting around 183, Where to stay 184,
Where to eat 186, Things to do 186

Chapter 14 **Ntchisi and Surrounds** 189
Climate 189, Getting around 189, Ntchisi Forest
Reserve 191, Ntchisi 192, Nkhotakota Wildlife Reserve 192

Chapter 15 **The M1 between Lilongwe and Mzuzu** 195
Climate 195, Getting around 195, Kasungu 195, Kasungu
National Park 196, Mzimba 198, Forestry resthouses
around Mzimba 199

Chapter 16 **The Lakeshore from Nkhotakota to Nkhata Bay** 203
Climate 203, Getting around 203, Nkhotakota 203, The
lakeshore between Nkhotakota and Chintheche 206,
Chintheche 207, Nkhata Bay 210

Chapter 17 **The Lake Ferry and the Islands** 213
The Lake ferry 213, Likoma Island 215, Chizumulu Island
219

Chapter 18 **Mzuzu, Nyika and Vwaza Marsh Wildlife Reserve** 221
Climate 221, Getting around 221, Mzuzu 223,
Rumphi 226, Nyika National Park 227, Vwaza Marsh
Wildlife Reserve 234

Chapter 19   **Livingstonia and the Northern Lakeshore**   **237**
              Climate 237, Getting around 237, Between Rumphi and
              Chitimba 237, The lakeshore around Chitimba 239,
              Livingstonia (Khondowe) 241, Chilumba 243,
              Karonga 243

Appendix 1   **Language**   **247**

Appendix 2   **Further Reading**   **250**

Index   **253**

LIST OF MAPS

Blantyre Orientation	100	Liwonde National Park	144
Blantyre	104	Mangochi	151
Chintheche	208	Mulanje	124
Dedza	163	Mulanje Massif	126
Dedza and surrounds	162	Mzimba	199
Karonga	243	Mzuzu	224
Kasungu	196	Mzuzu, Nyika and Vwaza	222
Kasungu to Mzuzu (M1)		Nkhata Bay	211
and Nkhotakota to		Nkhotakota	202
Nkhata Bay	194	Ntchisi and surrounds	190
Lake Malawi National Park	156	Nyika National Park	228
Lakeshore: Mangochi to		Rumphi	226
Cape Maclear	148	Salima Lakeshore	182
Likoma Island	216	Shire Valley: Blantyre to	
Lilongwe Old Town Centre	172	Nsanje	112
Lilongwe Orientation	168	Zomba, Chilwa, Liwonde	
Livingstonia and		and North Shire Valley	132
Northern Lakeshore	238	Zomba Plateau	136
Liwonde	142	Zomba Town	134

Acknowledgements

During the time I spent collecting update material for this third edition, I was supported by my wife Patsy, whose opinions and impressions contribute significantly to this guide.

While travelling and researching, I received assistance from a number of companies and individuals. I'd like to extend my thanks and best wishes to Chris Badger (Central African Wilderness Safaris), Jake Da Motta (Flatdogs Camp), Pim and Marga (Kiboka Camp and Safaris), Bryn Evans (Big Blue), Billy and Mark (Doogles Backpacker Lodge), Mark Sprong (Land and Lake Safaris), Chip and Dawn Cathcart Kay (Satemwa Tea Estates), the management and staff of Chinteche Inn, the management and staff of Mvuu Camp, Prof. Friedemann Shrenck and Stephanie Mueller of Karonga, Maky (Chez Maky) and John Grosart (Njobvu Safari Lodge).

Many thanks also to all the travellers who wrote with their impressions of Malawi: Tom Heffer, Gerrienne and Johan, Antonia Hamilton, Lonneke van der Kamp, Claudia Gamperle, Annalinda and Robin Robinson; and to all the Malawians and travellers who kept us company along the way, shared their experiences and impressions with us, and helped in countless small but significant ways while we were in Malawi.

Finally, my thanks to Philip Briggs and to the Bradt team for their invaluable advice and support.

KEY TO STANDARD SYMBOLS

—·—·—	International boundary		🏛	Historic building
------	District boundary		†	Church or cathedral
-----	National park boundary		🔔	Buddhist temple
✈	Airport (international)		🏠	Buddhist monastery
✈	Airport (other)		🛕	Hindu temple
✛	Airstrip		☪	Mosque
🚁	Helicopter service		⛳	Golf course
▬	Railway		🤾	Stadium
....	Footpath		▲	Summit
--⛴--	Car ferry		△	Boundary beacon
--⛴--	Passenger ferry		◉	Outpost
⛽	Petrol station or garage		⊠—⊠	Border post
🅿	Car park		(⌂)	Rock shelter
🚌	Bus station etc		🚡	Cable car, funicular
🚲	Cycle hire		=	Mountain pass
Ⓜ	Underground station		o	Waterhole
⌂	Hotel, inn etc		☼	Scenic viewpoint
⛺	Campsite		✤	Botanical site
♠	Hut		♧	Specific woodland feature
♀	Wine bar		🗼	Lighthouse
✕	Restaurant, café etc		⚊	Marsh
✉	Post office		♈	Mangrove
ℓ	Telephone		🕊	Bird nesting site
℮	Internet café		🐢	Turtle nesting site
✚	Hospital, clinic etc		～～	Coral reef
🏺	Museum		➢	Beach
🐘	Zoo		✎	Scuba diving
🄸	Tourist information		🐟	Fishing sites
$	Bank			
⚲	Statue or monument		*Other map symbols are sometimes shown in separate key boxes with individual explanations for their meanings.*	
∴	Archaeological or historic site			

Introduction

'The Land of the Lake', 'The Warm Heart of Africa', 'Africa for Beginners' ...
Malawi certainly attracts its share of snappy catch phrases, and these three sum
up much of what makes this small African country so well liked by all who
visit it.

Few countries are so dominated by a single geographical feature as the Land
of the Lake. Lake Malawi follows the dramatic contours of the Great Rift
Valley for a distance of 585km; it is up to 100km wide in parts, and it covers
more than 15% of Malawi's surface area. Enclosed by sheer mountains and
edged by seemingly endless palm-fringed sandy beaches, Lake Malawi is the
most beautiful of Africa's great lakes, and the indisputable focal point of
Malawi's tourist industry.

There is much truth in the phrase 'The Warm Heart of Africa'. Not only do
the climate and lush vegetation of the lakeshore conform effortlessly to every
stereotype image of tropical Africa, but the people of Malawi exude a warmth
and friendliness that make most visitors feel instantly at home. Malawi may
well be the most laid-back nation on earth.

And 'Africa for Beginners'? Well, certainly, Malawi would lie near the top
of any list of African countries I'd recommend to a nervous novice traveller.
Although crime *is* on the increase, Malawi remains as safe as anywhere on the
continent, and it is one of a handful of African countries where English is
widely spoken. The country's small size, relatively well-maintained roads and
unusually nippy public transport combine to spare visitors from the arduous
all-day bus trips that are part and parcel of travel elsewhere on the continent.
Malawi is remarkably compact, cheap and hassle-free – with one qualification:
the high incidence of malaria on the lakeshore.

Tourism in Malawi has developed along rather unusual lines. The country
lacks the vast game reserves of East Africa and the world-class tourist facilities
of southern Africa; as a result, it sees little in the way of fly-in tourism. Instead,
Lake Malawi has become the ultimate venue for backpackers crossing between
East and southern Africa. It also relies on being included in the itineraries of
tourists visiting neighbouring countries, and in 2002 was suffering, as
Zimbabwe's troubles kept visitors away from the region.

Within Malawi, tourist patterns are oddly schizophrenic. Travellers gather
in their hundreds at lakeshore retreats like Cape Maclear and Nkhata Bay, yet
away from the lake there are many attractive and accessible destinations which
regularly go weeks on end without seeing a non-resident visitor. There is

more to Malawi than a lake, and with the publication of this guide, I hope to draw attention to several exciting destinations which have previously been overlooked by visitors.

Malawi boasts a wealth of forest and mountain reserves, ranging from the relatively well-known Mulanje and Zomba Plateaux to the little-visited but highly accessible mountains around Dedza, Ntchisi and Mzimba. Malawi's wildlife reserves may not compare to the very best in Africa, but several – Nyika, Vwaza, Nkhotakota and Liwonde – are easy and cheap to visit, and they have an untrammelled and unpretentious appeal, which, combined with the opportunity to watch big game on foot, should make them popular fixtures on the overland travel circuit. Add to this such currently obscure gems as Lake Chilwa and the Elephant Marsh, and you realise it is one of the anomalies of African travel patterns that a country which attracts such consistently heavy traveller traffic has so much unrealised travel potential.

Perhaps the greatest of Malawi's attractions is a low-key charm that most visitors find thoroughly addictive. Many travellers fly into Africa barely aware that Malawi exists; by the time they return home, a high proportion have come to regard it as their favourite African country.

Whether you're content to relax at the lake or prefer actively to explore little-visited mountains, forests and game reserves, it is difficult to think of a more agreeable place for easy, unstructured travel than Malawi.

FEEDBACK REQUEST

Every effort has been made to ensure that the details contained within this book are as accurate and up to date as possible. Inevitably, however, things move on. Any information regarding such changes, or relating to your experiences in Malawi – good or bad – would be very gratefully received. Such feedback is priceless when compiling further editions, and in ensuring pleasant stays for future visitors.

Happy holidays!

Bradt Travel Guides Ltd, 19 High St, Chalfont St Peter, Bucks, SL9 9QE
Tel: 01753 893444; fax: 01753 892333
Email: info@bradt-travelguides.com
Web: www.bradt-travelguides.com

Part One

General Information

MALAWI AT A GLANCE

Area 118,484 km^2

Population 10,701,824 (July 2002)

Location Southern Africa, east of Zambia

Time GMT +2

International dialling code +265

Electricity AC 240V

Border countries Zambia, Tanzania, Mozambique

Flag Three equal horizontal bands of black (top), red, and green with a radiant, rising, red sun centred in the black band.

Capital Lilongwe

Other main towns Blantyre, Mzuzu, Zomba and Karonga

Climate November to April, hot and wet; May to August, moderate and dry; September to October, very hot and dry.

National parks Lake Malawi, Liwonde, Nyika, Kasungu, Lengwe

Game reserves Vwaza, Nkhotakota, Majete and Mwabvi

Currency Malawian Kwacha (MWK)

Official language English (indigenous languages important regionally)

Religion Approximately 50% Christian, 12% Islamic and the remainder a selection of other faiths and sects.

Ethnic divisions There are about ten groups. The Chewa are found in the central region, the Yaos along the lakeshore districts of the central and southern regions. Lomwes are mainly found in the Shire highlands, while the Nkhonde, Lambya, Tonga and Tumbuka are found in the northern region. The Ngoni are in the north and centre, the Sena in Chikwawa and the Nsanje in the south.

Type of government Democratic republic

Head of state Dr Bakili Muluzi (president)

Ruling party United Democratic Front (UDF)

Independence July 6 1964 (from UK)

Economy The economy is predominately agricultural. The economy depends on substantial inflows of economic assistance from the IMF, the World Bank, and individual donor nations. The performance of the tobacco sector is key to short-term growth.

Inflation 14.8%

Background and History

FACTS AND FIGURES

Location
Malawi is a landlocked country in south central Africa falling between 33° and 36° east and 9° and 18° south. It is bordered by Tanzania to the north, Zambia to the west and Mozambique to the east and south.

Size
Covering an area of only 118,484km², Malawi is one of the smallest countries in Africa, smaller even than England. It is 840km long from north to south, and nowhere more than 160km wide.

Capital
In 1975, the centrally situated city of Lilongwe replaced Zomba as the capital of Malawi. In most practical respects, the city of Blantyre is of more importance than Lilongwe, with double the population of the official capital.

Population
The population of Malawi is estimated to stand at close to 12 million people, making it one of the most densely populated countries in Africa, especially in the south. Despite this, most of the population lives in rural areas. The most populous city in Malawi is Blantyre, followed by Lilongwe, Zomba and Mzuzu.

Administrative regions
Malawi is divided into three administrative regions: Southern, Central and Northern provinces, the capitals of which are respectively Blantyre, Lilongwe and Mzuzu.

Government
Malawi is a democratic republic, with elections every five years. In 1970, Hastings Kamuzu Banda, Malawi's president since independence in 1964, amended the constitution to declare himself Life President, a position he retained until 1994. During these years Malawi was a one-party state, and the only people who were allowed to stand for election were members of Banda's Malawi Congress Party (MCP). The first truly democratic election took place in May 1994, bringing the United Democratic Front (UDF) to

power, with Dr Bakili Muluzi as president. Re-elected in 1999, President Muluzi was, at the time of researching this third edition, attempting to change Malawi's constitution to allow him to seek re-election for a third term. The MCP and AFORD, as the main opposition parties, were contesting this.

Languages

The official language of Malawi is English. The indigenous languages of Malawi all belong to the Bantu group. The most widely spoken of these, especially in the southern and central regions, and the joint official language until 1994, is Chichewa. In the north, the most widely spoken language is Chitumbuka. There are many other linguistic groups in the country, some of the more important being Yao, Ngoni and Nyanja.

Religion

Organised religion has played a major role in the history of Malawi. It's influence started with the slave-trading Yao tribe that settled in southern Malawi after being converted to Islam by Zanzibari Arabs, and picked up when the Christian Portuguese arrived on the scene in the first half of the 19th century to share in the spoils of this evil trade. The arrival of the Scottish missionary, David Livingstone, in 1859 was the catalyst that put an end to the slave trade and the string of mission stations that followed, opened up the country for trade and colonisation. The missionaries were a strict bunch and offered a high standard of education to all, a tradition which, to this day, ensures that Malawians are well-educated and well-disciplined.

The modern Malawi government allows freedom of religion and believes in co-operation between the state and religious organisations for assistance in the socio-economic upliftment of the people – the missions are still very involved in education. It is estimated that about half the country's population is Christian and 12% are Islamic; various other faiths and sects make up the remaining 38%. There is a high degree of religious tolerance between all religions, which contributes to the generally peaceful state of affairs in Malawi.

Culture

With about ten different ethnic groups in the country, Malawi has a mosaic of cultural norms and practices. Unique traditional dances and rituals as well as arts and crafts identify the groups. The Museum of Malawi recognises the importance of these traditions, and promotes appropriate activities in schools and other public places. Above all though, it is the tradition of hospitality, friendship and courtesy that permeates the entire country and warrants the claim 'Africa's Warm Heart'.

HISTORY

History has scant regard for the arbitrary political boundaries of modern Africa, and the history of Malawi in particular throws up several problems of definition. Malawi took its modern shape only in 1907, for which reason it is misleading to think of it as a discrete entity prior to the 20th century, and it's questionable whether one can write meaningfully about the history of Malawi in isolation of events that took place outside its modern boundaries.

Between 1907 and 1964, Malawi was known as Nyasaland and Lake Malawi was called Lake Nyasa (the name that is still in use today in Tanzania). In the history that follows, I have used the name Nyasaland where appropriate, but I have referred to Lake Malawi by its modern name throughout.

At different times I refer to Malawi as a part of southern Africa, East Africa and Central Africa. This is simply because Malawi doesn't fit convincingly into any of these regions. Geographically, the country follows the southern end of the East African Rift Valley, and in prehistoric and geographical terms it seems to me to be a part of East Africa. In the 19th century, northern Malawi was most often influenced by events further north, and southern Malawi by events further south. During the colonial era, the term Central Africa was generally applied to the grouping of Nyasaland and northern and southern Rhodesia (ignoring any geographical reality). In modern Malawi, you sense a society and economy that looks south to Johannesburg rather than north to Nairobi, and I would thus tend to think of Malawi as part of southern Africa.

For the sake of clarity, when I refer to East Africa I generally mean Kenya, Uganda, Tanzania, Malawi and Mozambique north of the Zambezi River; when I refer to Central Africa, I generally mean Zambia, Zimbabwe and Malawi; and when I refer to southern Africa I generally mean Malawi, Zambia, Mozambique and those countries south of the Zambezi River.

Prehistory

It is widely agreed that the entire drama of human evolution was enacted in the Rift Valley and plains of East Africa. The details of human evolution are obscured by the patchy nature of the fossil record, but the combination of DNA evidence and two recent 'missing link' discoveries (the fossils of a 4.4-million-year-old hominid in the Ethiopian Rift Valley and a 5.6-million-year-old jawbone unearthed in the Turkana Basin in northern Kenya) suggest that the ancestors of modern humans and modern chimpanzees diverged roughly five to six million years ago.

Malawi has not thrown up hominid remains of a comparable antiquity to those unearthed in Kenya, Tanzania and Ethiopia. Nevertheless, it is reasonable to assume that Malawi has supported hominid life for as long as any other part of East Africa, an assumption which is supported by the discovery near Karonga in 1993 of a 2.5-million-year-old hominid jawbone of the species *Homo rudolfensis*.

Stone age implements over one million years old have been discovered throughout East Africa, and it is highly probable that this earliest of human technologies arose in the region. For a quarter of a million years prior to around 8000BC, stone age technology was spread throughout Africa, Europe and Asia, and the design of common implements such as the stone axe was identical throughout this area. Little is known about the early stone age hunter-gatherers who occupied Central Africa, but the only known skull of this period, found at Broken Hill in Zambia, suggests they were of completely different stock from the modern peoples of the region.

The absence of written records means that the origin and classification of the modern peoples of East and southern Africa is a subject of some academic debate. Broadly speaking, it is probable that East and southern Africa have incurred two major human influxes in the last 3,000 years, on both occasions by people from West Africa.

The first of these influxes probably originated somewhere in modern-day Zaire, about 3,000 years ago. The descendants of these people, remembered locally as the Akafula or Batwa, are thought to have been similar in appearance to the pygmies of West Africa and the Khoisan of southwestern Africa. In other words, they were slightly built hunter-gatherers, much shorter in stature than the modern occupants of the region. The rock paintings which are found throughout East and southern Africa are generally credited to people whose social customs derived from this early human influx. By the time the first Europeans settled in Malawi, it is probable that the Batwa had been exterminated in Malawi, although rumours that a few still lived on the Mulanje Massif suggest that they may have survived in small numbers into the 19th century.

The second human influx started in roughly AD100, and it apparently coincided with the spread of iron age technology in the region. The earliest known iron age site in Malawi, dated to AD300, is on the South Rukuru River near Phopo Hill. There is good reason to suppose that the people who brought iron-working techniques into the region were the ancestors of the Bantu-speakers who, by AD500, probably occupied most of sub-equatorial Africa with the major exception of the arid southwest, which was still occupied by the Khoisan when the Cape was settled by Europeans in 1652.

East and Central Africa before the 19th century

It is impossible to discuss events in Malawi prior to European colonisation without first having a general grasp of the regional history.

The eastern coast of Africa has been a hub of international trade for millennia. It is not known when this trade started, but the region was certainly known to the Phoenicians at around the time of Christ. By AD1000, trade between East Africa and the Shirazi Arabs of Persia was well established; by AD1300, more than 30 Swahili city-states had been established along the coast between Mogadishu in Somalia and Sofala in Mozambique. The most important of these cities was Kilwa, which lay on a small island 2km off the shore of what is now southern Tanzania.

The cornerstone of Kilwa's medieval trading empire was gold, and the source of this gold was the powerful Shona Kingdom of Great Zimbabwe. The nature of trade between Great Zimbabwe and Kilwa is obscure, but the absence of Arabic influences on Shona architecture suggests it was the Shona who organised trade as far as the coast. Great Zimbabwe alone is evidence enough that this was a well-organised and technologically impressive society. Founded in around AD1250 and abandoned 250 years later (when its inhabitants moved into the Zambezi Valley to form the Mwene Matupa Empire), the old Shona capital near Masvingo (in modern-day Zimbabwe) remains the most compelling and impressive ruin anywhere in sub-equatorial Africa.

The amiable trading relationship between the Shona, the Swahili and the Shirazi was shattered by the arrival of the Portuguese in the early 16th century. Portugal's interest in East Africa was driven to some extent by the desire to check the spread of Islam, which had become the predominant religion on the coast. But this motive was rapidly sublimated to simple greed: Portugal wanted to control the gold trade, not only on the coast (which it did by razing Kilwa and moving the main trading centre to Sofala near the Zambezi mouth) but at the source of the Zambezi in the interior.

After the Portuguese captured Sofala in 1505, they decided to seek out the gold fields of Mwene Matupa, which they believed to be the fabled mines of King Solomon. In 1513, a Portuguese emissary called Antonio Fernandez was sent inland up the Zambezi Valley to locate the source of the gold. By 1540, Portugal had established official trading posts at Tete and Sena, the result of which was that the Zambezi Valley rapidly became a hotbed of religious tensions, with the Christian Portuguese and Islamic Swahili vying for trade with Mwene Matupa, and for converts. King Sebastian's first military incursion into the Zambezi Valley in 1569 met with dismal failure – only one-fifth of the 1,000 soldiers sent inland returned to the coast alive. A second attempt at colonisation in 1574 was only marginally more productive.

In 1596, Portugal took control of the Zambezi Valley by placing a puppet king on the Shona throne. This led to a brief flourishing of coastal trade, but also to civil war in Mwene Matupa and the eventual split of the Shona in 1665. The Portuguese were never prepared to pay fair prices to local gold traders and so production slowly dropped. Up until 1680, the Zambezi Valley produced around 16,000 ounces of gold annually. By 1800, this figure had dropped to less than 200 ounces per year. Portuguese expansion into the plateau south of the Zambezi was halted in the 1590s by the Changamire Empire, a Shona offshoot, but the Portuguese remained in control of the Zambezi Valley right up until Mozambique's independence in 1974. The net result of Portuguese interference in East Africa was the destruction of a trade network that had existed for centuries.

Coastal trade probably prompted the change in Malawi's social structures from loosely related clans to more centralised kingdoms. The process of centralisation started in the 14th century, as Malawi became an increasingly important source of ivory to coastal traders, and it gathered momentum under Portuguese influence. The most important kingdom, Maravi (from which the name Malawi derives), was formed in around 1480 and covered much of what is now southern Malawi, northern Mozambique and eastern Zambia. It was an agriculture and trade based empire, ruled by a dynastic king or Kalonga from a capital in central Malawi. The Kalonga dynasty reached its peak under Chief Masula, who ruled from about 1600 to 1650. Masula formed a strong alliance with Portugal, at one time sending 4,000 warriors to help quell a rebellion in

Mwene Matupa, and by the time of Masula's death the empire extended all the way to the coast near Mozambique Island. This vast kingdom was feared and respected by the Portuguese, but it gradually collapsed after 1650, and by 1700 it had split into several less powerful groups united under a breakaway Kalonga known as Undi. Many of Malawi's modern ethnic groups, most notably the Chewa, share a common Maravi heritage.

Centralisation was less of a feature in northern Malawi, where the Tumbuka people lived in loosely related clans, united by language and culture rather than politics. In around 1775, a group called the Balowoka established a major trading post in Tumbuka territory, but they had no imperial ambitions and were regarded by the Tumbuka as fair and honest in their dealings. The Balowoka were probably Swahili people from the Kilwa area, whose main interest was to maintain the ivory trade between northern Malawi and the coast.

Although Portugal had no sustained physical presence in what is now Malawi, a Portuguese trader called Gasper Boccaro was probably the first European to enter the country. In 1616, Boccaro marched the 1,000km stretch between Tete and Kilwa in seven weeks, a remarkable if now largely forgotten feat of exploration. Boccaro crossed the Shire River near Chiromo and he also passed close to Lake Chilwa. His journals mention 'a lake which looks like the sea, from which issues the river Nhanha, which flows into the Zambezi below Sena and there it is called the Chiry', a clear reference to Lake Malawi and the Shire River. It is uncertain whether Boccaro ever saw the lake, and, rather oddly, the Portuguese showed no apparent interest in his report, though after his journey Lake Malawi appeared on several of their maps.

The slave trade

The 19th century was a period of rapid and destructive change in Malawi, as the previous relative stability of the region was shattered by brutal incursions from all sides.

In 1824, Sultan Said of Muscat captured Mombasa and effectively ended Portugal's dominance of the East African coast north of Mozambique. By 1840, when the sultan moved his capital from Muscat to Zanzibar, coastal trade and commerce was dominated by newly arrived Omani Arabs, who established trade routes deep into the interior: most significantly from Bagamoyo to Lake Tanganyika and from Kilwa to Lake Malawi.

Slavery had always played a role in East Africa's coastal trade, both under the Shirazi-Swahili and later under the Portuguese, but prior to the 19th century it was subservient to the trade in gold and ivory. Under Omani rule, which coincided not only with the abolition of slavery in the Atlantic but also with the decline of gold output from Zimbabwe, the slave trade took on fresh and quite horrific dimensions. By 1839, over 40,000 slaves were sold annually at Zanzibar's slave market, and perhaps five times as many Africans died every year in slave raids and on the long march from the Rift Valley lakes to the coast.

Several coastal slave traders established themselves in what is now Malawi. The most important was Jumbe, who moved to Nkhotakota in around 1845, founding a dynasty which ruled over the local Tonga for three generations. Under the Jumbe dynasty, Nkhotakota became the main slave terminus out of Malawi, shipping thousands of slaves annually across the lake to Kilwa.

The Omani slavers were methodical and ruthless. Their night raids, known as *chifwamba*, were initiated by letting off a volley of gun shots around the targeted village. The slavers would then wait outside hut entrances to club or spear to death the village's men, who would rush from their huts to see what was happening. The fittest and healthiest women and children were selected as captives and tethered together using iron neck bracelets; the rest were killed on the spot. The captives would be herded to the nearest slave stockade until they numbered around 1,000, when they were shipped across the lake. After crossing Lake Malawi, the captives were forced to march for three or four months to Kilwa, generally carrying heavy loads of ivory and other goods. If any of the captives became ill or expressed tiredness along the way, they were instantly beheaded so that their neck bracelet could be reused. At Kilwa, males were castrated, because eunuchs fetched higher prices. Eventually, the captives would be shipped to Zanzibar in conditions so crowded and dirty that a cargo of 300 people might be reduced to fewer than 20 on arrival.

The devastation that was caused to East African societies by the Omani slave trade cannot be underestimated. For Malawi, it was exacerbated by the arrival of the Yao, an itinerant group who originally came from the Ruvumu River Valley east of the lake. In the 1840s, the Yao were converted to Islam by Zanzibari Arabs, who also gave them weapons and agreed to buy any slaves they could capture. From 1850 onwards, many Yao settled in southern Malawi operating as a kind of fifth column, repaying the hospitality shown to them by the local Maganja and Chewa by capturing and killing them in their hundreds, and in a manner only slightly less ruthless than that of their mentors. The Yao also sold their captives to the Portuguese, whose trade in slaves grew greatly after about 1850.

The *mfecane*

Nineteenth-century Malawi was further rocked by the aftermath of events in what is now the Zululand region of the KwaZulu-Natal province of South Africa. Prior to the turn of the 19th century, Zululand was populated by around 20 small, decentralised Nguni-speaking clans. Between 1800 and 1830, the nature of this society was transformed by the cataclysmic series of events which became known as the *mfecane* – 'The Crushing'. The roots of the *mfecane* remain a subject of debate, but modern theorists believe they had more to do with the influence of the Portuguese slave and gold trade in what is now Mozambique than with the more distant European settlement in the Cape. For whatever reason, there is no doubt that the first few years of the 19th century saw Nguni society become highly militarised, the result of which was the formation of three centralised kingdoms: Ngwane, Mdwandwe and Mthethwe.

In 1816, the Mthethwe Kingdom fell under the rule of Shaka, a member of the previously insignificant Zulu clan. Shaka revolutionised Nguni warfare by replacing the traditional throwing spear with a shorter stabbing spear, and instructing his troops to surround their foes in a U-formation and stab them to death. The result was an extended massacre which reverberated across the country and depopulated vast tracts of the southern African interior. As many as two million people died in the *mfecane*, and those who were not killed by Shaka's marauding army either joined its ranks or fled, taking with them the Zulu's frenzied militarism and deadly tactics.

In 1818, the Mdwandwe Kingdom collapsed beneath Shaka's military onslaught. Under the leadership of Zwangendaba, a Jere chief, various Mdwandwe clans fled north into Mozambique, where they attacked and co-opted the local Tonga people to form a mighty migrating army known as the Jere-Ngoni. Northwards they marched, into the Zambezi Valley, where they ran riot over the Portuguese settlements at Tete and Sena, and destroyed the powerful Changamire Empire. The Ngoni raided every village they passed through, killing everybody but young men (who were drafted into their army) and women of marriageable age. Their methods of killing were without mercy: men were bludgeoned to death and unwanted women had their breasts lopped off and were left to die of blood loss.

The Jere-Ngoni crossed the Zambezi in November 1825, settling for many years in the area west of Lake Malawi, where they terrorised the Tumbuka of the highlands and the Tonga of the lakeshore. This period is still remembered by the people of northern Malawi as 'The Time of Killing'. In 1845, Zwangendaba died on the southern tip of Lake Tanganyika. After his death, the Ngoni split into several factions, two of which returned to what is now Malawi. The most significant of these, the Mombera-Ngoni, subjugated the Tumbuka, Tonga and Nkonde people of northern Malawi, killing their chiefs and massacring huge numbers of people at the first sign of rebellion.

Livingstone and the Zambezi Expedition

By the middle of the 19th century, the combined efforts of the Ngoni, the Yao, and the Omani and Portuguese slave traders had turned Malawi into something of a bloodbath. And so it might have remained but for the arrival in 1859 of David Livingstone, a Scottish missionary who, perhaps more than any one man until Banda, was to shape the future course of events in Malawi.

David Livingstone was born at Blantyre, Scotland in 1813. He trained as a medical doctor at Glasgow University and then as a missionary at the London Missionary School. In 1840, he joined Robert Moffat's mission station at Kuruman in South Africa, where he married Moffat's daughter Mary. While at Kuruman, Livingstone came to perceive his role in Africa as something grander than merely making a few more converts: his ambition was to open up the African interior so that other missionaries might follow in his wake.

Between 1853 and 1856, Livingstone became the first European to cross Africa from west to east, starting at Luanda in Angola and then following the course of the Zambezi to its mouth in Mozambique. Livingstone was a first-hand witness to the suffering caused by the brutal slave trade; he became convinced that the only way to curb slavery was to open Africa to Christianity, colonisation and commerce. Livingstone's faith in the so-called 'three Cs' was not untypical of Victorian attitudes to Africa, but, more unusually, Livingstone was fuelled neither by greed nor by arrogance, but by plain altruism.

In 1858, Livingstone convinced the British government to finance an expedition to search for a navigable river highway upon which European influences might be brought to the African interior. Livingstone's firm belief that the Zambezi would prove to be this highway was crushed by the end of 1858, when the Kebrabasa Rapids west of Tete proved to be impassable by steamer.

In 1859, Livingstone turned his attention to the Shire, a tributary of the Zambezi and, though he did not know it at the time, the sole outlet from Lake Malawi. Livingstone's steamer made several trips up the river, but his projected highway to the interior was again blocked, this time by the Kapichira Rapids. Nevertheless, Livingstone, together with his companion John Kirk, explored much of southern Malawi on foot in 1859, including mounts Mulanje and Zomba, as well as Lake Chilwa and the southern part of Lake Malawi.

In 1861, Livingstone was sent a new boat by the British government. It arrived at the Mozambican coast carrying a party of clergymen, who had been sent by the Universities' Mission to Central Africa (UMCA) at Livingstone's request to establish the first mission in Central Africa. Livingstone deposited the party, led by Bishop Mackenzie, at Mogomero near Chiradzulu Mountain (between the modern towns of Blantyre and Zomba).

On September 2 1861, Livingstone sailed up Lake Malawi in a local boat, a trip that John Kirk was to describe as 'the hardest, most trying and most disagreeable of all our journeys'. Livingstone stopped at Jumbe's slaving emporium at Nkhotakota, which he called 'an abode of bloodshed and lawlessness'. Further north, the lakeshore was 'strewed with human skeletons and putrid bodies', victims of the marauding Ngoni. By the time he reached Nkhata Bay, the depressed and exhausted doctor feared for his life, and he decided to turn back south, thus underestimating the length of the lake by 100km.

From here on, the Zambezi Expedition went from disaster to disaster. Disease claimed the lives of several of the Mogomero missionaries, including Bishop Mackenzie himself in late 1861, and the UMCA eventually withdrew the mission to Zanzibar. Days after Bishop Mackenzie's death, Mary Livingstone, who had only shortly before joined her husband in Central Africa, died of malaria. In 1863, the last time Livingstone sailed up the Shire, the river was described by a member of the expedition as 'literally a river of death'. The boat's paddles had to be cleared of bloated corpses every morning. Livingstone realised that in attempting to open the Shire to the three Cs, he had unwittingly opened the way for Portuguese slave raids. The British government withdrew their support for the expedition in 1864, and Livingstone returned to Britain.

Livingstone is now best remembered as the recipient of Henry Stanley's immortal greeting, 'Doctor Livingstone I presume', and as one of the many explorers of his era obsessed with the search for the source of the Nile. Neither memory does him justice: Livingstone had been exploring Africa for more than two decades before he turned his thoughts to the Nile (on his last African trip between 1867 and 1874), and the posthumous reward for his earlier efforts was indeed the abolition of slavery through the influence of the three Cs. Somewhat ironically, it was only after Livingstone's death near Lake Bangweula in 1874 and his emotional funeral at Westminster Abbey that Britain finally made serious efforts to end the slave trade around Lake Malawi.

Christianity, commerce and colonialism

Livingstone's Zambezi Expedition was, on the face of it, an unmitigated disaster. In time, however, it was to prove the catalyst that put an end to the slave trade. Livingstone's published descriptions of the atrocities he had witnessed in Malawi heightened public awareness in Britain. In the year that Livingstone died, John Kirk, a leading member of the Zambezi Expedition, persuaded the Sultan of Zanzibar to close Zanzibar's slave market.

The UMCA returned to Malawi in 1875, establishing a chain of missions, the most important of which was on Likoma Island. In 1874, the Free Church of Scotland established the Livingstonia Mission at Cape Maclear under the leadership of Dr Robert Laws, but due to the high incidence of malaria at Cape Maclear, the mission moved to Bandawe in 1881, where Dr Laws made the significant breakthrough of persuading the Ngoni to cease their endless harassment of the more peaceable Tonga. The Livingstonia Mission moved to its current position on the Rift Valley Escarpment above the lake in 1894. The other important mission established in 1875 was the Blantyre Mission in the Shire Highlands, eventually to become the site of Malawi's largest city.

As a rule, the arrival of missionaries in Africa was at best a mixed blessing. Many were unbelievably arrogant in their handling of Africans. Often they collaborated with would-be colonisers against the interests of their purported congregation, and the use of violence to create converts was commonplace. The Scottish Missions in Malawi were a happy exception. Inspired by Livingstone's humanitarian values and his respectful attitude towards Africans, they made great efforts to end local wars and to curb slavery, often risking their lives in the process.

The Scottish missionaries offered education to thousands of Africans. Malawi's Northern Province had at one time the highest educational standards anywhere in Central Africa, and Likoma Island boasted the only 100% literacy rate on the continent. The missionaries introduced new crops and farming methods as well as passing on practical skills such as carpentry and tailoring. Reverend Scott, who ran the Blantyre Mission for 30 years from 1881, said that 'Africa for the Africans has been our policy from the first'. And it is true that many of the graduates of the mission schools at Blantyre and Livingstonia played a significant role in the eventual rise of Malawian nationalism, as well as in the struggles for equality in Zambia, Zimbabwe and South Africa. Banda himself once referred to Livingstonia as the 'seed-bed' of his Malawi Congress Party.

Livingstone's prediction that legitimate trade might slow the slave trade encouraged two Scottish brothers, John and Frederick Muir, to form the African Lakes Company (ALC) in 1878. The ALC not only provided an important source of materials for the missions, but it rapidly became a major trading force on Lake Malawi and the Shire River, and was to prove instrumental in controlling and eventually killing Mlozi, the sultan of a vast slaving empire around Karonga.

The so-called 'Scramble for Africa' (1885–95) was precipitated by Germany's unexpected claim to a vast portion of East Africa, firstly Tanganyika (what is now mainland Tanzania) and then parts of Malawi, Uganda, Kenya and Zanzibar. In 1890, Germany relinquished all its claims (except for Tanganyika) in exchange for Heligoland, a tiny but strategic North Sea island. In 1891, the vast British territory north of the Zambezi and south of Tanganyika was given the rather unwieldy name of the British Central African Protectorate, and Harry Johnston was appointed as its first commissioner.

Johnston's overriding concern was to stamp out the slave trade, which, despite its abolition on Zanzibar, was still operating between Lake Malawi and Kilwa. In 1891, Fort Johnston was built near the village of the dominant Yao slave trader, Mpondo. Mpondo's village was destroyed and 270 slaves were released from imprisonment. The Yao slave traders hit back several times, but Johnston was eventually able to stop their shipments across the lake. The south of Malawi was finally freed of slave raids when the last two Yao traders were defeated in 1895, and Fort Lister was built near Mulanje to block the last usable route to the coast. In northern Malawi, Johnston persuaded Jumbe, the overlord of Nkhotakota, to give up the slave trade in exchange for British protection. His attempts at negotiating with Mlozi, the self-styled Sultan of Nkondeland (near Karonga), were less successful. After several battles, Mlozi was captured by Johnston in 1895 and sentenced to death.

Twenty-one years after his death, Livingstone was proved to have been correct – Christianity, commerce and colonialism had ended the slave trade. They had also brought inter-tribal peace to Malawi, as the Yao and Ngoni abandoned their spears for the education offered by the Scottish Missions. Colonialism in Malawi was eventually to take on the more nefarious character it did elsewhere in Africa, though never perhaps to the same degree. Again, the paternalistic Scottish missionaries must take much credit for this: in the words of one of the most fondly remembered missionaries, William Johnson, they 'did not come here necessarily to subjugate [but] to protect and instruct'. Ultimately, it is difficult to argue with the assertion that British intervention was the best thing that happened to Malawi in the troubled 19th century.

Nyasaland

In 1907, the British Central African Protectorate was divided into two separate territories: Northern Rhodesia (now Zambia) and Nyasaland (the colonial name for Malawi). Throughout the colonial era, there were strong ties between Nyasaland, Northern Rhodesia and Southern Rhodesia (now Zimbabwe), culminating in the federation of the three colonies in 1953.

Nyasaland was the least developed of the three colonies, due to the absence of any significant mineral deposits and also because the region was so densely populated that large-scale cash-crop farming was not a realistic option. A coffee boom at the turn of the 20th century turned out to be short lived when production fell by 95% between 1900 and 1915. Tea was the only settler-dominated agricultural product that really took off, but its production was restricted to the hills around Thyolo and Mulanje.

Together with this lack of development went a low level of alien settlement. By 1953, the settler population, comprised mainly of European administrators and Indian traders, numbered little more than 10,000. The indigenous population, on the other hand, had by this time grown to 2.5 million, creating a population density six times greater than that of Southern Rhodesia, and ten times greater than that of Northern Rhodesia.

The lack of development had its good and bad sides. At no point in the colonial era was more than 15% of the land under colonial or settler ownership, in large part due to the unusually scrupulous attitude of early governors such as Johnston and his successor Sharpe in ratifying settlers' claims to having 'bought' land from local chiefs. By 1953, a series of government actions had guaranteed that 90% of the land was for the communal use of Africans, while the remaining 10% was protected in forest reserves or occupied by cities or settler farms. This meant that, unlike many other British colonies where the majority of good land was used by settlers to produce cash crops, Africans in Nyasaland were in theory free to continue their traditional subsistence lifestyle.

The obstacle that prevented theory from becoming actuality was the system of taxation introduced by the colonial administration. This was called a poll tax: something of a misnomer as there was no related poll. It was not good enough for the people of Nyasaland merely to subsist; they were forced by the colonial administration to pay for the privilege. A small number of local farmers got around the need to earn money by growing cash crops such as tobacco and cotton. Far more Africans entered into the migrant labour system: they were in effect forced to leave their homes and to work for puny wages and in miserable conditions in the copper mines of Northern Rhodesia and at the gold and coal reefs of South Africa and Southern Rhodesia. In the 1930s, it was estimated that 20% of the men of Nyasaland spent a part of any given year working outside of the country. Villages were thus robbed of their most able workers for months at a stretch, while traditional family structures collapsed under the stress of long periods of separation. Worse still, in 1938 it was estimated that 5% of the men of Nyasaland had been lost permanently to migrant labour – either victims of the filthy living conditions on the mines, or seduced by the big cities.

Ethiopianism and the rise of nationalism
Protest against colonial rule surfaced in Nyasaland even before World War I, in large part due to the influence of Scottish missionaries, notably Dr Robert Laws, who presided over the Livingstonia Mission for half a century, and the Rev Joseph Booth, a noted denomination hopper whose outspoken pro-African politics forced him to leave Nyasaland in 1902.

The early protests in Malawi were strongly linked to the Ethiopianist churches which emerged in America and South Africa in the wake of Ethiopia's victory over Italy at Adwa in 1896 (the victory which resulted in Ethiopia remaining independent for all but five years of the colonial era). Ethiopianist churches attempted to reconcile Christianity with traditional African customs and beliefs, producing a distinctly African brand of religion with a strongly Baptist flavour. By taking a pro-African stance at a time when few people of African descent had political power, Ethiopianism was an inherently political movement, and it became strongly aligned with the 'Africa for the Africans' philosophy of the Jamaican visionary Marcus Garvey.

The first indigenous Nyasa to challenge colonial rule was Edward Kamwama, a product of Laws' Mission School in Bandawe. Kamwama worked in the gold fields of South Africa for several years, where he met the Rev Booth, who introduced him to the Ethiopianist Watch Tower Church. Kamwama returned to his home in Bandawe in 1908, and formed his own Watch Tower Church, organising the first public protests to forced taxation. He was driven into exile by the colonial administration, but the Watch Tower Church grew all the same. Growing out of this movement, and with the encouragement of Dr Laws, the first of a number of Native Associations was formed in 1912. In alliance with so-called 'Tribal Councils', the Native Associations made repeated demands to government to improve educational levels and end taxation.

The first martyr to the cause of liberation was the Rev John Chilembwe, yet another product of the mission schools. Chilembwe was born near Chiradzulu in 1871 and worked as a kitchen boy for the Rev Booth for several years. He was baptised by Booth in 1893 and then travelled with him in the USA, where he too was influenced by Ethiopianism. On his return to Chiradzulu in 1900, Chilembwe bought a farm close to the original site of the Mogomero Mission, where he founded the Provident Industry Mission (PIM). By 1912, over 800 converts lived in the mission grounds.

Adjoining the PIM, the Bruce Estate was owned by a stepson of David Livingstone and managed by another member of the clan, William Livingstone. Chilembwe came into frequent conflict with the adjoining estate over Livingstone's bullying of his labourers and his dismissive attitude to Africans. Chilembwe's full indignation at European racism was invoked when many African soldiers died in the battle between Britain and Germany at Karonga. In his final correspondence, which appeared in *The Nyasaland Times*, Chilembwe asserted that 'In times of peace, everything for the European only … but in times of war, it is found we are needed to share hardships and shed blood in equality.'

On January 23 1915, three armed columns marched out of the PIM, two to different points on the Bruce Estate, where they were ordered to kill all the European men they found, and the third to Blantyre, in order to raid the arsenal. The raid on the Bruce Estate was succesful enough: William Livingstone and two other European men were killed, and all the women and children were captured alive. The raid on Blantyre failed, and colonial troops descended on the

PIM. After a manhunt that lasted several days, Chilembwe was shot dead near Mulanje, and many of his supporters were jailed or executed. The PIM, along with several other Ethiopian churches, was revived at the end of World War I, but the ensuing decades saw little in the way of organised protest.

After the end of World War II, protests against colonialism in Nyasaland and elsewhere in Africa became more militant. Thousands upon thousands of African conscripts had been shipped around the world to fight for the freedom of their colonisers; those who returned found their own liberty as restricted as ever. The first major uprising against colonialism took place in February 1948 in the Gold Coast, when a group of returned war veterans started a riot in Accra. As a result, Britain granted the Gold Coast self-government in 1953 and full independence in 1957, when the country was renamed Ghana.

Kwame Nkrumah, Ghana's first president, declared the moment of independence to be 'the turning point on the continent' and indeed it was. In 1957, Ghana joined Ethiopia and Liberia as one of only three African countries with black rule. A decade later, this picture had been reversed. By 1968, only three of Africa's 50 countries (those colonised by Portugal) remained European dependencies, and three others (South Africa, South West Africa, and UDI Rhodesia) remained under white rule.

Hastings Kamuzu Banda

During the heady years from 1953 to 1957, the Ashanti town of Kumasi in the Gold Coast housed the practice of the Nyasa-born Dr Hastings K Banda. In the year that the Gold Coast became Ghana, Banda returned to the land of his birth after more than 40 years abroad; despite being only a year shy of his 60th birthday, he was destined to dominate every aspect of his homeland's politics for nearly four decades.

Hastings Kamuzu Banda was born at Chiwenga near Kasungu. The most likely year of his birth was 1898, a mere three years after the Chewa chief of Kasungu signed a treaty of protectorateship with Britain. Banda was educated in the mission schools; by 1914 he had passed his Standard Three examinations. In 1915, after being accused of cheating in an examination, Banda decided to leave Nyasaland. He walked 800km via Mozambique to Southern Rhodesia, where he worked for a year as a sweeper in a hospital at Hartley. He then obtained a contract to work at a colliery in Natal, the only way he could legally gain entrance to South Africa, but after three months he deserted his job to live in Johannesburg.

It was in Johannesburg that Banda first took an interest in politics. Like many educated Africans of his era, he fell under the influence of the Ethiopianists, joining the AME Church in Johannesburg in 1922. In 1925, the AME sent Banda to the US to receive further education. For three years he studied at the AME's Wilberforce Institute in Ohio. From 1928 to 1929 he studied at the University of Indiana, then in 1930 he moved to the University of Chicago, where he obtained a Bachelor of Philosophy degree. Finally, in 1932, Banda fulfilled his dream by enrolling at the Mihary Medical College in Nashville, Tennessee, where he was awarded his Doctorate of Medicine in 1937.

Banda's dream was to return to Nyasaland to serve his compatriots as a doctor; in 1938 he moved to Edinburgh where he studied for a licence to practise medicine in the British Empire. But when, in 1941, he tried to find medical work in Nyasaland, his applications were repeatedly snubbed. The nurses at Livingstonia refused to serve under a black doctor, while the colonial administration in Zomba, after much deliberation, would offer him work only if he agreed not to attempt to seek social contact with white doctors. Banda declined the offer and instead set up in private practice in Liverpool.

In 1945, Banda moved his practice to London. The benevolence of spirit that was noted by his patients in London also stretched back to his homeland. He made generous donations to the Nyasaland African Congress (NAC), and he financed the education of 40 Africans over a period of seven years. His Harlesden home became a meeting ground for African nationalist leaders based in London; regular visitors included Kwame Nkrumah and Jomo Kenyatta, the future leaders of independent Ghana and Kenya respectively. It seems likely that Banda would have stayed in London indefinitely had it not been for the humiliation of being named as the co-respondent in a divorce suit filed by Major French against his wife Margaret. In August 1953, the respected Dr Banda of Harlesden closed his practice, packed his bags, and, at the urging of Nkrumah, the newly installed prime minister of the Gold Coast, Banda and Mrs French moved to Kumasi.

The federation saga

The idea of federating Nyasaland with Northern and Southern Rhodesia surfaced as early as the 1890s and it was raised several times before World War II without ever coming to anything. After the war, however, the white settlers of Southern Rhodesia made a more concerted appeal for federation, knowing that it would give them practical sovereignty over the other two colonies in the face of growing African nationalism. The Africans of Nyasaland and Northern Rhodesia were opposed to federation for precisely the same reason that the white settlers favoured it. As Banda pointed out, under a colonial government 'the relationship between [Africans] and the authorities [was] one of ward and warden', but under a government provided by Southern Rhodesia it would become 'one of slaves and masters'.

The issue of federation became the focal point of protest in Nyasaland. The Nyasaland African Congress (NAC), formed in 1943, became the most vocal opponent of Rhodesian rule, and in alliance with Banda in London it entered into negotiation with Britain and Southern Rhodesia to prevent federation. Yet, despite the clear opposition of the African people of Nyasaland and Northern Rhodesia, Britain agreed to federation in 1953 (ironically, the same year in which the Gold Coast was granted self-government), thereby placing the future of Nyasaland under the overtly racist and, to all intents and purposes, self-governing settlers of Southern Rhodesia. Banda described this enshrinement of white dominance in Central Africa as a 'cold, calculated, callous and cynical betrayal' and he vowed not to return to Nyasaland until the federation was dissolved.

In August and September of 1953, a series of spontaneous protests against federation took place in Nyasaland, starting in Thyolo and spreading to Chiradzulu, Mulanje and Nkhata Bay. Eleven Africans were killed in these protests and a further 72 were injured. The relatively conservative NAC leadership responded to the protests with some ambiguity, and as a result the organisation fell increasingly under the influence of a group of radical young leaders, the most prominent of whom were Henry Chipembere and the Chisiza brothers, Dunduzu and Yatutu. In 1957, Chipembere asked Dr Banda to return to Nyasaland. After some vacillation, Banda agreed.

Chipembere and his cohorts built Banda up as a messianic symbol of resistance. However, they saw him not as the potential leader of an independent Nyasaland, but as the figurehead through which their more radical views could dominate NAC policy. Banda had rather different ideas. On his return to Nyasaland in 1958, he took over the NAC presidency and urged its 60,000 members to non-violent protest. The first official riot took place in Zomba on January 20 1959, when 400 people spontaneously rushed the police station after an NAC rally. They were fired on with tear gas and forced to disperse, but the incident marked the start of a spate of riots during which 48 Africans were killed in police fire. The most serious of these incidents took place at Nkhata Bay, where 20 rioters were killed by police reservists.

On March 3 1959, a State of Emergency was declared, and the NAC was banned. Banda and over a thousand of his most prominent supporters were arrested. Immediately the NAC was banned, one of its more prominent members, Orton Chirwa, founded the Malawi Congress Party (MCP). Banda became MCP president on his release from jail in April 1960. By releasing Banda, Britain had signalled recognition of the need for change. At the Lancaster House conference of August 1960, Britain disregarded the protests of the Southern Rhodesians and allowed Nyasaland greater autonomy within the federation. And significantly, the colonial administration awarded a selective vote to Africans, so that in the election of August 1961 the MCP won 94% of the national vote and all but six of the 28 seats in parliament.

In January 1962, Banda became Minister of Natural Resources and Local Government in a government headed by the colonial governor, Glyn Jones. In November 1962, at the Marlborough House talks in London, Britain agreed to a two-phase plan for self-government in Nyasaland, and on December 19 the House of Commons announced that Nyasaland could withdraw from the federation. On February 1 1963, Banda was sworn in as the Prime Minister of Nyasaland; on the final day of the same year, the federation was formally dissolved, and on July 6 1964, Nyasaland was granted full independence and renamed Malawi.

Malawi under Banda

Even before independence, Banda had demonstrated to his cabinet a reluctance to accept constructive criticism and other people's ideas. His autocratic tendencies were emphasised when, at the Organisation of African Unity (OAU) summit in Cairo exactly three weeks after independence, he announced that Malawi had 'one party, one leader, one government and no nonsense about it'. It was this sort of statement, as well as a sudden reversal on foreign policy (in 1960, Banda had issued a joint statement with the future president of Tanzania, Julius Nyerere, to the effect that both countries would boycott white-ruled African states, but after independence he showed an unexpected enthusiasm to strike a trade deal with Portuguese Mozambique) that prompted the fateful 'Cabinet Crisis' little more than a month after independence.

On August 16 1964, following Banda's return from the OAU conference, a group of cabinet members, led by Orton Chirwa, confronted Banda regarding his inflexible leadership and foreign policy. Banda offered to resign, but the cabinet asked him to continue as president on the condition that he would consider their grievances. Instead, Banda dismissed Chirwa and two other ministers from his cabinet. Three other ministers resigned in protest, including Henry Chipembere and the surviving Chisiza brother (in 1961, Dunduzu Chisiza, widely regarded as the most intellectually capable and far-sighted politician of his generation, had become the first of many Malawian politicians to die in a suspicious car 'accident'). The highly talented independence cabinet was overnight transformed into a bunch of yes-men.

Banda faced two more challenges to his rule. In February 1965, Henry Chipembere led a rebellion which was foiled by the army at Liwonde. Chipembere escaped to America, but many of his supporters were killed. In 1967, Yatutu Chisiza, another of the Cabinet Crisis discards, led several supporters into Malawi from a base in Tanzania. Chisiza was killed by soldiers. Remnants of Chipembere's rebels used guerrilla tactics to destabilize Banda's government for several years, but by the end of 1970 they had all been rounded up. After the Chipembere Rebellion, Banda formally declared Malawi to be a one-party state, and on July 6 1971, he made himself Life President.

It is often said that Banda was a benign dictator. True enough, he was not in the murderous class of somebody like Amin; nevertheless, he was entirely ruthless in his quest to obtain and maintain absolute power. It is estimated conservatively that 250,000 Malawians were detained without trial during his rule. Prisoners were underfed and in many cases brutally tortured. Banda's perceived political opponents, if they were not killed by the security police in jail, were victims of suspicious car accidents, or else – as Banda was proud of boasting – became 'meat for crocodiles' in the Shire River. Several exiled Malawians died in explosive blasts strikingly reminiscent of those used by the South African security police.

To say that Banda was intolerant of criticism is an understatement. Critics were jailed, and not just political critics: it was, for instance, a detainable offence to discuss the president's age or his past relationships and medical activities. Gossip was not tolerated regarding his relationship with the MCP's 'Official Hostess', Cecelia Tamanda Kadzamira, who became Banda's mistress in 1958. Other illegal subjects included family planning (Malawi's population tripled under Banda) and, naturally enough, politics of any variety. Jehovah's Witnesses were persecuted (20,000 fled the country and many who remained or returned were detained or tortured to death) and Muslims were only barely tolerated, probably because they were so numerically strong in areas like Mangochi that even Banda wasn't prepared to stoop to the required scale of genocide.

Censorship was rife under Banda. Thousands of films, books and periodicals were banned, often for absurd reasons. Banda's whimsical dictates even covered personal dress – from 1968 to 1993, Malawian women were banned from wearing mini-skirts or trousers. Perhaps no other episode illustrates the absurd vanity, megalomania and paranoia of Banda as his banning of an innocuous Simon & Garfunkel song: its release coincided with a rocky patch in Banda's love life and the lyrics ('Cecilia, you're breaking my heart …') were more than he could bear.

That Banda was perceived as benign is partly because so little information about Malawi reached the outside world. Most of all, though, it is because it was in Western interests to support the status quo in Malawi. In a climate of socialist-inspired African nationalism, Banda was an arch-conservative, openly Anglophilic, and cynical enough to deal openly with the South African government throughout the apartheid era. Banda was acceptable simply because he was co-operative. As recently as 1989, Margaret Thatcher and the Pope both visited Malawi, praising Banda's achievements and uttering not one public word of criticism of what had become the longest-lived dictatorship of its sort in Africa.

What did Banda achieve during his rule? Peace and stability, for one – though it can be argued that his ruthless dictatorship allowed for little else, and that Malawians are not a people given to civil disorder. Economic growth, for another – but again, Malawi was so underdeveloped at the time of independence that the growth rate he achieved (around 5% per annum on average) might easily have occurred under a genuinely benign leadership. Banda built Malawi its new and more centrally positioned capital at Lilongwe – a capital city funded almost entirely by the South African government. He improved the infrastructure and in particular the road system immeasurably – using Western aid given in exchange for his pro-Western policies. In short, Banda achieved little that might not have been achieved by a more consensual government. And, in 1993, Malawi remained as it had been at the time of independence: one of Africa's poorest countries.

Banda did much to stir latent ethnic conflict in Malawi. His dream was to restore the ideal of the Maravi Empire, to which end he dressed his speeches in traditional Chewa symbolism and made Chichewa the official language, despite the fact that less than 30% of Malawians spoke it as their mother tongue. At the same time, he used the Messianic build-up to his return to Malawi and the authority which Africans traditionally invest in a man of his age to create a powerful personality cult. He carried with him at all times a fly-whisk, the traditional symbol of the *sangoma* (witchdoctor). On his return to Malawi, he insisted on using a name which he had reduced to a middle initial in Britain and Ghana – Hastings K Banda became Kamuzu (meaning 'the little root', roots being the primary source of traditional Malawian medicines). By using this traditional symbolism, and by emphasising his background as a Western doctor, Banda set himself up, especially in the eyes of village elders, as the new Kalonga of a revived Maravi Empire. Banda was a dictator; he was no fool.

The road to democracy

In the last decade or so of his rule, Banda's was increasingly a puppet presidency, largely due to his advanced years (Banda turned 80 in 1978 and he was 95 when he finally relinquished power). From the mid-1980s onwards, Malawi was to all intents and purposes ruled by Banda's shadowy official hostess and her much-reviled uncle, John Tembo.

John Tembo was born in Dedza in 1932. He went to university in Lesotho and worked as a schoolmaster before he was appointed to Banda's cabinet as finance secretary in 1963, an appointment which was unpopular with other cabinet members for its strong air of nepotism. In the early years, Tembo played a sycophantic role in parliament, using his position primarily to acquire a personal fortune (by 1990, he was a director of a major firm in practically every business sector that dealt with government, including Malawi's main bank). Tembo came to be seen as Banda's natural successor, and in January 1992 he finally became, in name, the Minister of State in the Office of the President. In effect, John Tembo was appointed the executive president of Malawi.

One of the reasons why Malawians tolerated Banda for so long was that, for all his failings, he commanded respect, particularly from the rural population. Another was that nobody could have predicted how long he would live: there was always hope that his replacement would have more democratic inclinations. Tembo neither commanded respect (he was widely seen as the mastermind behind Banda's greatest excesses) nor, at 60, was he particularly old, and his appointment in 1992 made it clear that he was Banda's chosen successor.

Even without Tembo, it is probable that Banda's days as Life President of Malawi were numbered. The end of the Cold War meant that supporting the West was no longer enough to ensure Banda a good international press and generous aid packages. In 1989, the British prime minister praised Banda for his 'wise leadership'; two years later, Britain made the belated and hypocritical gesture of withdrawing all non-humanitarian aid to Malawi in protest at Banda's abuse of human rights. The neighbourhood, too, was changing. By the end of 1992, Kenya and Zambia had held their first multi-party elections, Tanzania and Uganda were talking about them, South West Africa had become independent Namibia, and in South Africa the previously unthinkable was fast becoming an eventuality. Banda had become a man out of time.

But despite the change in the external climate, Tembo's appointment was probably the main impetus behind the Catholic bishops' galvanising *Lenten Letter*, which documented in graphic detail the failings and abuses of power of the Banda administration. The *Lenten Letter* was read aloud on March 3 1992 and then faxed to the BBC. Banda's response to the letter was to place the bishops under house arrest. But for once the world was watching. Banda was condemned by governments and church bodies world-wide, and within

Malawi, for the first time since independence, there was a climate of open dissent. May 1992 saw Malawi gripped by strikes and protests, culminating in the Lilongwe Riot of May 7 in which 40 people were shot dead by police. In October 1992, Orton Chirwa, the founder of the MCP and a leading member of the short-lived independence cabinet, died in suspicious circumstances in the Zomba Prison where he had been detained since 1981.

Banda's growing unpopularity left him little option but to announce a referendum on the question of a multi-party election. The referendum took place in March 1993, and it drew an overwhelming majority of votes in favour of change, a popular pro-referendum slogan being 'Votey smarty, votey multi-party'. Two new parties of note emerged: AFORD and the UDF, the latter led by Bakili Muluzi, a Muslim businessman who had once briefly served in Banda's cabinet before resigning.

Polling took place on March 17 1994. The election was declared substantially free and fair, which in the strict sense it probably was, though the final results were a reflection less of policies and popularity than of regional and ethnic differences. The MCP won by a landslide in the central region, AFORD achieved a similar result in the northern region, and the UDF won overwhelmingly in the south. The southern region being the most populous part of Malawi, the overall election was won by the UDF. Bakili Muluzi was made the second president of Malawi.

The general election of 1999 was again won by the UDF and Dr Muluzi was installed for a second presidential term. Although Muluzi has proved to be a democratic ruler, he and his party were attempting in 2002 to alter the constitution to allow him a third term as president, a move that was causing controversy and dissent. Freedom of speech is a reality, as is a free press, and many Malawians are openly critical of Muluzi's leadership, something that would never have been allowed under Banda.

Perhaps the greatest crisis facing Malawi is poverty. As in many African countries, democracy comes hand-in-hand with economic liberalisation, and the artificially high exchange rates of the 1980s have collapsed, causing prices to rocket while incomes stay the same. In Malawi, the devaluation against the US dollar was to the order of 100% in the 18 months following the 1994 elections, a further 70% between 1995 and 1998 and a massive 200% to 2002. Crime, too, has increased dramatically in the last few years, and allegations of government corruption are rife. Many of the Malawians we spoke to query the benefits of democracy, and we noted a widespread nostalgia for the relative prosperity and social stability of the Banda era.

Banda himself died of natural causes in 1997, aged somewhere between 97 and 101, depending on which of the several possible dates given for his birth you believe. In 1995, the former Life President was tried for the alleged murder of three cabinet ministers and an MP who died in a 'car accident' near Mwanza in 1983. Both he and his co-defendants, John Tembo and Mama Cecelia, were acquitted on all charges. This alone says much about the new Malawi: a legal trial was a privilege given to few opponents in the despotic days of Banda and Tembo.

The Natural World

GEOGRAPHY

The Malawian landscape is dominated by the Great Rift Valley, which runs through the eastern side of Africa from the Red Sea in the north to the Zambezi Valley in the south. The Malawian sector of the Rift Valley is dominated by Lake Malawi, which, at 585km long and up to 100km wide, is the third largest lake in Africa and the eleventh largest in the world. The only outlet from Lake Malawi is the Shire River, which flows out of the southern tip of the lake near Mangochi and then follows the course of the Rift Valley southwards, descending to an altitude of 38m above sea level near Nsanje, before it crosses into Mozambique where it drains into southern Africa's largest river, the Zambezi.

In addition to Lake Malawi, there are three other sizeable lakes in Malawi. Lake Malombe lies in the Rift Valley south of Mangochi along the Shire River, and it can thus be seen as part of the Lake Malawi system. Lakes Chilwa and Chiuta are shallow bodies of water east of the Rift Valley near the border with Mozambique. Altogether, some 20% of Malawi's surface area is covered by water.

The Rift Valley Escarpment rises sharply to the west of the lake, in some areas reaching altitudes of above 1,500m (about 1km higher than the lake shore). The highest and most extensive mountain range in northern Malawi is Nyika, protected in the national park of the same name, followed by the Viphya Plateau around Mzimba. Southern Malawi is also rather mountainous. Mulanje and Zomba are the most important mountains in the south, but there are also several smaller peaks in the Dedza and Thyolo areas. The highest peak in central Africa, Sapitwa (3,002m), is part of the Mulanje Massif in southeastern Malawi.

CLIMATE

Malawi's climate is typical of tropical Africa. Days are hot and humid, particularly at altitudes of below 1,000m, while night-time temperatures are generally quite moderate. Within Malawi, temperature variations are influenced greatly by altitude. The hottest parts of the country are Lake Malawi and the Shire Valley, which lie below 500m. Highland regions such as Mulanje, Zomba, Nyika, Dedza and Viphya are more temperate, and they can be very chilly at night.

There are three seasons in Malawi. The months between November and April are hot and wet, the months between May and August are moderate and dry, while the months of September and October are very hot and dry. Despite the large amounts of surface water in Malawi, much of the country is prone to drought; the absence of any irrigation schemes means that local famines are a serious threat in years of low rainfall.

VEGETATION

The dominant vegetation type in Malawi is *brachystegia* woodland (also known as miombo woodland), which naturally covers around 70% of the country's surface area, though it has been degraded in many areas. Brachystegia woodland is found at altitudes up to 1,500m in areas with an average annual rainfall of over 1,000mm. In areas of higher rainfall, such as the Viphya Mountains, the *brachystegia* woodland often has a closed canopy and consists of tall trees, while in areas with a rainfall between 1,000mm and 1,300mm, trees are more stunted and the canopy is open.

Brachystegia woodland is, as the name suggests, dominated by trees of the *brachystegia* family. These trees are highly resistant to fire and, although they are technically deciduous, they only lose their leaves briefly in September and October. Several other woodland types (again named after the most common type of tree) occur in Malawi, mostly at altitudes below 500m. Mopane woodland is dominant in the Liwonde area, while *terminalia* woodland is common in the area east of Zomba and west of Lake Chilwa. The mixed woodland of the Shire Valley and Lilongwe area holds trees of the *brachystegia*, *acacia*, *combretum* and *bauhinia* families.

The unmistakable baobab tree (*Adansonia digitalia*) is a characteristic feature of low-lying parts of Malawi, particularly the Lake Malawi shore and the Shire Valley. The unusual, bulbous shape of the baobab tree makes it one of the most photogenic features of the African landscape, and it has given rise to the belief in many parts of Africa that the tree was planted upside down by God. It is thought that some baobab trees grow to be over 3,000 years old. The spongy wood of the baobab (it is related to the balsa tree) is rich in calcium, making it an important food source for elephants in times of drought.

Palm trees are characteristic of low-lying and well-watered parts of Malawi, and together with the baobabs they give places like Liwonde National Park and the Elephant Marsh much of their character. Four types of palm occur naturally in Malawi. The borassus palm (*Borassus aethiopum*) is a tall tree growing up to 20m in height, and is characterised by a distinctive swelling halfway up its stem, and by fan-shaped leaves. It is common along rivers in northern Malawi, such as in Vwaza Marsh Wildlife Reserve, and on the southern lakeshore around Salima and Monkey Bay.

The doum palm (*Hyphaene benguallensis*) grows to a similar height as the borassus, but it has a thinner stem without a swelling, and more frond-like leaves. Doum palms are common on the Lake Malawi shore and in the Shire Valley, particularly in Liwonde National Park and around the Elephant Marsh.

The much smaller wild date palm (*Phoenix relinata*) occurs along rivers, where it may take one of two forms: that of a dense bush, or of a tree hanging over the water. The wild date palm can be recognised by its feathery fronds. It is common along the Shire River (you'll see plenty in Liwonde National Park) and in highland areas such as Thyolo, Viphya and Nyika.

The raffia palm is noted for its large leaves: at up to 18m in length, they are the largest found on any plant in the world. The raffia may have a stem of up to 10m in height, or its leaves may grow straight out of the ground in a cluster. Raffia palms are generally found along streams to an altitude of 1,500m; they are common in the Shire Highlands and in Nkhotakota Wildlife Reserve.

Evergreen forests, though they have been reduced to covering a mere 1% of the country's surface area through deforestation, provide Malawi's most biologically diverse habitat in terms of plants, birds and insects. Evergreen forest is distinguished from woodland by having a high interlocking canopy and by being composed mostly of non-deciduous trees. What evergreen forest still occurs in Malawi is confined to remnant pockets in montane areas. Among the more accessible areas of evergreen forest are those on Ntchisi, Mulanje, Viphya, Nyika, Dedza and Zomba mountains.

Semi-evergreen forest covers around 2% of Malawi's surface area. The canopy of this forest is generally formed by *Brachystegia spiciformis* trees, underneath which lies a dense undergrowth of herbs and shrubs. Forest of this type is found on the slopes of Mulanje and Zomba mountains, as well as in the Thyolo and Nkhata Bay areas. It is also common along some rivers.

The most common type of forest in Malawi is probably exotic plantation forest, comprised mainly of pine and eucalyptus trees. Though such plantations play an important role in preventing the further loss of indigenous forest, they have little aesthetic appeal and generally hold few birds and mammals. Many plantations are interspersed with areas of indigenous riverine forest and fringing scrub, which can be very rewarding for seeing animals.

Montane grassland and moorland covers about 5% of Malawi's surface area. It is the predominant vegetation type on the plateaux of Nyika, Mulanje and Viphya mountains. These plateaux support a mixture of grasses, heathers and heaths, and are particularly rich in wild flowers, especially after the rains.

A notable feature of Malawi's flora is the high number of orchid species. Around 280 terrestrial and 120 epiphytic orchid species have been recorded in Malawi, with the greatest variety to be found in Nyika National Park and on Mulanje and Zomba mountains. The best time for seeing orchids in bloom is between November and March, though exact flowering times vary from year to year and area to area, depending on local rainfall.

CONSERVATION AREAS
National parks and wildlife reserves
Malawi has five national parks and four wildlife reserves, all of which fall under the jurisdiction of the Department of National Parks and Wildlife (PO Box 30131, Lilongwe; tel: 01 753232; fax: 01 754427; email: tourism@malawi.net).

The largest and most northerly of these reserves is **Nyika National Park**, which protects the vast Nyika Plateau and its northern slopes. Nyika is primarily a scenic reserve, but it does offer some good game viewing, with the advantage that it can be explored on foot or horseback. Access to the reserve is a problem for those without private transport.

Vwaza Marsh Wildlife Reserve lies a short way south of Nyika. Access to the tented camp at Lake Kazuni couldn't be simpler, and there is excellent game viewing from the camp. All in all, an independent traveller's dream come true.

Kasungu National Park lies along the Zambian border between Nyika and Lilongwe. It is the largest 'bush' reserve in the country, and supports the widest selection of large mammals, but game viewing is highly seasonal. The lodge at Lifupa has accommodation for all tastes and budgets, which combined with ease of access makes it a good target for independent travellers on a budget.

Nkhotakota Wildlife Reserve, near the town of the same name, is the oldest reserve in Malawi. A wide variety of game species are present, but few animals are seen due to the rough terrain and the limited road network. Chipata Camp is now closed following a bad fire, and the only feasible access is via Bua River Camp, off the Nkhotakota–Nkhata Bay road at Mphonde.

Lake Malawi National Park protects the Cape Maclear area on the southern lakeshore. Though a few game species are present, the park is mostly of interest for its marine and birdlife. Lake Malawi National Park is highly accessible to independent travellers.

Liwonde National Park, which lies along the Shire River south of Liwonde, is richly atmospheric and well stocked with animals. Hippo and elephant in particular are abundant, there is a chance of seeing lions and leopards, and the birds are simply fantastic. In the centre of the park, Mvuu Camp offers bush luxury at reasonable rates, and it also allows camping at a price most budget travellers will be able to afford. Access is by boat from Liwonde town along the Shire River – a quite wonderful trip. In the south of the park, Chinguni Hills offers affordable accommodation, more suited to the younger traveller or backpacker. Unless you're seriously short of cash, this park is unmissable.

Majete Wildlife Reserve has been severely poached; there are now reported to be few animals left. There is only one short road into the reserve.

Lengwe National Park lies in the Shire Valley south of Blantyre. Game viewing here is good, despite a limited variety of large mammal species. Access is a problem without private transport. Once there, however, there's affordable accommodation and you'll probably have the place to yourself.

Mwabvi Wildlife Reserve lies in the far south of the country. It is rarely visited by tourists and the rough terrain makes wildlife viewing difficult, but the wilderness atmosphere makes up for that. There is a small, basic camp. Access is a problem without private transport.

Other conservation areas

The Department of Forestry (PO Box 30048, Lilongwe; tel: 01 771000) plays a valiant conservation role by preserving many of Malawi's evergreen and semi-evergreen forests in protected forest reserves. Entrance to these forest reserves is free and there are no restrictions on walking within them. In addition, some of the reserves have inexpensive accommodation in the form of Forestry resthouses, most of which also allow camping in their grounds.

Animals which are characteristic of Malawi's forest reserves include leopard, bushbuck, red, blue and grey duikers, klipspringer, bushpig, samango and vervet monkeys, baboon, and a variety of secretive nocturnal small predators. The forests are also notable for insects (most visibly butterflies), and are of special interest to birdwatchers.

Except for Zomba and Mulanje, Malawi's forest reserves have in the past received little attention from tourists. This is a shame, as several other forest reserves (most notably Viphya, Ntchisi, Dzalanyama, Chongoni, Dedza, Mua-Livulezi, Chiradzulu, Michuru and Thyolo) are in varying degrees accessible to independent travellers, and either have accommodation or else are close enough to a town to visit as a day trip.

Other parts of Malawi which are of interest for their wildlife include Lilongwe Nature Sanctuary and the Elephant Marsh.

WILDLIFE

Malawi boasts as wide a variety of large mammals as most African countries, and all the so-called 'big five' – buffalo, elephant, lion, leopard, rhinoceros – are present in the country. However, human population pressures mean that most big wildlife species are now restricted to reserves, none of which is really large enough to compare to the best in other African countries. That said, some parts of Malawi offer excellent game viewing, and it will be of particular interest to independent travellers that reserves such as Liwonde, Vwaza Marsh, Nyika and Nkhotakota are among the most easily and cheaply visited on the continent.

Large mammals

Several useful field guides to African mammals are available for the purpose of identification. What most such guides lack is detailed distribution details for individual countries, so the following notes should be seen as a Malawi-specific supplement to a regional or continental field guide.

Predators

The **lion** is the largest African cat, and the animal that every visitor to Africa hopes to see. Lions are sociable animals which live in family prides of up to 15 animals. They tend to hunt by night, favouring large and medium sized antelopes. By day, lions generally do little but find a shady spot and sleep the hours away. In Malawi, lions are now very rare. They are most likely to be seen in Kasungu National Park, and are recorded from time to time in Vwaza Marsh, Nyika, Nkhotakota and Liwonde.

Leopards are compact cats, marked with rosette-like spots, whose favoured habitats are forests and rocky hills. Leopards are still widespread in Malawi: they live in all the national parks and game reserves, most forest reserves and even in some hilly or wooded regions outside of conservation areas. The success of leopards in modern Africa is largely due to their secretive, solitary nature; they are very rarely seen even where they are common. Nyika National Park is said to have the most dense leopard population in central Africa, and sightings are quite commonplace in the vicinity of Chilinda Camp.

Leopard

Cheetahs are creatures of the open plains, normally seen on their own or in small family groups.

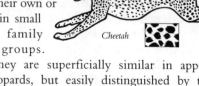

Cheetah

They are superficially similar in appearance to leopards, but easily distinguished by their more streamlined build, the black 'tear marks' running down their face, and their simple (as opposed to rosette) spots. If cheetahs are resident anywhere in Malawi, it is in Kasungu National Park.

Several smaller species of cat, such as **caracal**, **serval** and **African wild cat**, occur in Malawi, but they are rarely seen due to their nocturnal habits.

Caracal

The largest canine species found in Malawi, the **African hunting dog**, is unmistakable due to its cryptic black, brown and cream coat. Hunting dogs live and hunt in packs, normally about ten animals strong. The introduction to Africa of canine diseases such as rabies has caused a severe decline in hunting dog numbers in recent years, and they are now classified as an endangered species. The status of hunting dogs in Malawi is uncertain; they have been recorded from time to time in several reserves, but so infrequently that it is unlikely they are resident. Significantly, most records come from reserves on the Zambian or Mozambican borders, with several recent sightings in Vwaza Marsh and Kasungu.

African hunting dog

Jackals are lightly built dogs, nocturnal in habit and generally solitary by nature. Several species are recognised, but only one – the side-striped jackal – is present in Malawi, and can be recognised by its grey or sometimes yellowish coat, indistinct black side stripe, and white-tipped tail. The side-striped jackal has been recorded in Nyika, Liwonde and Lengwe national parks, and in Vwaza Marsh and Nkhotakota wildlife reserves.

Spotted hyena

The **spotted hyena** is a large, bulky predator with a sloping back, black-on-brown lightly spotted coat and dog-like face. Contrary to popular myth, hyenas are not a type of dog, nor are they exclusively scavengers (when you see hyenas hanging around a 'lion kill', it may well be that they are waiting to reclaim what the lions have hijacked), but rather they are opportunistic feeders whose complex social structure and innate curiosity makes them perhaps the most fascinating creatures to watch in the wild. Spotted hyenas are widespread throughout Africa, often living near human habitation, and can be found in all of Malawi's national parks and wildlife reserves, as well as in many forest reserves and even outside conservation areas. The spotted hyena is nocturnal in habit, but because it is not as retiring as most night hunters, it is often seen around dusk and dawn.

The *viverridae* is a group of small predators that includes **mongooses** and the cat-like **civets** and **genets**. At least nine mongoose species have been recorded in Malawi, most of which can be readily observed in the right habitat. The African civet, tree civet and large-spotted genet are all present in Malawi, but they are rarely seen due to their nocturnal habits. The best chance of seeing these animals is on a night game drive in Liwonde National Park.

Four representatives of the *mustelidae* occur in Malawi: the **ratel**, **Cape clawless otter**, **spotted necked otter** and **striped polecat**. Otters are occasionally seen at Otter Point in Lake Malawi National Park.

Primates

The most common primate in Malawi is probably the **vervet monkey**, a small, grey animal with a black face and, in the male, blue genitals. Vervet monkeys live in large troops in most habitats except desert and evergreen forest. They are frequently seen outside of reserves. The closely related **samango** or **blue monkey** is a less common species, with a darker, more cryptic coat. Samango monkeys are always associated with evergreen and well-developed riverine forests.

Vervet monkey

Blue monkey

The **yellow baboon** is common throughout Malawi. Like vervet monkeys, baboons are highly sociable animals with a wide habitat tolerance. They are most frequently seen in the vicinity of rocky hills. The greyer **chacma baboon** exists alongside the yellow baboon south of Lake Malawi. The nocturnal bushbabies (or *galogoes*) are small arboreal primates more often heard than seen. The **thick-tailed bushbaby** generally occurs in true forest, and it can be distinguished from the **lesser bushbaby**, a species of woodland

Lesser bushbaby

and savannah habitats, by its much larger size and bushy tail. The best way to see a bushbaby is to follow its distinctive, piercing call to a tree and then shine a torch to find its large eyes.

Antelope
Large antelope
All the antelope described below have an average shoulder height of above 120cm, roughly the same height as a zebra.

Common eland

The **eland** is Africa's largest antelope, with a lightly striped fawn-brown coat, short spiral horns and a slightly bovine appearance accentuated by its large dewlap. In Malawi, eland are most likely to be seen on the Nyika Plateau, where they are seasonally common, but they occur in all reserves and parks north of Lilongwe.

The **greater kudu** is another very large antelope, with a greyish coat marked by thin, white stripes. The small dewlap and immense spiralling horns of the male greater kudu render it unmistakable. The female might just be confused with the female bushbuck, though it is much larger and has no spotting. Greater kudus are generally found in small groups in woodland habitats. They are present in all of Malawi's national parks and wildlife reserves. Note that the similar but smaller lesser kudu of East Africa does not extend its range as far south as Malawi.

Greater kudu

The male **sable antelope** is unmistakable with its large, backward-curving horns and black coat. The female has smaller horns and is chestnut-brown in colour. Both sexes have a well-defined white belly and rump. The sable antelope is reasonably common in Lengwe and Kasungu national parks, and it has been recorded in all Malawi's wildlife reserves.

Sable antelope

The related **roan antelope** is an equally handsome animal, with a uniform reddish-brown coat and short backward-curving horns. The roan is the most common large antelope on the Nyika Plateau, and it also occurs in Kasungu, Vwaza Marsh and Nkhotakota.

The **common waterbuck** has a shaggy coat and a distinctive white horseshoe on its rump. It is always associated with water, and is particularly common along the Shire River in Liwonde National Park. It also occurs in Kasungu, Majete, Vwaza Marsh and Nkhotakota.

Liechtenstein's hartebeest is an ungainly antelope, closely related to the wildebeest (which, incidentally, does not occur in Malawi), with a red-yellow coat and short stubby horns. It is seen occasionally on the Nyika Plateau and is reasonably common in Kasungu and Vwaza Marsh.

Medium-sized antelope

All the antelope described below have a shoulder height of between 75cm and 95cm, except for the male nyala, which has a shoulder height of slightly over 1m.

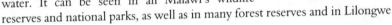

Common bushbuck

The most widespread medium-sized antelope in Malawi is the **bushbuck**. The male bushbuck has a dark chestnut coat marked with white stripes and spots, while the female is lighter with similar markings to the male, giving it an appearance much like a European deer. The bushbuck is common in most forested habitats and in thick woodland near water. It can be seen in all Malawi's wildlife reserves and national parks, as well as in many forest reserves and in Lilongwe Nature Sanctuary.

The closely-related **nyala** is a southern African species that reaches the northern extreme of its range in Majete Wildlife Reserve and Lengwe National Park, where it is common. The nyala can easily be confused with the bushbuck, though the exceptionally handsome male is much larger and shaggier in appearance, with a distinctive white crest running along its spine.

The **impala** is a highly gregarious and photogenic antelope found in most woodland habitats. It has a bright chestnut coat, distinctive white and black stripes on its rump, and the male has large lyre-shaped horns. The impala is present in Vwaza Marsh, Liwonde, Lengwe, Mwabvi and Kasungu.

Impala

The **southern reedbuck** is a lightly coloured, rather nondescript antelope almost always associated with water. It is present in small numbers in most of Malawi's reserves and national parks, as well as on other mountain plateaux, but it is only common in Kasungu and Nyika national parks.

Reedbuck

The related **puku**, a golden-brown antelope with no distinguishing features, is found in marshy habitats. It is essentially an animal of Zambia and southern Zaire, but it occasionally strays into those Malawian reserves which border Zambia.

Small antelope

All the antelope described below have a shoulder height of below 60cm.

The **klipspringer** has a grey, bristly coat which gives it a mildly speckled appearance. Klipspringers live exclusively on rocky outcrops, and are normally

Klipspringer

seen in pairs. They occur throughout Malawi wherever there are suitable habitats, which include all the national parks and wildlife reserves except Lengwe, as well as most rocky mountains outside of national parks.

The **oribi** is a tan-coloured antelope with a white belly, black tail and a diagnostic black patch beneath its ears. It generally occurs in open woodland and grassland, but it is rare and secretive in Malawi, where it has only been recorded in Kasungu and Liwonde national parks.

Sharpe's grysbok is widespread in Malawi, occurring in all national parks and wildlife reserves, but it is rarely seen due to its retiring nature and nocturnal habits. It is similar in overall appearance to an oribi, though it lacks any distinctive features and is considerably smaller. Sharpe's grysbok occurs in thicket and scrub rather than open grassland.

Livingstone's suni is a tiny and rather nondescript grey antelope, which in Malawi occurs only in Lengwe and other reserves in the Shire Valley south of Blantyre. In this area, it is only likely to be confused with the significantly larger and more robust grey duiker.

Three duiker species occur in Malawi. The most widespread is the **grey** or **common duiker**, a greyish antelope with a white belly and a tuft between its small horns. The grey duiker is common in almost all woodland habitats. The other two duiker species are forest animals and are thus very rarely seen. The **Natal red duiker** is a tiny antelope with a reddish coat and no distinguishing markings. The even tinier **blue duiker**, the smallest antelope found in Malawi, is grey with a white tail.

Common duiker

Other herbivores

Back with animals you're unlikely to have much trouble identifying, **elephants**, despite the heavy poaching of the 1980s, are still reasonably common in many of Malawi's reserves. The largest elephant herds occur in Kasungu, Liwonde and Vwaza Marsh, but there are also elephants in Nkhotakota, Nyika and possibly Majete.

Black rhinoceros, too, are easy enough to identify – if you can find one. Intense poaching has killed even the remnant herds which once occurred in Kasungu and Mwabvi. A herd of rhino from South Africa has recently been reintroduced into Liwonde National Park, but it is fenced off in a part of the park.

Hippos have also suffered from poaching in the last few years, mostly by villagers affected by famine. Nonetheless, hippos are still common on most major rivers and lakes, particularly on the part of the Shire River that runs

Black rhino

through Liwonde National Park, where some 2,000 individuals are present. Outside of reserves, hippo can be seen in the Salima area, in the Elephant Marsh, and in the Shire River near Sucoma Sugar Estate.

Of relevance here is the other common large aquatic creature in Malawi, the **crocodile** (not, of course, a mammal or a herbivore, but a reptile). Crocodiles are common along the Shire River, particularly in Liwonde National Park and in the Elephant Marsh. They are also present in many other rivers and lakes, including Lake Malawi.

Another unmistakable large animal is the **African buffalo**, which occurs in all Malawi's wildlife reserves and national parks except for Lake Malawi and Liwonde national parks.

African buffalo

Burchell's zebra is the only equine species found in Malawi. It is common in Kasungu and Nyika national parks, and a few have been re-introduced to Lake Malawi National Park. It occurs in small numbers in all the wildlife reserves except Mwabvi.

Two swine species occur in Malawi. The **warthog** is a diurnal swine with a uniform bristly grey coat and the distinctive habit of holding its tail erect when it runs. Warthogs are normally seen in pairs or family groups in savannah and woodland habitats. They are common in all Malawi's wildlife reserves and national parks excluding Nyika and Lake Malawi. The nocturnal **bushpig** has a red-brown coat and a hairier appearance than that of the warthog. It is widespread in forest and riverine woodland, and occurs in all Malawi's national parks and wildlife and forest reserves, but it is very rarely seen by visitors due to its retiring nature.

Warthog

Several other nocturnal animals are widespread in Malawi, but unlikely to be seen by tourists. The **porcupine**, for instance, occurs in every national park and wildlife reserve and most forests, but the most you are likely to see of a porcupine is a discarded quill on a forest path. The insectivorous **aardvark** occurs in most reserves and national parks, but if you see one you can rank yourself among the luckiest people on the planet.

Hyraxes (dassies) are small mammals which have a guinea pig-like appearance, though they are considered to be more closely related to elephants than any other living animal. The rock hyrax is commonly seen on koppies and other rocky areas throughout Malawi. The tree hyrax is a more uncommon animal, and strictly nocturnal. It is more likely to be heard than seen – it has a quite outrageous shrieking call.

Rock hyrax

One characteristic African mammal which is entirely absent from Malawi is the giraffe.

Birds

A total of 649 bird species have been recorded in Malawi, a highly impressive total for a country smaller than Great Britain. Though Malawi does not boast the diversity of birds of East African countries like Kenya and Uganda, serious birdwatchers who visit Malawi are likely to find it a less frustrating country, for no other reason than that it is served by excellent and comprehensive field guides (see *Further Reading*), which means that identification is rarely the problem it can be in East Africa.

Malawi is a particularly rewarding destination for South African birdwatchers. Roughly 10% of the species recorded in Malawi are not found on the southern African list. It is also the case that several birds which do appear on the southern African list as vagrants or rarities are more easily seen in Malawi – African skimmer, racquet-tailed roller, Boehm's bee-eater, wattled crane and green-headed oriole being obvious examples.

National parks and wildlife reserves are the best places to see a good variety of birds. Liwonde National Park in particular is excellent – the birdlife along the river is stunning, and guided morning walks from Mvuu Camp almost always yield a few localised species. The forests in Nyika National Park are probably the best place to see birds which occur in Malawi but not in southern Africa: many East African species extend their range no further south than Nyika or the nearby Viphya Plateau.

Evergreen forest is a particularly rich bird habitat, and, unlike game reserves, many of Malawi's forest reserves can be explored on foot. Among the more accessible forest habitats in Malawi are the Viphya and Zomba plateaux, Mulanje Massif, and Ntchisi, Chiradzulu and Thyolo mountains.

Brachystegia woodland also holds several characteristic birds, many of which are found in no other type of woodland, for instance Stierling's woodpecker, miombo pied barbet, white-winged starling, red-and-blue sunbird, pale-billed hornbill and chestnut-mantled sparrow weaver. As *brachystegia* woodland is the dominant vegetation type in Malawi, most *brachystegia* birds are widespread in Malawi.

Malawi boasts an exceptional range of water habitats. Oddly enough, Lake Malawi itself isn't particularly rewarding for birds, because it has few shallows – Lake Chilwa has a far greater number of birds. The marshes that form around several rivers during the rainy season (known in Malawi as *dambos*) are also excellent for birds – one of the best and most accessible is Mpatsanjoka Dambo near Salima. For waterbirds in general, few places I've visited compare to the Elephant Marsh in southern Malawi, where you're likely to see such unusual species as purple heron, African skimmer and pygmy goose.

Really, though, in a country as rich in birdlife as Malawi, almost anywhere is likely to prove rewarding to birdwatchers. Don't ignore the obvious – even a morning walk through Lilongwe Nature Sanctuary can throw up a variety of robins, kingfishers and the gorgeous Schalow's turaco, while, over a ten-year period, more than 100 species were recorded in one garden in Blantyre.

Fish

Each of Africa's three great lakes (Victoria, Tanganyika and Malawi) contains more species of fish than any other lake in the world. It is not yet known which of the three lakes is home to the greatest number of species, because more species are discovered every year and large parts of all three lakes have still to be explored. The most conservative estimate for the number of fish species in Lake Malawi is 500 – a greater number of freshwater species than are found in Europe and North America combined – and the real total may well be closer to 1,000. No less remarkable is the fact that only a handful of fish species are known to occur in all three of the great lakes – most of them are endemic to one particular lake.

The vast majority of Lake Malawi's fish belong to the cichlid group, one of the few types of fish that cares for its offspring – all but one of Malawi's cichlids are mouth brooders, meaning that the eggs and fry are held in the mother's mouth until they are large enough to fend for themselves. The Lake Malawi cichlids are divided into four major groups: the small plankton eating *utaka*, the large, pike-like and generally predatory *ncheni*, the bottom-feeding *chisawasawa*, and the brightly coloured, algae-eating *mbuna*.

The *mbuna* are the best known of Lake Malawi's cichlids, not least for their spectacular colours, a source of constant delight to snorkellers and scuba divers. Of more biological importance, however, is that the *mbuna* formed the subject of Dr Geoffrey Fryer's classic study of adaptive radiation in the 1950s. Adaptive radiation is when one species 'explodes' into a variety of closely related species, each of which evolves different modifications to allow it to specialise in some or other aspect of its lifestyle (it is the adaptive radiation that occurred among the finches of the Galapagos Islands which led Charles Darwin to propose the Theory of Evolution through Natural Selection). Interestingly, such species explosions have occurred independently among the cichlids in all three of Africa's great lakes, and possibly even within each lake – the *mbuna* of Lake Malawi stick so closely to the rocks on which they feed that two rocky stretches of shore separated by a sandy beach may hold completely different *mbuna* species filling identical ecological niches.

A group of *ncheni* cichlids, belonging to the *oreochromis* genus of tilapia, are known collectively in Malawi as *chambo*, and are regarded as the finest eating fish to be found in the lake.

Although cichlids are by far the most important fish in the lake, both in terms of species and actual fish tonnage, and the *mbuna* specifically are the family that is of most interest to snorkellers and divers, several other fish families occur in the lake.

The *usipa* is a small sardine-like fish that occurs in large shoals, and which forms the backbone of the local fishing industry. Dried *usipa* are sold in bulk at practically every market in Malawi.

The carp family is well represented in Lake Malawi. The *ngumbo*, a type of barbel, is a large silvery fish reaching up to 60cm in length and occurring in shoals on rocky stretches of shore such as Otter Point at Cape Maclear.

Another well-known carp is the *mpasa* or 'lake salmon', which is common in the northern part of the lake, where it is an important source of food.

The African catfish is probably the most widespread fish in Africa. It occurs in practically all freshwater habits, largely due to its ability to move across land during wet conditions. The African catfish is common in Lake Malawi. The genus of catfish known collectively as *bombe* or *sapuwa* are all evolved from the African catfish but, since they have lost the ability to cross land, they are endemic to the lake. The *bombe* catfish are the largest fish found in the lake, measuring up to 1.5m in length and weighing up to 30kg. Belonging to a separate genus of catfish, the predatory *kampango* is a popular eating fish throughout Malawi.

Overfishing in Lake Malawi is becoming a major problem. Fish like *chambo*, once plentiful and a crucial source of food, are now becoming scarce. In addition, overfishing is thought to be responsible for the presence of bilharzia in the lake. For treatment of bilharzia, see page 92.

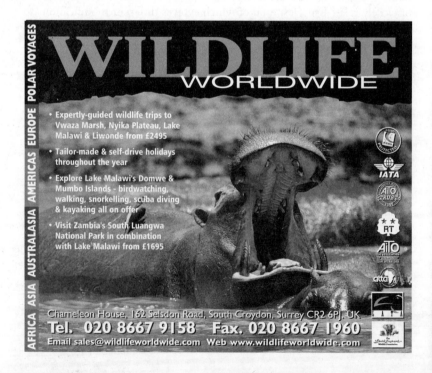

Previous page Colourful aloes are a feature of the Nyika Plateau in the southern hemisphere winter

Above Water monitor (lizard), Liwonde National Park

Right White-breasted cormorant breeding colony, *Phalocrocorax carbo*, Liwonde National Park

Below Hippos, *Hippopotamus amphibius*, on Shire River, Liwonde National Park

Planning and Preparations

This chapter covers most practical aspects of planning a trip to Malawi, with the exception of things like vaccinations and medical kits, which are covered in *Health* (see page 81).

WHEN TO VISIT

There is no major obstacle to visiting Malawi at any time of year. Lake Malawi is the focal point of tourism, and its attractions are unaffected by seasons. Likewise, most of the main hiking and walking areas in Malawi are good throughout the year. That said, there are reasons why general visitors and those with special interests might try to avoid certain seasons.

There are several disadvantages to travelling in Malawi during the hot, wet months between November and April. Malaria is more widespread during this period, and even in parts of Malawi where malaria is present all through the year, the chance of catching it is far greater during the rains. Game viewing is never as good during the rainy season, as the vegetation is higher and the animals tend to disperse away from perennial water sources. In addition, many roads in reserves and national parks will be closed after heavy rain. And, even though rain in most parts of Malawi tends to take the form of swift storms rather than protracted drizzling, hiking and camping are generally more pleasant in dry weather.

None of which means it is an overwhelmingly bad idea to visit Malawi during the rainy season, only that where you have the choice there are definite advantages in visiting during the drier months. In fact, there are a couple of definite plus points attached to visiting during the rains. High-lying areas will be much warmer at night, the countryside is a lot more green and attractive, and a greater variety of fruits and vegetables is available. A special-interest group who will definitely want to visit during the rainy season are birdwatchers – between November and April the variety of species present is boosted considerably by Palearctic and intra-African migrants.

GETTING TO MALAWI
By air

The only European airlines which fly directly to Malawi are KLM and British Airways. Within Africa, airlines that fly to Malawi are Air Zimbabwe, Ethiopian Airlines, Kenya Airways and South African Airways. Almost all international flights land at Lilongwe International Airport, 26km from Lilongwe, the exception being some flights from Johannesburg (South Africa), which land at Chileka Airport, 16km north of Blantyre. Air Malawi has been taken over by a consortium led by South African Airways and Crown Aviations. Air Malawi's most frequent international destinations from Blantyre are the capital cities Johannesburg and Nairobi (Kenya). They are now flying into Liwonde National Park, an extension of the current service between Lilongwe or Blantyre and Club Makola.

An airport tax of US$30 is charged to all non-residents upon flying out of Malawi. This must be paid in cash, in US dollars. If you don't have dollars cash to hand, you can exchange travellers' cheques for cash at the foreign exchange kiosk at the airport. Domestic departures tax is K100. Passengers transiting through Lilongwe and Blantyre airports are exempt from departures and pass through the transit routes at international airports.

Getting a flight that lets you feel as if you've got a good deal is becoming more daunting as local flight specialists fight with global flight consolidators. Put everybody on the internet and the competition just gets hotter. Below is a list of operators who give good service at a reasonable price. Getting the lowest price will require several calls and may result in some rather complicated rerouting of the plane.

From the UK

Bridge the World targets the independent traveller. Their offices are at 47 Chalk Farm Rd, Camden Town, London NW1 8AJ; tel: 0870 444 7474; email: sales@bridge-the-world.co.uk; web: www.b-t-w.co.uk.

Flight Centre is an independent flight provider with over 450 outlets worldwide. The UK head office is at Level 3, Broadway House, Wimbledon SW19 1RL; tel: 0990 666677; fax: 0181 541 5120. Offices in Australia, New Zealand, South Africa and Canada.

STA Travel 6 Wrights Lane, London W8 6TA; tel: 0870 1600599; email: enquiries@statravel.co.uk; web: www.statravel.co.uk. STA has 12 branches in London and 25 or so around the country and at a different university sites. STA also has several branches and associate organisation around the world.

Trailfinders has several offices around the UK. The main office is in London at 194 Kensington High St, London W8 7RG; tel: 020 7938 3939; web: www.trailfinders.com. Provides a one-stop travel service including visa and passport service, travel clinic and foreign exchange.

Travel Bag provides tailor-made flight schedules and holidays for destinations throughout the world. Their main office is at 12 High St, Alton, Hants GU34 1BN; tel: 0870 8901456; email: freequote3@travelbag.co.uk; web: www.travelbag.co.uk.

From the USA

Airtech 588 Broadway, Suite 204, New York, NY 10012; tel: 212 219 7000; email: fly@airtech.com; web: www.airtech.com. Standby seat broker that also deals in consolidator fares, courier flights and a host of other travel-related services.

Council Travel sells cheap tickets at over 60 offices around the US. The New York office is at 205 East 42nd St, New York, NY 10017-5706; tel: 1 800 2 COUNCIL; web: www.counciltravel.com.

STA Travel has several branches around the country. Freephone on 800 777 0112.
Worldtek Travel operates a network of rapidly growing travel agencies. For your
nearest office contact 111 Water St, New Haven, CT 06511; tel: 800 243 1723 or 203
777 1483; email: dave.smith@worldtek.com; web: www.worldtek.com.

Organised tours

Although Malawi has not really caught on as a major package-tour destination,
a number of companies in the UK and elsewhere offer tours, often in
conjunction with neighbouring countries.

UK

Aardvark Safaris Tel: 01980 849160; fax: 01980 849161; email;
mail@aardvarksafaris.com; web: www.aardvarksafaris.com. Uses mostly small,
owner-run properties, to tailor trips that take in the best of the wildlife and scenery on
offer.
Abercrombie and Kent Tel: 0845 0700611 (for UK reservations); web:
www.abercrombiekent.co.uk. A specialist in luxury and adventure travel with over 40
years of experience.
Art Safari Tel: 01394 382235 or 07780 927560 and ask for Mary-Anne for
provisional bookings and more information. Tailor-made for those who want to
spend time observing nature and learning the skills which will help them paint and
draw what they see, an art safari is ideal for creative travellers of all ages.
Cazenove and Loyd Safaris Tel: 020 73842332; fax: 020 73842399; web: www.caz-
loyd.com. Specialists in tailor-made private travel in Africa and the Indian Ocean.
Cox and Kings Travel Ltd Tel: (brochure requests) 01235 824404, (reservations)
020 78735000; fax: 020 76306038; email: cox.kings@coxandkings.co.uk. Offers
comprehensive tours for both groups and individuals, taking in wildlife and culture.
Gane and Marshall Tel: 020 8441 9592; fax: 020 8441 7376; email:
holidays@ganeandmarshall.co.uk. Tailor-made itineraries including cycling.
In the Saddle Tel: 08700 133983; email: malawi@inthesaddle.com; web:
www.inthesaddle.com. Specialises in horse-riding safaris on the Nyika Plateau in
Malawi. Malawi specialist: James Sales.
Roxton Bailey Robinson Worldwide Tel: 01488 689700; fax: 01488 681973; email:
safaris@rbrww.com web: www.rbrww.com. Specialises in top-end safaris to East and
southern Africa.
Safari Consultants Ltd Tel: 01787 228494; fax: 01787 228096; email:
bill@safariconsultants.com; web: www.safari-consultants.co.uk or
www.safariconsultantuk.com. Established in 1983, a specialised safari company
dealing with tailor-made and small group departures to East and South Africa.
Safarilink Tel: 0870 3332150; fax: 0870 3332151; email: henry@safarilink.com; web:
www.safarilink.com. A one-stop website covering all things 'safari' in Africa. Does not
sell safaris – provides links to the best resources to help plan a safari.
Sunvil Discovery Tel: 020 8232 9777; email: africa@sunvil.co.uk; web:
www.sunvil.co.uk. Flexible trips for all travellers.
Volcanoes Safaris UK Tel: 0870 8708480; fax: 0870 8708481; email:
salesuk@volcanoessafaris.com; web: www.volcanoessafaris.com

Wildlife Worldwide Tel: 020 86679158; fax: 020 86671960; email: sales@wildlifeworldwide.com; web: www.wildlifeworldwide.com. Specialising in tailor-made and small group wildlife holidays worldwide.

Germany

Livingstone Tours is a Germany-based company specialising in set departure two- and three-week camping tours for small groups of German speakers. The owner has worked in Malawi for several years and leads the tour himself. Contact details are Muhlwiesenstr 3, D-72555 Metzengen, Germany; tel: 07123 920943; fax: 07123 920944; email: livingstone.tours@t-online.de; web: http://home.t-online.de/home/livingstone.tours/malawi.htm.

South Africa

South Africans developed a taste for Malawi during the apartheid years when Banda was very welcoming and it was one of the few African countries that they could visit. It's still a popular destination and there are a number of tour operators.

Animaltracks Tel: 27 11 4540543; fax: 27 11 4540544; email: ati@intekom.co.za; web: www.animaltracks.co.za

Getaway Travel Tel: 27 21 5516552; fax: 27 21 5516594; email: info.getaway@galileosa.co.za or log on to www.getawaytravel.co.za

Pulse Africa Tel: 27 11 3252290; fax: 27 11 3252226; email: info@ africansafari.co.za or pulseafricauk@easynet.co.uk ; web: www.africansafari.co.za or www.pulseafrica.com. Specialises in tailor-made safaris/holidays to Lake Malawi's mountains, lakes and national parks.

Thompsons Tours Tel: 27 11 7707677; email: africaj@thompsons.co.za or visit the website at www.thompsons.co.za

Touraco Travel Services Tel/fax: 27 12 8038585; email: touraco@intekom.co.za; web: www.touraco.co.za

Malawi

Several good tour companies operate out of Lilongwe and Blantyre. For personalised travel arrangements, we've heard nothing but praise about Central African Wilderness Safaris, a Lilongwe-based offshoot of the highly regarded Wilderness Safari Group which operates in several southern African countries. Also recommended are the Nyika Safari Company, Lake and Land Safaris, Soche Tours and Travel, Kiboko Safaris, Ulendo Safaris, Jambo Africa and several other companies listed under the appropriate heading in the chapters on Lilongwe (page 178) and Blantyre (page 108).

Overland

Malawi lies on the most popular backpackers' route between South Africa and Kenya, and so it is highly likely that more tourists arrive in Malawi overland than by air. For this reason, it's worth going into some detail on the main overland routes to Malawi from South Africa and East Africa.

If you are heading to Malawi as part of a larger trans-African trip, Bradt Travel Guides Ltd has recently publish *East and Southern Africa: The Backpackers' Manual*, by Philip Briggs. Also look out for Getaway's new publication, *Cape to Cairo*, by Mike Copeland.

From South Africa

Several routes can be used to get between South Africa and Malawi. The quickest route is to head for Blantyre via Harare in Zimbabwe and the Tete Corridor in Mozambique, but from Harare it is equally possible to head directly to Lilongwe via Zambia. If you literally just want to get to Malawi as quickly and cheaply as you can, the Intercape coach service between Johannesburg and Blantyre leaves four times weekly in either direction and costs around US$70 one way. For details of coaches out of Johannesburg, contact the Intercape reservations office on tel: 27 11 3340350; web: www.intercape.co.za. Translux operates a similar service; tel: 27 11 7743333; web: www.translux.co.za.

Otherwise, if working your way up slowly, getting from **Johannesburg to Harare** couldn't be more straightforward. Trains run once a week, leaving Johannesburg every Monday at 18.15 and arriving in Harare roughly 24 hours later. Tickets cost approximately US$90/60 first/second class (web: www.spoornet.co.za). Greyhound buses run every night between Johannesburg and Harare, leaving from Johannesburg Rotunda (opposite the railway station) at 22.30 and arriving in Harare 16 hours later. A ticket costs around US$35 (web: www.greyhound.co.za). It is also reasonably easy to hitch between Johannesburg and Harare. There are several backpackers' hostels from which to choose in Harare, with dormitory rooms costing around US$4 per person – among the best are Wayfarers (tel: 14 572125), Backpackers and Overlanders (tel: 14 575715), The Rocks (tel: 14 576371) and It's a Small World (tel: 14 335341). You can call any of these places from the city centre for a lift.

The route from **Harare to Blantyre via the Tete Corridor** was very dangerous in the early 1990s as a result of the civil war in Mozambique. It is now reasonably safe and several bus services do the run every day, leaving Harare at 06.00 and arriving in Blantyre at nightfall, though timings are dependent on the border crossings, which, if your bus is the last to arrive at the border, can take several hours. Express buses have the reputation of being the quickest – and thus the first to reach every border. A ticket between Harare and Blantyre will cost around US$16. Note that you will need a Mozambique transit visa to cross through Tete. These are very expensive in South Africa, and take several days to issue, so it's better to do it in Harare.

The alternative to using the Tete Corridor is to travel from **Harare to Lilongwe via Lusaka** in Zambia. This route is not as popular as it was in the days when the Tete Corridor was known as the gun run, and it is much slower. The only real advantage, at least for citizens of some Commonwealth states, is that you don't need a visa to travel through Zambia (British citizens should take note that they do now require a visa to enter Zambia, and this costs US$50). The trip between Harare and Lusaka takes around ten hours by bus, depending on how busy the border is. In fact, although there are buses all the way to Lusaka, there is a strong case for bussing only as far as the border and either hitching or else boarding another bus once you've crossed into Zambia – you could cut two hours off your travelling time by doing this.

Rather than go all the way to Lusaka – a capital with few charms, even fewer affordable accommodation options, and an abundance of pickpockets – you might think about spending the night in **Kafue**, a small town about 50km south of Lusaka. The Bayi Hotel in Kafue is a reasonable place with self-contained rooms for US$12/20 single/double, and there are regular minibuses between Kafue and Lusaka when you're ready to move on. A popular alternative is to stay at Eureka Farm, 7km out of Lusaka on the Kafue Road, where you can pitch your own tent, or hire one. In Lusaka itself, the recently moved and reopened Chachacha Backpackers (161 Mulombo Close; tel: 02 222257; email: cha@zamtel.zm; web: www.zambiatourism.com/chachacha) provides a much-needed base for backpackers passing through the Zambian capital. The owner will pick up travellers from anywhere in town at no charge; just give him a ring when you arrive. Camping costs US$3 per person, dorms are US$6 per person, and private rooms cost US$12/14 single/double. Meals are available all day, and there is a kitchen for self catering. Other facilities include a bar with cold beers, email, and a public phone. Trips can be arranged to an African village outside Lusaka, and there is cultural dancing three nights a week.

Buses from Lusaka to Chipata (the nearest town to the Malawi border) leave until around midday, though buses leaving much after 08.00 are unlikely to reach Chipata before nightfall. If you're still trundling along after dark, you might think about stopping over at Patauke or Betete, both of which have basic hotels for around US$4 per room. It is easy enough to pick up local transport from these towns on to Chipata. For good accommodation at Petauke turnoff, try Zulu's Kraal – camping is US$3 and chalets cost US$4 per person. Great accommodation is available 10km out on the Malawian side of Chipata at the Yellow Chicken Camp where camping costs US$4, nicely furnished huts US$10 per person, and good home-grown vegetable meals US$5.

The Malawi border is 30km from Chipata. The best way to get there is by shared taxi. It's at least 5km between the Zambian and Malawian border posts, so do try for a lift. Both border posts are very relaxed. Once you cross into Malawi, it's only a few minutes' walk to **Mchinji**, where there are several basic resthouses, and Joe's Motel has good, self-contained rooms with hot showers for US$5/7 single/double.

Many people who travel between South Africa and Malawi will prefer not to go directly via Harare but instead to travel **via Bulawayo and the Victoria Falls**. This, again, is straightforward enough: there is a train once a week and a Greyhound bus every night between Johannesburg and Bulawayo, from where you can either catch the overnight train or else bus on through to Victoria Falls. From Victoria Falls you have the option of returning to Bulawayo and then continuing to Blantyre via Harare and Tete. It is probably easier to head on through Zambia to Lilongwe: first cross the border at the falls into Zambia, then hitch through to Livingstone,

14km away. From Livingstone there are trains to Lusaka (notoriously unreliable) and also buses leaving at around 06.00, but it's as easy as anything to hitch; you should get through in a day. The roads to Lusaka from Livingstone and Harare connect just south of Kafue. There is plenty of choice when it comes to budget accommodation in Bulawayo and Victoria Falls, but the best option in Livingstone is Fawlty Towers (216 Mosi-oa-Tunya Road; tel: 03 323432).

If you are driving yourself, be warned that officials along the Tete Corridor have a reputation for fining drivers for transgressing a variety of obscure or non-existent road regulations, though the danger of being attacked or hijacked has diminished a lot since Mozambique's civil war quietened down. Zimbabwe was going through a bad time in 2002 and one hopes that it does not become dangerous to traverse that country. Already police and traffic officials are starting to get greedy and corrupt.

You cross into Mozambique and the Tete corridor from Zimbabwe at the Nyamapanda border post 240km from Harare. Mozambique charges you an outrageous US$2 just to stamp your passport, another US$10 to issue a temporary import permit, and US$30 for one month's vehicle insurance (even though you can traverse the corridor in a few hours). You'll save a lot if using a *carnet de passage*. The 145km to Tete is a good road and fuel, food and accommodation are available there. Pay US$0.50 toll to cross the bridge over the mighty Zambezi, but watch out for the traffic police and other scam artists there. The remaining 120km to the border at Zobue and on into Malawi is also a good road.

The trip up from South Africa to Malawi requires several currency changes. There are no banks or forex bureaux at any of the border crossings, but it is easy enough to exchange with private individuals. This is quite open at most borders and there is no real danger of being queried by a Customs official. A bigger threat (though not great) is that you will be short changed or pickpocketed in the process. To get around this, keep whatever notes you expect to change separate from the rest of your money.

Don't expect to get particularly good exchange rates at borders. The money changers at such places are not black market dealers of the sort you get in cities, but small businessmen performing a service to people crossing in both directions. Understandably, they need to exchange money below the official rate to make a livelihood. In my opinion, it's worth changing money at a slightly lower rate simply to avoid the hassle of arriving in a city without local currency. My advice is to change as much as you think you'll need to get you through your first night in the country you are entering, or through to Monday if you arrive over the weekend.

In Zimbabwe, Zambia, Malawi and Mozambique, the South African rand used to be as popular with money changers as the US dollar. The slide of the rand means that this is not quite as true as it used to be, though you'll have no difficulty getting rid of rands. As it's easy to pick up small denomination rand notes in South Africa, and rather more difficult to get cash US dollars, the rand is probably the best currency to use on the trip up. Bear in mind, however, that the rand isn't widely recognised in East Africa, so once in Malawi you should get rid of any excess rands in somewhere like Blantyre or Lilongwe.

Note that if you are bussing through the Tete Corridor, there is absolutely no need to carry any Mozambican currency. You'll have no call to use it.

From East Africa

By far the most popular route from East Africa to Malawi is from Dar es Salaam on the Tanzanian coast straight through to Mbeya in southern Tanzania, then to the Malawi border at Songwe via Tukuyu and bypassing Kyela. The best way to cover the long haul between Dar es Salaam and Mbeya is by rail: trains run five days a week. There are also plenty of buses, though you are advised not to take overnight buses due to the high risk of theft.

If you arrive in Mbeya late in the day, there is no shortage of cheap hotels to choose from. Otherwise, you could continue straight on towards the Malawi border by boarding a bus heading to Kyela (you could break the trip to Kyela at the beautifully positioned town of Tukuyu, where the Langiboss Hotel offers cheap and congenial accommodation). Ask the bus to drop you at the turn-off to the border, which lies a few kilometres before Kyela. From the turn-off, you can either walk or else hire a bicycle taxi to cover the 6km to the border post. Bear in mind, though, that transport on the Malawi side of the border is quite thin on the ground; if you get to the turn-off towards mid-afternoon, it's probably a better idea to find a hotel in Kyela (there are plenty) and cross into Malawi the next day.

Once you've crossed into Malawi, you'll find that there are no hotels at the border. Fortunately there are now a good number of *matola* pick-up trucks and buses running between the border post and Karonga, so unless you arrive ridiculously late in the day, the chance of getting stuck at the border is minimal.

Although the overwhelming majority of overland travellers come from East Africa via Dar es Salaam and Mbeya, a small number use the more obscure route via Lake Tanganyika and Zambia. The Lake Tanganyika ferry runs once a week between Bujumbura in Burundi, Kigoma in Tanzania and Mpulungu in Zambia. If you're heading south, it leaves Bujumbura at 16.00 every Monday and Kigoma at 16.00 every Wednesday, and it arrives in Mpulungu at roughly 10.00 every Friday. From Mpulungu, it is roughly 320km via Mbala and Makonde to the Malawi border post at Nyala. This is rough road and transport is erratic, so it's wise to allow at least two days to get through. From the Nyala border post it's easy to find a vehicle to Chitipa, the first major town in Malawi.

Crossing to Mozambique

Due to its extensive Indian Ocean coastline, noted for numerous idyllic beaches and atmospherically crumbling colonial ports, the former Portuguese colony of Mozambique has generated a great deal of interest among adventurous travellers since the protracted civil war ended in 1994. And, while the relatively developed part of Mozambique lying south of the Zambezi River can be visited with ease from several countries, the more remote and rewarding northern half is readily accessible only from Malawi.

Of the four options open to travellers who intend to visit northern Mozambique from Malawi, the most straightforward is the road crossing between Mangochi and Mandimba. Regular transport to the border leaves Mangochi from the bus station a few hundred metres from the PTC supermarket, stopping en route at Namwera, a small town with plenty of resthouses. If you can't get a lift along the 7km road between the two border posts, your options are walking or hiring a bicycle-taxi – and if you opt for the latter you won't regret splashing out on a separate bike for your luggage. The Mozambican border post at Mandimba lies on the main road between Lichinga and Cuamba – arrive before 14.00 and you should find transport in either direction – but there is a basic resthouse in Mandimba if you get stuck.

Also worth considering is the train service connecting Liwonde to Cuamba via Nayuchi border. Trains to Nayuchi leave Liwonde at 06.00 Monday to Friday and take about three hours. In Interlagos on the Mozambican side of the border there's a restaurant and resthouse, though if everything runs to schedule you should pick up the train to Cuamba on the same day, a four-hour trip which might take twice as long on a bad day.

More remote is the crossing between Likoma Island and Cobue on Lake Malawi (or Lago Niassa as Mozambicans call it). The ferry, MV *Ilala* of the Malawi Lake Services, calls in at the ports of Cobue and Metangula on its way up and down the lake (see page 215 for timetable and details). There's a good hostel and campsite in Cobue, but it's easier to get transport out of Metangula.

The Milanje border between Mulanje and Mocuba is worth considering only if you're determined to visit Quelimane. It's easy to get a bus from Mulanje to Milange, where there's basic accommodation at Pensão Esplanada, but transport on to Mocuba is more erratic.

Those who are confining their Mozambican travels to the south can use the Zobue border post between Blantyre and Tete. Buses to Harare (in Zimbabwe), which leave Blantyre at 06.00 daily, will drop you in Tete, no problem, though they do charge the full fare of roughly US$15 to Harare. Alternatively, local buses connect Blantyre to the border town of Mwanza, and at Zobue on the Mozambican side there are regular *chapas* (the Mozambican equivalent of *matola* vehicles) on to Tete.

All visitors to Mozambique *must* buy a visa in advance. Most backpackers get a visa at the Mozambican Consulate in Blantyre, but there is also an embassy in Lilongwe. Tourist visas cost about US$35 and take three working days to issue, whereas cheaper transit visas can be issued within four hours. It's worth knowing that a transit visa is valid for seven days after issue and there is nothing stopping you from entering Mozambique on the first of those days and exiting it on the last!

For comprehensive travel information about Mozambique, see Philip Briggs's *Guide to Mozambique*, researched in late 1996 and published by Bradt Publications in July 1997.

RED TAPE
Passport

A valid passport is required to enter Malawi. The date of expiry should be at least six months after you intend to end your travels; if your passport is likely to expire before that, get a new one.

Visas

At the time of writing, visas are required by everyone except passport holders of the following nationalities: Bahamas, Bangladesh, Barbados, Belgium, Botswana, Brunei, Canada, Cyprus, Denmark, Fiji, Finland, Gambia, Germany, Ghana, Grenada, Iceland, Ireland, Israel, Jamaica, Kenya, Lesotho, Luxembourg, Malaysia, Malta, Mauritius, Netherlands, New Zealand, Nigeria, Norway, Portugal, San Marino, Sierra Leone, Singapore, South Africa, Sri Lanka, Swaziland, Sweden, Trinidad and Tobago, UK, USA, Zambia and Zimbabwe. Such rulings are always subject to change, so even those people who are currently exempt from visa requirements are advised to confirm that this is still the case before embarking for Malawi.

Malawi has an embassy or high commission in the following countries:

Belgium Third floor, 15 rue de la Roi, Brussels; tel: 231 0960; fax: 231 1066
Canada 7 Clemow Av, Ottowa; tel: 236 8931/2
Ethiopia PO Box 2361, Addis Ababa; tel: 129 4440/1
France 20 rue Euler, Paris; tel: 4720 2027
Germany Mainzert Strasse 1234, Bonn; tel: 34 3016; fax: 34 0619
Kenya PO Box 30453, Nairobi; tel: 02 221174
Mozambique 75 Kenneth Kaunda Av, Maputo; tel: 1741 468
Namibia PO Box 23384, Windhoek; tel: 22 1391; fax: 22 7056
South Africa PO Box 11172, Brooklyn, Pretoria; tel: 47 7827
Tanzania PO Box 7616, Dar es Salaam; tel: 51 37260/1
UK 33 Grosvenor St, London; tel: 020 7491 4172; fax: 020 7491 9916
USA 1400-20th St, NW, Washington DC; tel: 223 4814
Zambia PO Box 5025, Lusaka; tel: 121 3750
Zimbabwe PO Box 231, Harare; tel: 70 5611; fax: 70 5604

Immigration and customs
Arriving by air

Provided that you have a valid passport (and a visa if required) and an onward ticket out of Malawi, you should whizz through the entrance formalities with no hassle. The only reason that fly-in visitors would be likely to arrive in Malawi without an onward ticket is if they were using Malawi as a starting point for broader African travels, which is fairly uncommon (I've yet to meet someone who has done this).

Nevertheless, if you are arriving in Malawi on a one-way ticket, there is a possibility (my gut feeling is that it is only a slight possibility) that you will be given a rough time. Basically, what immigration officials are worried about is that you won't have funds to buy a flight out of the country. Obviously, the more money you have, the less likely they are to query your finances. And a credit card will almost certainly convince them to let you in. Finally, assuming that you do intend to travel to neighbouring countries, you can underline this intention by arranging a visa or visitors' pass for the next country you plan to visit *before* you land in Malawi.

The very worst that will happen if you arrive in Malawi without an onward ticket is that you will have to buy a ticket back to your home country before being allowed entry. Assuming you intend to leave Malawi overland, it is important you check with the relevant airline that this ticket will be refundable once you have left Malawi, and also that you buy it for a date that will give you time to get to a country where you can organise the refund.

Arriving by land
Malawi's land borders are generally very relaxed. Provided that your papers are in order, you should have no problem, nor is there much likelihood of being asked about onward tickets or funds. At one point, the Malawian customs workers had a slightly Draconian reputation, mainly for enforcing Banda-era restrictions such as the ban on the travel guide *Africa on a Shoestring*, and a ruling requiring men with hair over their shoulders to have a trim on the spot. These regulations went out with Banda; these days, about the worst you can expect at Malawian customs is a cursory search of your luggage.

If arriving in your own vehicle, you will need its registration documents and, if it's not registered in your name, an official letter giving you permission to drive the vehicle and cross borders with it. It will cost US$1 for a temporary import permit and US$11 per car for insurance for one month (US$26 for light trucks). All vehicles pay US$20 road-toll tax per entry into Malawi. If you add this to what it costs to bring a vehicle through Mozambique, it might make you wish you'd taken the bus instead.

MONEY MATTERS
Organising your finances
Bring the bulk of your money in the form of travellers' cheques, as these can be refunded if they are lost or stolen. The most widely recognised currency is the US dollar, followed by the South African rand and, to a lesser extent, the pound sterling. Other currencies are fine in major cities, but may cause some confusion at banks in smaller centres.

It is advisable to bring a small amount of money (say around US$200) in US dollars cash, preferably small denominations, in case you need to change money on the street when banks are closed. If you can't get hold of US dollars cash, South African rands are also quite widely accepted. Most other currencies (including pounds sterling) are as good as useless outside of banks. Note that US$100 notes are not accepted by some hotels and banks due to the large number of forgeries in circulation in Malawi.

No matter how long you are travelling in Malawi (or elsewhere in Africa except South Africa) make sure that you bring enough money with you, so that you won't need to have any more transferred or drafted. This is a notoriously tedious process and there is a real risk the money will never arrive. Even if it does arrive safely, it will be a battle to obtain it in hard currency.

Credit cards are accepted in most tourist-class hotels and in many shops and restaurants in Blantyre and Lilongwe. In the main branches of banks in Lilongwe, Blantyre and Mzuzu, you can also draw a limited amount of cash against an internationally recognised credit card, though this can be a time-consuming process. Outside major cities, credit cards are close to useless, except at upmarket game lodges and resorts.

Carrying your money and valuables

It is advisable to carry all your hard currency as well as your passport and other important documentation in a money-belt. The ideal money-belt for Africa is one that can be hidden beneath your clothing. Externally-worn money-belts may be fashionable, but wearing one in Africa is as good as telling thieves that all your valuables are there for the taking.

Use a money-belt made of cotton or another natural fabric, bearing in mind that such fabrics tend to soak up a lot of sweat, so you will need to wrap plastic around everything inside the money-belt.

Currency Declaration Forms

At one point, Currency Declaration Forms (CDFs) were the bane of African travel. On entering the country, all your currency had to be declared on a CDF. You were then required to have every foreign exchange transaction noted on the form. When you left the country, the initial total you declared minus the sum of all your transactions had to tally with the amount of foreign currency you had left on you. The purpose of this rigmarole was to prevent travellers using the black market (which was almost unavoidable in many countries due to an absurdly low bank rate). Fortunately, the liberalisation of most African economies in the last few years has discouraged people from using the black market, the result of which is that CDFs are by and large a thing of the past.

The reason for this long-winded exposition is that you may still be required to fill in a CDF at some Malawi borders, something which might instil some trepidation in people who have travelled in Africa before. But fear not – the form you fill in is kept by Customs and you'll never hear about it again.

Budgeting

A budget is a personal thing, dependent on how much time you are spending in the country, what you are doing while you are there, and how much money you can afford to spend.

If you use facilities that are mainly geared to locals, Malawi is a very inexpensive country, even by African standards. You can generally find a room in a local hotel for around US$3–4 per person and you can normally buy a meal for a similar price. Buses are cheap, as are drinks. Rigidly budget-conscious travellers can probably keep costs down to US$10 per day per person, but US$15 gives you considerably more flexibility. At US$20 per day, you can, within reason, do what you like.

If you are on a restricted budget, it is often a useful idea to separate your daily budget from one-off expenses. This is less the case in Malawi than most African countries, because few travellers will be doing expensive one-offs such as going on safari, visiting gorilla reserves or climbing Kilimanjaro. Nevertheless, there are always going to be days which a variety of factors conspire to make expensive. At current prices, a daily budget of around US$15 with a few hundred dollars spare for one-offs would be very comfortable for most travellers.

WHAT TO TAKE

As I have travelled almost exclusively on public transport, both in Malawi and elsewhere in Africa, the following advice is probably slanted towards people travelling in a similar manner.

Carrying your luggage

If you intend using public transport or to do any hiking, you will want to carry your luggage on your back. There are three ways of doing this: with a purpose-made backpack, with a suitcase that converts to a rucksack, or with a large daypack.

The choice between a convertible suitcase or a purpose-built backpack rests mainly on your style of travel. If you intend doing a lot of hiking, you're definitely best off with a proper backpack. If, on the other hand, you'll be doing things where it might be a good idea to shake off the sometimes negative image attached to backpackers, there are obvious advantages in being able to convert your backpack to a conventional suitcase. Otherwise, it doesn't really matter much which you use.

After several African trips, my own preference is for a large daypack. The advantages of keeping your luggage as light and compact as possible are manifold. For a start, you can rest it on your lap on buses, thus avoiding complications such as extra charges for luggage, arguments about where your bag should be stored, and the slight but real risk of theft if your luggage ends up on the roof. A compact bag also makes for greater mobility, whether you're hiking or looking for a hotel in town.

The sacrifice you need to make in order to carry a daypack is essentially camping equipment and a sleeping bag. In a country where accommodation is as cheap as Malawi, camping equipment won't save you a great deal of money, nor will you often be forced to use it. And for most purposes, a light sheet sleeping bag is as useful as the real thing (a sheet sleeping bag still performs the important role of enclosing and insulating your body; it is only in really cold conditions that it will fail you – then you can just cover up with extra clothing). During my last two African trips, I've managed to fit everything I truly need as well as a few luxuries in a 35l daypack weighing around 8kg. And, having made the conversion from a bulkier, heavier rucksack, I can only recommend it to other travellers.

If you find that your luggage won't squeeze into a daypack, a sensible compromise is to carry a large daypack in your rucksack. That way, you can carry a tent and other camping equipment when you need it (for instance, the

PHOTOGRAPHIC TIPS
Ariadne Van Zandbergen
Equipment

Although with some thought and an eye for composition you can take reasonable photos with a 'point and shoot' camera, you need an SLR camera with one or more lenses if you are at all serious about photography. If you carry only one lens in Malawi, a 28–70mm or similar zoom should be ideal for anything but wildlife photography, whereas a 80–200mm or 70–300mm or similar will be better for candid shots and wildlife. Carrying both will allow you to play more with composition. If you're serious about wildlife photography a higher magnification than 300 is useful but expensive and bulky. For a small loss of quality, tele-converters are a cheap and compact way to increase magnification: a 300 lens with a 1.4x converter becomes 420mm, and with a 2x it becomes 600mm. Note that tele-converters reduce the speed of your lens by 1.4 and 2 stops respectively. For wildlife photography from a safari vehicle, a solid beanbag, which you can make yourself very cheaply, will be necessary to avoid blurred images and is more useful than a tripod.

Film

Print film is the preference of most casual photographers, slide film of professionals and some dedicated amateurs. Slide film is more expensive than print film, but this is broadly compensated for by cheaper development costs. Most photographers working outdoors in Africa favour Fujichrome slide film, in particular Sensia 100, Provia 100 (the professional equivalent to Sensia) or Velvia 50. Slow films (ie: those with a low ASA [ISO] rating) produce less grainy and sharper images than fast films, but can be tricky without a tripod or beanbag in low light. Velvia 50 is extremely fine-grained and shows stunning colour saturation; it is the film I normally use in soft, even light or overcast weather. Sensia or Provia may be preferable in low light, since 100 ASA allows you to work at a faster shutter speed than 50 ASA. Because 100 ASA is more tolerant of contrast, it is also preferable in harsh light. For extreme situations it is always good to carry some faster films. Provia 400 ASA is a relatively fine-grained fast film.

For print photography, a combination of 100 or 200 ASA film should be ideal. For the best results it is advisable to stick to recognised brands. Fujicolor produces excellent print films, with the Superia 100 and 200 recommended.

Some basics

The automatic programmes provided with many cameras are limited in the sense that the camera cannot think, but only make calculations. A better investment than any amount of electronic wizardry would be to read a photographic manual for beginners and get to grips with such basics as the relationship between aperture and shutter speed.

Beginners should also note photographs taken at a low shutter speed are often affected by camera shake, resulting in a fuzzy image. For hand-held photographs of static subjects using a low magnification lens such as 28–70mm, select a shutter speed of at least 1/60th of a second. When hand-holding lenses of higher magnification, the rule of thumb is that the shutter speed should be at least the inverse of the highest magnification of the lens (for instance, a speed of 1/300 or faster on a 70–300mm lens). You can use far lower shutter speeds with a tripod or beanbag.

Most modern cameras include a built-in light meter, and allow a choice of three different types of metering, ie: matrix, centre-weighted, or spot metering. You will need to understand how these different systems work to make proper use of them. Built-in light meters are reliable in most circumstances, but in uneven light, or where there is a lot of sky, you may want to take your metering selectively, for instance by taking a spot reading on the main subject. The meter will tend to under- or overexpose when pointed at an almost white or black subject. This can be countered by taking a reading against an 18% grey card, or a substitute such as grass or light grey rocks – basically anything that isn't almost black, almost white or highly reflective.

Dust and heat
Dust and heat are often a problem in Africa. Keep your equipment in a sealed bag, stow films in an airtight container (such as a small cooler bag), leave used films in your hotel room, and avoid changing film in dusty conditions. On rough roads, I always carry my camera equipment on my lap to protect against vibration and bumps. Never stow camera equipment or film in a car boot (it will bake), or let it stand in direct sunlight.

Light
The light in Africa is much harsher than in Europe or North America, for which reason the most striking outdoor photographs are often taken during the hour or two of 'golden light' after dawn and before sunset. Shooting in low light may enforce the use of very low shutter speeds, in which case a beanbag (from a vehicle) or tripod (on foot) or monopod (lighter but less steady than a tripod) will be required to avoid camera shake. Be alert to the long shadows cast by a low sun; these show up more on photographs than to the naked eye.

With careful handling, side lighting and back lighting can produce stunning effects, especially in soft light and at sunrise or sunset. Generally, however, it is best to shoot with the sun behind you. Because of this, most buildings and landscapes are essentially a 'morning shot' or 'afternoon shot', depending on the direction in which they face. When you spend a couple of nights in one place, you'll improve your results by planning the best time to take pictures of static subjects (a compass can come in handy).

When photographing people or animals in the harsh midday sun, images taken in light but even shade are likely to look nicer than those taken in direct sunlight or patchy shade, since the latter conditions create too much contrast. Fill-in flash is almost essential if you want to capture facial detail of dark-skinned people in harsh or contrasting light.

Protocol
Except in general street or market scenes, it is unacceptable to photograph people without permission. Expect some people to refuse or to ask for a donation. Don't try to sneak photographs as you might get yourself into trouble, especially where the Maasai are concerned. Even the most willing subject will often pose stiffly when a camera is pointed at them; relax them by making a joke, and take a few shots in quick succession to improve the odds of capturing a natural pose.

Zomba Plateau), but at other times you can reduce your luggage to fit into a daypack and leave what you're not using in storage.

Clothing

If you're carrying your luggage on your back, you will want to restrict your clothes to the minimum. In my opinion, this is one or two pairs of trousers and/or skirts, and one pair of shorts; three shirts or T-shirts; at least one sweater (or similar) depending on when you are visiting the country and where you intend to go; enough socks and underwear to last five to seven days; and one or two pairs of shoes.

Trousers Jeans are not ideal for African travel. They are bulky and heavy to carry, hot to wear, and they take ages to dry. Far better to bring light cotton trousers. If you intend spending a while in montane regions, you might prefer to carry tracksuit bottoms rather than bring a second pair of trousers. These can serve as thermal underwear and as extra cover on chilly nights, and they can also be worn over shorts on chilly mornings. There is no longer a law against women wearing trousers in Malawi.

Skirts Like trousers, these are best made of a light natural fabric such as cotton. For reasons of protocol, it is advisable to wear skirts that go below the knee: short skirts will cause needless offence to many Malawians (especially Muslims) and, whether you like it or not, they may be perceived as provocative in some quarters.

Shirts T-shirts are a better idea than button-up shirts, because they are lighter and less bulky. That said, I've found that the top pocket of a shirt (particularly if the pocket buttons up) is a good place to carry my spending money in markets and bus stations, as it's easier to keep an eye on than trouser pockets.

Sweaters Those parts of Malawi at an altitude of 1,500m or higher tend to be cold at night. In winter, even places at more moderate altitudes (Lilongwe and Blantyre, for instance) can be surprisingly cool after dusk. For general purposes, one warm sweater or sweatshirt should be adequate in Malawi. If you intend hiking in Mulanje and other highland areas, you'll be grateful for a second sweater or sweatshirt, particularly during winter. During the rainy season, it's worth carrying a light waterproof jacket.

Socks and underwear These *must* be made from natural fabrics, and bear in mind that re-using them when sweaty will encourage fungal infections such as athlete's foot, as well as prickly heat in the groin region. Socks and underpants are light and compact enough to make it worth bringing a week's supply.

Shoes Unless you're serious about off-road hiking, bulky hiking boots are probably over the top in Malawi. They're also very heavy, whether they are on your feet or in your pack. A good pair of walking shoes, preferably made of leather and with some ankle support, is a good compromise. It's also useful to carry sandals, thongs or other light shoes.

Camping equipment

As with most countries in southern Africa, there is a case for carrying a tent to Malawi, particularly if you are on a tight budget. Campsites exist in most of Malawi's national parks and reserves, and camping is permitted at most lakeside resorts, backpackers' hostels and forestry resthouses. Travellers who intend doing a fair bit of off-the-beaten track hiking will find a tent a useful fallback where no other accommodation exists.

That said, there are few parts of Malawi where a tent is an absolute necessity, and cheap rooms are so widely available that the costs saved by camping are not immense. For travellers using public transport, the disadvantage of carrying a tent (and other camping equipment) is that it will add considerably to the weight, bulk and unmanageability of your luggage. There are plenty of interesting off-the-beaten-track places in Malawi where affordable rooms exist and which involve a walk of anything up to 15km to reach. In such circumstances, the extra bulk and 4–5kg added by carrying camping equipment can turn a pleasant walk into a real slog.

If you decide to carry camping equipment, the key is to look for the lightest available gear. It is now possible to buy a lightweight tent weighing little more than 2kg, but make sure that it is reasonably mosquito proof. Usable sleeping bags weighing even less than 2kg can be bought, but, especially as many lightweight sleeping bags are not particularly warm, my own preference is for a sheet sleeping bag, supplemented by wearing heavy clothes in cold weather. Also essential is a roll-mat, which will serve both as insulation and padding. In Malawi, there is no real need to carry a stove, as firewood is available at most campsites where meals cannot be bought. If you do carry a stove, it's worth knowing that Camping Gaz cylinders are not readily available in Malawi. It would, however, be advisable to carry a pot, plate, cup and cutlery: lightweight cooking utensils are available at most camping shops.

Other useful items

A torch is essential if you are camping or staying in towns where there is no electricity.

Binoculars are essential for birdwatching and to get a good look at animals in wildlife reserves. Compact binoculars have a crisper image than the traditional variety, they are much more backpack-friendly, and these days you can find adequate brands that are not significantly more expensive than traditional binoculars. The one drawback of compact binoculars is their restricted field of vision, which can make it difficult to pick up birds and animals in thick bush. For most purposes, 7x35 traditional binoculars or 7x21 compact binoculars are fine, but birdwatchers might find a 10x magnification more useful.

If you stay in local hotels, it is best to carry your own padlock – many places don't supply them. You should also carry a towel, soap, shampoo, toilet paper and any other toiletries you need. A travel alarm clock is essential for catching early morning buses.

People who wear contact lenses should be aware that the various fluids are not readily available in Malawi. Bring enough to last the whole trip. Many people find the intense sun and dry African climate irritates their eyes, so you could also think about reverting to glasses for the duration of your trip.

English-language reading material of any description is difficult to get hold of outside the two main cities, and even in the cities you'll find the range of fiction books is limited. Books are also very expensive, and there are few secondhand book stalls around, so bring a good stock with you. If you're remotely interested in what's happening in the world, think about carrying a short-wave radio. Another useful item is a Swiss knife or multi-purpose tool.

If travelling in your own vehicle, make sure you have a good set of tools, a selection of wire, string and rope, your driver's licence and the vehicle's registration papers (and a letter of permission to use the vehicle if not registered in your name). You might also consider spare engine oil, a jerry can for fuel, a fan belt, spare fuses and a fluorescent light that plugs into the cigarette lighter.

Medical kits and other health-related subjects are discussed in *Health*.

Camera equipment

For photographs of people and scenery, an ordinary 50mm lens or – better for scenic shots – 35–70mm zoom should be adequate. If you are expecting to be taking photographs of animals or birds, a 70–210mm or similar zoom would be more appropriate. Low-speed 50, 64 or 100 ASA films are ideal for most circumstances. Although 400 ASA print film is widely available in Malawi, print film of other speeds and slide film are best brought with you.

I'm generally uncomfortable about taking photographs of people when I travel. Partly, this is because I've travelled so much in Muslim areas of East Africa, and partly because I think flashing cameras in any social situation is rude and obtrusive. Another factor is that I get so fed up with being asked to take people's photos, I actually can't be bothered to carry a camera most of the time. Malawi is something of an exception, as most Malawians apparently love having their photograph taken, so there is really very little risk of giving offence. All the same, you should always ask permission before taking a photograph of a person, and be prepared to pay in the unlikely event that payment is asked. Try to be sensitive about taking casual street shots in Muslim towns like Salima, Nkhotakota and Mangochi.

Maps

The 1:1,000,000 *Malawi Road and Tourist Map*, printed by the Department of Surveys in 1992, is the best general purpose map to the country. As far as I am aware, the only inaccuracies are that Chilumba (on the lakeshore near Livingstonia) is mistakenly called Khondowe, and that certain roads shown as dirt (the lakeshore road between Nkhata Bay and Nkhotakota, and the M14 between Lilongwe and Salima) have been surfaced since the map was printed.

This map is available through the map sales offices or tourist offices in Lilongwe and Blantyre and it costs around US$5.

The Department of Surveys has also produced excellent 1:50,000 and 1:25,000 maps covering the whole country. Except when individual maps are out of stock, these can be bought at any map sales office for US$3 per sheet. Good town plans of Blantyre, Lilongwe, Mzuzu and Zomba can be bought for the same price at any map sales office.

PLANNING AN ITINERARY

Any individual itinerary through Malawi is likely to be highly personal, based on your means of transport, your interests and budget, the season, as well as the amount of time you have available. Most readers of this guide will either be making personalised arrangements in advance through a recognised tour operator, or will be travelling independently. In both cases, my advice is the same: go through this book picking out the places that are of greatest interest to you, and then base your itinerary around these, working out a rough route and adding other stops of interest along the way. I would tend to select first those places you want to visit away from the lake, since the lakeshore resorts, though not exactly interchangeable, are similar enough that it makes sense to visit those which slot most comfortably into the rest of your itinerary.

In the case of making prescribed travel arrangements, any reliable tour operator based in Malawi will be able to advise you on what is and isn't realistic, and to come up with an itinerary that suits your requirements. One factor influencing those who require their creature comforts will be the availability of upmarket accommodation, which is restricted to the main wildlife reserves, a few select places along the lake, and the three main cities. Another factor to be considered, especially by first-time visitors to Africa, is that travel in some parts of Malawi will be unexpectedly time consuming, for which reason it is advisable to allow yourself ample time at those places you do particularly want to visit. As a rule, you'll have a more relaxing holiday if you settle on a relatively compact itinerary rather than one that tries to cram in the whole country over a couple of weeks.

As a rule, independent travellers have the flexibility to adjust their itinerary as they go along, so that the obvious way of planning their travels is to pick out a rough circuit and follow it at a pace dictated by events. Even more than those visitors who are on organised tours, travellers using public transport shouldn't attempt to take on too much in a limited space of time, or their dominant memory of the country will be of sitting in buses. As a rule of thumb, travellers using public transport are advised to allow themselves at least one day 'off' between travelling days. It is a matter of preference, I realise, but if I had only two weeks or so in which to explore Malawi using public transport, I would prefer to spend a few nights at any one lake resort than to attempt visiting several for one or two nights each.

In my opinion, the sort of itineraries reproduced in most travel guides are somewhat restrictive and serve little practical purpose, since there are so many variables for which they cannot allow, not only regarding the interests of the individual traveller, but also the manner in which they intend to travel.

What follows is not a suggested itinerary, then, but an annotated south-to-north list of some of Malawi's most alluring spots, some well known, others more obscure, all of them worth visiting.

Elephant Marsh (pages 117–19) — Inexpensive, little-visited, atmospheric, prolific waterbirds, ideal for adventurous backpackers.

Majete Wildlife Reserve (pages 114–15) — A relatively obscure reserve, with decent game viewing and affordable accommodation; a good overnight excursion from Blantyre in private transport.

Mulanje Massif (pages 125–9) — The best montane hiking in Malawi, accessible and affordable to those on a limited budget.

Zomba Plateau (pages 135–9) — The most accessible of Malawi's large mountains, with good walking, camping facilities, and an excellent tourist-class hotel.

Lake Chilwa (pages 139–41) — A great and surprisingly accessible off-the-beaten-track excursion for backpackers on a tight budget.

Liwonde National Park (pages 143–7) — Best game viewing in Malawi, stunning birds, wonderful atmosphere, and excellent facilities ranging from a campsite to the country's top game lodge.

Nkopola (page 153) — Here you'll find the major cluster of tourist-class hotels on the southern lakeshore.

Cape Maclear (pages 154–9) — Legendary backpackers' hangout, good affordable facilities; these days it receives mixed reviews.

Dedza and surrounds (pages 161–4) — Hikers could spend a cheap week exploring this underrated area.

Senga Bay (pages 184–7) — Boasts plenty of cheap rooms and the superlative Livingstonia Beach Hotel, hippo and breeding colonies of birds, very close to Lilongwe.

Ntchisi (page 189) — Main town on one of the country's least used and most rewarding backroads.

Kasungu National Park (pages 196–8) — Seasonally good game viewing, good lodge and camping facilities, easy access, great stopover for those heading north on the M1 from Lilongwe.

Viphya Plateau (page 200) — Hiking and birding not as good as in some other montane areas, but a lovely spot, infrequently visited by travellers, and very accessible and affordable.

Likoma Island (pages 215–19) — Good place to get away from it all, with a friendly atmosphere, attractive scenery, and some historical interest.

Chintheche (pages 207–9)

The Chintheche Inn is the most upmarket hotel on the northern lakeshore, while nearby Kande Beach is one of the country's busiest and best campsites.

Nkhata Bay (pages 210–12)

The 'new' Cape Maclear, with a thriving backpackers' scene, cheap SCUBA courses, and a habit of transforming short visits into extended stays.

Vwaza Marsh Wildlife Reserve (pages 234–6)

The most underrated game reserve in the country – plenty of animals, very accessible and affordable, and a new upmarket lodge.

Nyika National Park (pages 227–34)

Malawi's largest national park, offering walking and horseback excursions in fantastic scenery. Good game viewing, too.

Livingstonia (page 241)

Site of a turn-of-the-20th-century mission on the Rift Valley Escarpment, overlooking the lake and close to the beautiful Machewe Falls.

Travelling in Malawi

TOURIST INFORMATION

There are tourist offices in Lilongwe, Blantyre and Mzuzu. The Blantyre office is most accessible and a good source of pamphlets and advice. It also sells several books useful to visitors. The Lilongwe office has a more limited range of books. The less said about the Mzuzu office the better. To contact the head office from outside the country, write to the Malawi Department of Tourism, PO Box 402, Blantyre (tel: 01 620902; email: tourism@malawi.net).

Tour companies, other travellers and notice boards at various backpacker hostels are often the most useful source of practical travel information.

PUBLIC HOLIDAYS

Visitors to Malawi should be alert to the fact that banks, government offices and many shops and businesses close on public holidays, and also that when a holiday falls on a Saturday or Sunday it is taken on the subsequent Monday. Malawi's relatively small Muslim population celebrates the normal Muslim holidays, but this will have no significant practical effect on travellers. In addition to Easter, which falls on a different date every year, the following public holidays are taken in Malawi.

New Year's Day	1 January
John Chilembwe Day	16 January
Martyrs' Day	3 March
Labour Day	1 May
Freedom Day	14 June
Independence Day	6 July
Mothers' Day	Second Monday in October
National Tree Planting Day	Second Monday in December
Christmas Day	25 December
Boxing Day	26 December

MONEY

The unit of currency is the Malawi *kwacha*, divided into 100 *tambala*. Notes are printed in denominations of K200, K100, K50, K20, K10 and K5, while smaller denominations are coins only. The rate of exchange to major international currencies has dropped steadily in recent years. In mid-2002, the rate against the US dollar was approximately US$1 = K75.

Foreign exchange

Foreign currency can be converted to *kwachas* at any branch of the Commercial Bank of Malawi or National Bank of Malawi, as well as at many upmarket hotels and at any of several private bureaux de change (generally called forex bureaux) in Lilongwe or Blantyre. The most widely recognised international currency is the US dollar, followed by the South African rand and British pound sterling, but most major currencies will be accepted by banks. Banking hours are from 08.00 to 14.00 Monday to Friday. Banks are not open on Saturdays, Sundays or public holidays.

Changing money is generally a reasonably swift and straightforward transaction in Lilongwe, Blantyre and other large towns such as Mzuzu, Mangochi and Zomba. It may be more tedious in small towns, especially those which see few tourists. It is important to note that there are no facilities for foreign exchange (not even a black market) in many popular tourist spots, most notably Nkhata Bay, Cape Maclear and Monkey Bay, so it's advisable to change what you expect you'll need while you're still in a large town. In any case, the best exchange rates are generally available in Lilongwe and Blantyre. As a rule, private forex bureaux offer a better rate than upmarket hotels and banks. This does vary, however, and you may come across forex bureaux that offer very poor rates, so it's worth shopping around, especially when you want to change a large sum. When comparing rates, allow for the commission that is charged by banks but not by forex bureaux and hotels.

The black market which once thrived in Malawi has declined in recent years as a result of liberalisation of exchange controls. If a steet tout offers you a rate that's significantly better than the best rate at a forex bureau, you're probably dealing with a con artist or a police informer. The one time it does make sense to change money on the streets is if you need *kwachas* after banking hours or over the weekends. Street touts will only accept cash, so it's worth carrying a few small denomination dollar bills for such eventualities. Except in Blantyre, Lilongwe and at border posts, it can be quite difficult to find somebody to change money with – upmarket hotels are your best bet, though they are often reluctant to change money with non-residents of the hotel.

Note that there are a large number of old counterfeit US$100 bills floating around Malawi. For this reason, you may find it difficult to exchange bills printed before 1992. Many banks have machines that test the authenticity of notes, but don't rely on this.

Prices quoted in this book

With a handful of exceptions, mostly some of the upmarket hotels, everything from national parks fees to meals in upmarket restaurants can be paid for in local currency. Nevertheless, given the instability of African currencies in general and the recent devaluation of the *kwacha* in particular, it is more reliable in the long term to quote prices at the US dollar equivalent. We noted that most prices had stayed remarkably constant in dollar terms between 1995 and 2002, even though the *kwacha* devalued from K15 to slightly more than

K75 during that period. For this edition, I've used an approximate exchange rate of US$1 to K75, and rounded up where necessary.

Prices quoted in this book were collected in mid-2002, and may be subject to inflation during the lifespan of this edition.

Here are some supermarket prices of common commodities (and an insight into some of my preferences):

Bread, loaf	US$0.45
Rice, 1kg	US$0.85
Sugar, 1kg	US$0.60
Rump steak, 1kg	US$4.00
Corned beef, can	US$2.50
Beer, 375ml bottle	US$0.45
Beer, in pub	US$0.80
Bunch of ten small bananas, in market	US$0.35
Petrol, 1 litre	US$0.75
Diesel, 1 litre	US$0.60

GETTING AROUND
Internal flights
Air Malawi runs domestic flights connecting Lilongwe to Blantyre, Karonga, Mzuzu and Club Makokola on the southern Lake Malawi shore. Any travel agent or tour operator can give further information about these flights, and there are Air Malawi offices in all three main cities.

Self drive
A number of car-hire companies operate out of Blantyre and Lilongwe, and some of the more reputable firms are listed in the chapters on these cities. If you decide to rent a vehicle, take a good look under the bonnet before you drive off, and check the state of all tyres including the spare. One reader has recommended you bring an aerosol puncture repair kit with you, for added security should you have to drive on your spare tyre on a poor road.

If arriving with your own vehicle, you've probably made sure it's tough and well kitted out, as driving *to* Malawi is worse than driving *around* Malawi. You don't need a 4WD, especially in the dry season, but a robust vehicle with high ground clearance is best.

What follows is the state of the roads in mid-2002. The M1 runs from south to north. From the southern border with Mozambique, the road is poor and pot-holed as far as Blantyre. Continuing up through Lilongwe, Kasungu, Mzuzu, Karonga and north to the Tanzanian border, it is good tar with some pot-holes between Mzuzu and Chiweta and roadworks between Chiweta and Karonga. The M2 east of Blantyre to the Mozambican border at Milanje is good tar, as is the M6 west from Blantyre to the Mozambican border at Mwanza. The M3 from Blantyre to Monkey Bay is well surfaced tar with some pot-holes north of Mangochi. The road on to Cape Maclear is a rough dirt road, as is the M10 west from there to the M5. The M14 from Lilongwe to Salima is a fine surfaced road, like the M12 west from Lilongwe to the Zambian border at Mchinji. The M5 which starts down near Balaka, runs up the lake shore to Nkhata Bay and Mzuzu, and has a good tarred surface, except where there is a temporary bridge across the Dwambazi river between Ngala Beach Lodge and Kande Beach. The M26 between Karonga and Chitipa is a very bad, steep and rocky road, but a start has been made on an upgrade. In and out of Nyika and Vwaza Marsh national parks is a reasonable dirt road from Rumphi as is the one into Kasungu National Park. The road between Kasungu and Nkhotakota was being rebuilt and should be a fine new tarred road by now.

Remember though that roads deteriorate fast – good tarred roads develop horrendous pot-holes with no maintenance and dirt roads become impassable if not graded regularly. Rain washes roads and bridges away, to stay like that for a year or more sometimes. This is Africa, not Europe or the States, and it's what you came for. So take care and, if in doubt, ask local advice.

Those who have never before driven in rural Africa will need to adjust their driving style for Malawi. Basically, this means driving more slowly than you might on a similar road in a Western country, and slowing down when you approach pedestrians or cyclists on the road or livestock on the verge. Drunken driving is a serious problem in Malawi, and minibus drivers tend to drive as if they might be drunk even when sober. Be alert to vehicles overtaking in tight situations, driving on the wrong side of the road (especially where there are pot-holes), pulling out behind you without warning, and generally behaving as if it's their last day on earth. Driving at night is even more hazardous, largely because so many vehicles in Malawi don't have functional headlights.

As in most former British colonies, driving is on the left side of the road, an additional adjustment for visitors from North America and mainland Europe. Petrol is widely available and costs about US$0.75 per litre. It is, however, blended with ethanol and has a low octane rating. Diesel is as freely available at US$0.60 per litre. One final tip – Malawians expect everyone to be driving from south to north, and position all signs to lodges and places of interest to face south. Frustrating if you're coming from the north.

Public transport and hitching

Malawi has a useful network of public transport, and we have always found the buses in particular to be well organised and quick by African standards. The rail network is limited to the south, and it is too slow and unreliable to be a practical alternative to bus transport. In practical terms, much the same can be said of the ferry which ploughs up and down Lake Malawi every week, but this is certainly worth using if you enjoy boat transport or you want to visit one of the islands which cannot be reached any other way.

Rail

The only railway lines in Malawi connect Lilongwe to Blantyre via Salima, Blantyre to Nsanje (near the Mozambican border in the south of the country) via Luchenza, and Liwonde to Nayuchi (on the Mozambican border northeast of Blantyre). Services are very slow, overcrowded and erratic, and as a rule they offer no practical advantages over road transport. I've yet to hear of a traveller using Malawi's internal railway services, but some travellers do use the train east from Liwonde to cross into Mozambique (see *Crossing to Mozambique* page 44).

Lake ferry
The MV *Ilala* is a popular means of travelling around the lake and to Likoma and Chizumulu islands; see *The Lake Ferry and the Islands*, page 213, for details.

Buses
By African standards, bus travel in Malawi can be an unqualified pleasure, provided you stick to the Coachline and express services. Buses are generally well maintained and driven with a relatively high level of sobriety, and most main roads are in good condition. Even on slower routes, you can expect express buses to cover between 40km and 50km per hour. Some routes are much quicker, for instance the express bus between Lilongwe and Blantyre can take as little as four hours to cover 311km. Express buses are inexpensive (in 2002, fares were typically in the region of US$1 per 40–50km) and overcharging tourists is most unusual. So is overcrowding. We were amazed at how often the buses we used were half full for much of the journey. Buses in Malawi generally leave throughout the day, which means that you are spared the endless early starts that characterise travelling on public transport in countries such as Tanzania and Ethiopia. Express buses almost always work on fixed departure times, as opposed to the fill-up-and-go system that is common in some other African countries, so it's always advisable to ask about your next day's travel in advance.

The main bus operator in Malawi, and the most reliable, is the newly privatised Shire Bus Company. Shire buses cover practically every conceivable road route in Malawi, and they run several different types of service. The most upmarket is the Coachline service, which runs four times daily non-stop between Lilongwe and Blantyre, costs US$18 per person, and takes little more than three hours in either direction. There is also a daily coach service between Lilongwe and Mzuzu, and international services connecting Blantyre to Harare (Zimbabwe) and Lilongwe to Lusaka (Zambia). Coachline buses are similar in standard to coach services elsewhere in the world, with steward service and on-board washroom and toilets. They leave from the normal bus station, and it is advisable to check current departure times a day in advance, when you can also buy your tickets.

A leap down from the coaches are the Express buses run between one and five times daily along most major routes, stopping only at large towns. Express buses covering the 311km between Lilongwe and Blantyre stop only at Dedza, Ntcheu, Balaka, Liwonde and Zomba, and typically they take four to five hours and cost US$6. Other useful Express services include Lilongwe to Karonga (via

CYCLING IN MALAWI

Taken from a letter by Wim van Hoom

We found that most parts of Malawi are very suitable for riding a bicycle. Since one of our bikes didn't arrive in Malawi, we had to buy a local mountain bike. This wasn't up to the standard of a European or American bike, but it was adequate and very cheap at around US$100. Generally, a mountain bike will cost a bit more than this (around US$120–150 including rear pannier and mudguards) and you will be able to arrange to sell it back to the shopkeeper at the end of your trip, so there's a good case for buying your bike after you arrive rather than flying one over to Malawi.

For long hauls, bicycles can easily be transported on the roof of a bus or minibus for a small fee, but you can expect minor damages to the paintwork, and should ask for help when you load and unload them. Suitable straps are available in the main bus stations, and we preferred to let a Malawian fasten the bike, because they are more aware of the do's and don'ts of handling baggage.

We did some cycling on surfaced roads, but we preferred not to, especially in the vicinity of large towns, because they can be very busy and some people drive like mad dogs. Drivers in Malawi expect a cyclist to make

Kasungu, Mzimba, Chikengawa, Mzuzu, Rumphi and Chilumba), Nkhata Bay to Blantyre (via Chintheche, Nkhotakota and Salima), Blantyre to Mulanje (via Thyolo) and Blantyre to Monkey Bay (via Zomba, Liwonde and Mangochi). As a rule, the Express buses are fast and efficient, but they do sometimes break down or suffer from problems that slow them down. A country bus may come to the rescue when an Express bus covering the same route breaks down, at which point you have to accept that it's not your day and that you've effectively paid an Express bus fare to be on a country bus.

Shire Bus Co country buses follow the same routes as Express buses, as well as several more obscure routes, but they are much slower because they stop at every bus stage (there's a stage every 2km or so in some parts of the country). As a rule of thumb, expect a country bus to take twice as long as an Express bus covering the same route. The difference in timing between Express and country buses is not normally significant over short distances, so my policy when hopping between nearby places was simply to take the first bus that left. Over longer distances, I'd wait for an Express bus wherever possible. Further details of country bus routes are given in the *Getting around* and *Getting there and away* sections throughout the regional part of this guide.

An increasing number of private buses operate main routes through Malawi. Based on our experience, these are generally even slower than country buses, stopping wherever anybody wants them to.

As a final note, a few people have told me horror stories about slow bus rides and breakdowns in Malawi, and some have moaned that this and other guides to Malawi haven't prepared them for this happening. Our general way for them by pulling over to the verge, a reflex we hadn't developed, and a habit that wastes time when you are trying to cover a lot of distance.

The dust roads were more interesting and enjoyable, and allow you to explore areas inacessible to travellers dependent on public transport. We passed through many small villages where travellers are a relative novelty, and were always met with great enthusiasm and hospitality. It was always easy to organise somewhere to pitch a tent, and often local people would help us find food. We normally paid the villagers the equivalent to what we would have paid for a room or meal in a basic local resthouse. The small resthouses along the way were also an unforgettable experience (not least because we regularly bumped our heads against the low door frames!).

The 1:250,000 maps we bought in Lilongwe and Blantyre proved to be excellent for route finding. Contrary to what we had been told (and to our own experiences in other countries), we were never pointed in the wrong direction by somebody who didn't want to 'disappoint' us. It happened more than once that somebody we stopped to ask for directions walked with us to show us a good short cut. The only navigational problem we had was that some village names are incorrect on the maps, but asking for another village in the same direction always solved this.

experience has been that buses are reliable in Malawi, but things can go wrong. Short of adding the clause 'but it could take longer if the vehicle breaks down' after every bus timing, there's not much that any travel guide can do about it.

Other road transport

On most routes in Malawi, and especially where there is no official public transport, bus services are replaced or supplemented by an informal *matola* system of paid lifts. The majority of *matola* vehicles are minibuses, which cover a route for the specific purpose of carrying passengers, making them the Malawian equivalent of the *matatu* and shared taxi transport you find elsewhere in Africa. *Matola* lifts may also come from private individuals who want to make a bit of extra cash from a journey that they're undertaking anyway. In both cases, there is normally a fixed fare for *matola* rides along any given route, and on routes where there are buses, this is generally the same as the bus fare. The main advantage of a *matola* lift is not that it is cheaper than a bus, but that you will get to your destination more quickly. In my opinion, this is outweighed by the reality that many private vehicles are in poor repair and minibuses in particular are frequently driven by drunken lunatics. Our policy in Malawi and elsewhere in Africa is to use buses where we can, and to hop in the death traps only where we have no other option.

Hitching

Hitchhiking is generally slow in Malawi, and many of the lifts you will be offered will expect payment. I met a few travellers who were quite indignant about this, so I should clarify that paying for lifts is the accepted custom in Malawi. The line between hitching and *matola* rides is at best blurred, and it is reasonable to expect that practically any lift you get with a Malawian will be on a paying basis.

If you get a free lift, it will probably be with an expatriate or an Asian or Malawian businessman. The only road in Malawi where it's very easy to get a free lift is the M1 between Blantyre and Lilongwe. The lakeshore road from Nkhata Bay to Mangochi can also be good for hitching, though my experience suggested that lifts on this road are very erratic and unpredictable. I found hitching along the M1 between Lilongwe and Karonga to be a dead loss. Unless it's a point of pride that you hitch everywhere, the sensible policy in Malawi is to flag down whatever vehicle passes your way, take the odd free lift when fortune favours you, but otherwise be prepared to pay.

ACCOMMODATION
Detailed accommodation listings for specific places of interest are given in the regional part of the guide, but the following overview should help readers be prepared for what to expect.

Tourist-class hotels
There has been a marked increase in options at this end of the range in recent years. Tourist-class hotels and lodges in Malawi are generally clean and well run, though by international standards some of them seem rather expensive for the facilities on offer.

The only chain of tourist-class hotels is the French-based Le Meridien Group, which has units in Blantyre, Lilongwe, Mzuzu, Zomba Plateau and at Nkopola (on the Lake Malawi shore between Mangochi and Monkey Bay). All these hotels offer air-conditioned accommodation with 24-hour room service, business facilities and satellite television. Other genuine tourist hotels include Mvuu Lodge (Liwonde National Park), Livingstonia Beach Hotel (Senga Bay), Club Makokola (on the lakeshore near Mangochi), Lifupa Lodge (Kasungu National Park), Chintheche Inn (Chintheche) and Chilinda Camp (Nyika National Park). All tourist-class hotels accept the major credit cards.

Cheaper accommodation
Most of the accommodation in Malawi comprises private resthouses aimed primarily at the local market. Typically, such resthouses offer cell-like rooms for around US$1–3, and as a rule they are rather scruffy and run-down, though no more so than similar accommodation elsewhere in Africa. Many local resthouses double as brothels, renting rooms not only by the night, but also by the hour (under the delightful euphemism of bed-resting). That said, a bit of grime and noise aside, there is no reason why travellers should have any qualms about staying in local resthouses: the risk of theft or catching sanitation-related diseases is negligible.

In addition to private resthouses, there is a council resthouse in most major towns in Malawi. It is difficult to make a general comparison between council and private resthouses, as standards and prices vary greatly. On the whole I would say that council resthouses offer poorer value for money, but there are plenty of exceptions.

In most larger towns, you'll find one or two motels which offer self-contained rooms with hot showers for around US$10 (sometimes a lot cheaper). Along the Lake Malawi shore, there are several resorts with rooms of a similar standard and at a similar price to motels in towns.

The ten or so resthouses run by the Forestry Department deserve highlighting. Not only do they offer wonderful value for money, but also they make excellent bases from which to explore Malawi's little-visited forest reserves. The Forestry resthouses generally have self-contained rooms at a cost of US$5 per person, and facilities include hot showers, a fridge, a fully-equipped kitchen, and the free services of a cook.

Malawi, as elsewhere in southern Africa, has several backpacker hostels, most of which are owned or managed by former travellers and overland truck divers. Most of these places offer a combination of private rooms and dormitories for around US$5 per person. Among the more popular hostels are Doogle's in Blantyre, and Kiboko in Lilongwe. There are also many backpacker-oriented hostels and resorts along the length of the Lake Malawi shore. So rapidly have these places sprouted up that a great many backpackers now manage to travel through Malawi using them exclusively.

Almost every Forestry resthouse, national park, backpackers' hostel and lakeshore resort in Malawi allows camping, typically at a cost of around US$3 per person.

EATING AND DRINKING
Restaurants
At tourist-class hotels and a few other restaurants in the major towns, you can eat food that comes close to international standards at a very reasonable price – there are few upmarket restaurants in Malawi where you can't eat well for under US$7 for a main course.

Otherwise, eating out in Malawi is a predictable and somewhat dull affair. The good thing about this is that meals are very inexpensive (at a local restaurant you'll rarely pay more than US$2), the bad thing that food is generally very bland and there is little in the way of variety.

The staple diet in Malawi is *nsima*, a stiff porridge made from pounded maize meal boiled in water. *Nsima* will be familiar to visitors from East Africa under the name of *ugali*, and to people from southern Africa as *mieliemeal*. Few travellers develop a taste for *nsima*, so it is fortunate that most local restaurants also serve rice and potato chips (or occasionally cassava or sweet potato chips).

Restaurants serve *nsima* or rice with a small serving of stew. This is most often made with chicken (*mkuku*) or beef (*nyama ngombe*). If you are hungry, you can ask for an extra serving of stew, though this will often double the price of the meal. Along with the meat stew, you will often get a sharp-tasting dollop of stewed cassava or pumpkin leaves (*chisisito*), or a heap of stewed beans.

Along the lake and in some larger towns, the monotony of bland chicken and beef stews is broken by fresh fish (*nsomba*), which may be served either in a stew or else fried whole. Popular fish include *chambo* (a type of tilapia), *kampango* (a type of catfish) and *mpasa* (a large cichlid with dark flesh that is often referred to as lake salmon). The most widely available fish in Malawi is *usipa*, a tiny fish which is generally sun-dried after it is caught. Few visitors to Malawi like the bitter taste of *usipa*.

Cooking for yourself

The alternative to eating at restaurants is to put together your own meals at markets and supermarkets. The variety of foodstuffs you can buy varies from season to season and from town to town, and sudden shortages of items which are normally readily available are to be expected. In most towns, you can buy fresh bread at the People's Trading Centre (PTC), the Kandodo supermarket, or at a bakery. PTC and Kandodo supermarkets also normally stock a variety of spreads: the locally manufactured jams are generally abysmal, but the peanut butter and honey are good, and you can also buy small sachets of Stork margarine. Other ready-to-eat food you can buy in most PTC and Kandodo supermarkets includes yoghurt, potato crisps, biscuits and sometimes cheese and cold meat.

Fruits and vegetables are best bought at markets, where they are very cheap. Potatoes, onions, tomatoes, bananas, sugar cane and some citrus fruits are available in most markets around the country. In larger towns and in agricultural areas a much wider selection of fruits and vegetables is available, for instance avocados, peas and beans, paw-paws, mangoes, coconuts and pineapples.

At most markets you can buy freshly fried potato chips for next to nothing. It is customary to try a couple of chips before you buy: do so, as sometimes they are very greasy. Grilled meat kebabs and chicken pieces are also cheap and tasty.

Fresh meat is very cheap in Malawi. A kilogram of beef costs around US$2–3 at most markets, and a whole chicken costs around US$4–5 depending on its size. Many PTC supermarkets sell frozen chickens and sausages, while supermarkets in larger towns sell high-grade meat at very reasonable prices (eg: fillet steak at around US$5/kg). A limited range of tinned goods (typically baked beans, soups and vegetables) is also available.

For hikers, packet soups are about the only dehydrated meals that are available throughout Malawi. I occasionally saw packets of dehydrated soya mince, which is tastier than the soups and makes for a more substantial meal. Dried staples such as rice, maize meal and pasta can be bought in supermarkets and markets.

Drinks

Brand-name soft drinks such as Pepsi, Coca-Cola and Fanta are widely available in Malawi and cheap by international standards. If the fizzy stuff doesn't appeal, you can buy imported South African fruit juices at most large supermarkets. Frozen fruit squashes are sold everywhere in Malawi for a few *tambala*; they're very sweet but otherwise quite refreshing on long walks and bus trips. Tap water is generally safe to drink in towns, but bottled mineral water is available if you prefer not to take the risk.

Traditional African beer is made of fermented maize or millet. It is brewed in villages for private consumption, and also brewed commercially to be sold in litre cartons. The most popular brand of traditional beer is the wonderfully titled *Chibuku Shake-Shake* (the latter half of the name refers to the need to shake the carton before opening), and special *Chibuku* bars can be found in most towns and villages. A carton of *Chibuku* is very cheap and, with its gruel-like texture, surprisingly rich in nutrients when compared with most alcoholic drinks. Unfortunately, African beer is something of an acquired taste: most travellers can't stand it, and it's taken me years of African travel to reach the point where I'll drink it with something approaching enjoyment when nothing else is available.

The Carlsberg Brewery in Blantyre produces a range of good, inexpensive bottled beers. Most visitors to Malawi settle on Carlsberg Green (named, like most Malawian beers, after the colour of its label), a light lager with 5% alcoholic content. A new Carlsberg beer which is proving popular is called Kuche Kuche (which means 'all night long'). It has a lower alcohol content of 3.7%, is sold in 500ml bottles and is cheaper than Green. Other visitors prefer the stronger Carlsberg Special Brew. Carlsberg produces two other brands of beer, Carlsberg Brown and Tuborg Red, both of which have a sweetish taste that doesn't appear to agree with many Western palates. Spirits such as cane, brandy and gin are manufactured locally, while a good variety of imported spirits is available in supermarkets and better bars.

South African wines are widely available in hotels, bars and supermarkets at prices which may faze most South Africans, but which will seem quite reasonable to overseas visitors.

BARGAINING AND OVERCHARGING

Tourists to Africa may sometimes need to bargain over prices, but this need is often exaggerated by guidebooks and travellers. In Malawi, there are very few situations where bargaining is necessary. Hotels, restaurants, supermarkets and buses charge fixed prices, and cases of overcharging are too unusual for it to be worth challenging a price unless it is blatantly ridiculous.

The main instance where bargaining is essential is when buying curios. What should be understood, however, is that the fact a curio seller is open to negotiation does not mean that you were initially being overcharged or ripped off. Curio sellers will generally quote a price knowing full well that you are going to bargain it down – they'd probably be startled if you didn't – and it is not necessary to respond aggressively or in an accusatory manner. It is impossible to say by how much you should bargain the initial price down (some people say that you should offer half the asking price and be prepared to settle at around two-thirds, but my experience is that curio sellers are far more whimsical than such advice suggests). The sensible approach, if you want to get a feel for prices, is to ask the price of similar items at a few different stalls before you actually contemplate buying anything.

Even when buying curios, it is possible to take bargaining too far. In Nkhotakota, I watched two travellers bargain with a Malawian who was selling a couple of statues he had almost certainly carved himself. The initial price asked (around US$1) was not unreasonable and the Malawian eventually settled on a much lower price. Still, the travellers weren't happy and they spent a full quarter of an hour beating him down by a further *kwacha*. It was evident to me that the carver's reluctant agreement to sell the statue at the lower price was motivated by desperation for cash. When dealing with individuals, as opposed to large curio stalls, I don't think it hurts to see the situation for what it is (somebody trying to scrape a living in difficult circumstances) and to be a little generous in your dealings.

It is normal for Africans to negotiate prices for market produce, though less so in Malawi than in most African countries. My experience in markets is that I was normally asked the going rate straight off. This doesn't mean you can't bargain prices down a little, but I would query whether it is really worth the effort – the general mentality in Malawi (unlike that in some other African countries) is not to overcharge tourists, and it seems appropriate to respond to this by being reasonably trusting.

Malawian hotels, like those in so many other countries these days, have a local residents' rate, a non-residents' rate and, sometimes, an in-between one for residents of other African countries. I found that these rates are often negotiable, especially if the hotel is almost empty.

HASSLES
Crime

In 1995, when the first edition of this guide was researched, Malawi was one of the most crime-free countries in Africa. Sadly this has changed, and while nowhere in Malawi is yet challenging Johannesburg or Nairobi as the regional crime capital, tourists do need to be alert to the risk of armed crime and casual theft. I've heard several explanations for this sudden increase in crime, but it is probably linked to the poverty created by the devaluation of the *kwacha* in recent years, as well as the breakdown of the migrant labour system to South Africa.

It is difficult to strike the right balance when discussing crime in a country such as Malawi. I firmly believe that an analytical understanding of how and where you are most likely to become a victim of crime in any given country serves not only to help you prevent being becoming a victim yourself, but also – and no less important – lets you relax in situations where crime really isn't a serious concern. It is important to recognise that African cultures are inherently honest, more so perhaps than ours, and that to the average Malawian theft is unspeakably wrong, to the extent that petty thieves are regularly killed by mob justice. The reason why tourists are often robbed is not because Malawi has a large criminal element, but because *wazungu* (white person, or foreigner) are easily identified as targets (and that includes backpackers, who habitually tell Africans that they are 'poor' travellers, oblivious to the simple truth that their extended travels are beyond the financial reach of practically every Malawian they meet, and that their backpack alone probably cost more money than would pass through the hands of many Malawians in a year). The point is that small-town and rural Malawi remains safe for travel, because Malawians in general wouldn't think of robbing a tourist, and that crime is largely restricted to large towns (where petty thieves often work the markets and bus stations targeting locals and tourists alike) and at a handful of places where large numbers of tourists congregate.

Unlike most African countries, crime against tourists doesn't yet seem to be a major problem in urban areas. Residents of Lilongwe and Blantyre say there has been a notable rise in house burglary and car hijacking in these cities, and the market area of Lilongwe is definitely dodgy. Otherwise, everybody we spoke to agreed that there was no significant risk attached to walking around the city centres by day, and we felt perfectly comfortable doing so. This will probably change, however, so ask local advice, and don't tempt fate by wandering alone along unlit streets or going out at night with more money than you need. In African cities generally, tourists are robbed and hassled on the streets far more often than expatriates; you are far less likely to draw attention by wearing trousers or a skirt with a button-up shirt or blouse than by donning the traveller 'uniform' of shorts and a T-shirt. And if you can, leave that give-away daypack in your hotel room – when we spend a few days in one African city, we are repeatedly struck by how much more hassle we attract on the days when we need to carry a daypack. Finally, when in doubt, *use a taxi* – they are very cheap in the cities.

In Malawi, crime against tourists occurs mostly in a few particular 'trouble spots' along the lakeshore. The pattern appears to be a sudden outbreak of mugging and snatch thefts in one particular resort, followed by a quiet period, indicating that these robberies are largely the work of one particular gang which is eventually arrested or moves on. Nkhata Bay, Cape Maclear and Salima have all experienced problems of this sort in the last year or two, so your best course of action is to be cautious when you first arrive at one of these places, and to ask local advice once you are settled in. Several travellers have been mugged of late on the way to Livingstonia; at the time of writing I would advise against hiking along this road. Camping wild on parts of the lakeshore is no longer advisable anywhere in Malawi, and we've heard of several instances of tents being broken into at 'proper' campsites.

You should be cautious of people who befriend you on buses and offer you food or drink, because it appears that the practice of doping travellers in this manner has spread into Malawi. We met somebody working in Nkhata Bay who was offered a sealed fruit juice carton by a fellow bus passenger, robbed of everything, and has no memory of the next three days. It's worth noting that a con trick of this sort is most likely to be perpetrated by a smartly dressed, smooth-talking guy who can easily build up a rapport with a traveller.

During our travels in Malawi, we've not heard of many incidents of casual theft and pickpocketing, but it does happen from time to time. Casual theft of this sort is largely confined to busy markets and bus stations, where you should keep a close watch on your possessions at all times and avoid having valuables or large amounts of money loose in your daypack or pocket. In any public area, it is advisable to carry all your valuables and the bulk of your money in a *hidden* money-belt. In order not to show your money-belt in public, remember to keep whatever spare cash you are likely to need elsewhere on your person. It is also a good idea to keep a small amount of hard currency hidden away somewhere in your luggage so that you have something to fall back on if your money-belt is stolen.

Many travellers carry their money-belt on their person at all times, even when they walk around a city at night. I must admit that I find this strange behaviour, and where I have the choice I generally feel safer leaving my valuables in a locked room than carrying them on me. Why? Because over the years I've been travelling in Africa, I've met hundreds of people who've been mugged or had their valuables snatched on the streets or on a beach, but I've heard of very few instances of a locked room being broken into. Obviously, an element of judgement comes into this, and if a room strikes me as being insecure or the hotel has a bad reputation, then I wouldn't leave anything of importance in it. When you leave stuff in a room, do remember to check that the windows are sealed and the door is properly locked. One factor to be considered here is that some travellers' cheque companies will not refund cheques which were stolen from a room. Finally, don't bring any jewellery of financial or sentimental value with you.

The last thing I would want is for the above to strike terror or evoke paranoia in travellers to Malawi. On the whole, Malawi remains a remarkably friendly and honest country, qualities which really did strike us afresh on our 2002 trip. Anybody can be unlucky when it comes to crime, but on the whole, so long as you conduct yourself sensibly and listen to local advice, you have little to fear. The reason for the detailed analysis above is that what most often gets travellers into trouble is one moment of recklessness – walking around Nkhata Bay at night with a money-belt on, wandering around Lilongwe market with a daypack dangling off your shoulder, dithering in a city bus station with a map in your hand and puzzled expression on your face, arriving in a city at night and not using a taxi to get to a hotel. Our policy, developed over years of African travel, is to focus our energy on recognising high-risk situations, particularly those where our valuables are at stake, and doing all we can to avoid them. The rest of the time, we don't worry about crime!

Women travellers

Sub-equatorial Africa as a whole is probably one of the safest places in the world for women to travel solo. Malawi in particular poses few, if any, risks specific to female travellers, provided that they apply the same sort of common sense they would at home. Women travelling alone may have to put up with some unwanted flirtation and the odd direct proposition, especially if they mingle with Malawians in bars, but a firm 'no' should defuse any potentially unpleasant situation. Men in Malawi probably constitute less of a sexual hassle than men in many Western countries, and for that matter than other male travellers.

Years ago, it was forbidden for women to wear trousers or short skirts in Malawi, and even today most Malawian women dress conservatively. We're not certain how much Malawians expect these dress customs to apply to tourists. Some foreigners working in Malawi feel that it would give offence for a woman to walk around in anything but a skirt or sarong. We tend towards the unfashionable but less patronising view that most Malawians, certainly those who are used to tourists, have better things to worry about than how we choose to dress ourselves. On the other hand, it would be insensitive for a woman traveller to wear shorts or a revealing top in an area where there is a strong Muslim presence, or where tourists are still relatively unusual. The difference is that to many Africans (and to Muslims in particular), exposing your knees or shoulders is indecent and offensive, in much the same way as displaying your breasts publicly would be in a Western society. By contrast, wearing trousers may go against custom, and may even raise a few eyebrows where people are unused to seeing it, but it doesn't amount to indecent exposure.

Any women readers (or men, for that matter) who are concerned about travelling alone in Malawi, but who can't find a travel companion, might be reassured by the thought that there are plenty of places in Malawi where it will be easy to meet with other travellers. You'll find plenty of kindred spirits at the hostels in Blantyre and Lilongwe, or at any of the lakeshore resorts, and there's a lot to be said for hooking up with people along the way – better, by far, than making an advance commitment to travelling with somebody who you don't know well enough to be sure they'll be a suitable travel companion.

Bribery, bureaucracy and the law

For all you hear about the subject, bribery is not the problem for travellers that it's often made out to be. The travellers who are most often asked for bribes are those with private transport; and even they only have a major problem at some borders and from traffic police in some countries (notably Mozambique and Kenya). If you are travelling on public transport or as part of a tour, or even if you are driving within Malawi, I wouldn't give the question of bribery serious thought.

There is a tendency to portray African bureaucrats as difficult and inefficient in their dealings with tourists. As a rule, this reputation says more about Western prejudices that it does about Malawi. Sure, you come across the odd unhelpful official, but then such is the nature of the beast everywhere in the world. The vast majority of officials in the African countries I've visited have been courteous and helpful in their dealings with tourists, often to a degree that is almost embarrassing. In Malawi, I encountered nothing but friendliness from almost every government official I had dealings with, whether they were border officials, policemen or game reserve staff. This, I can assure you, is far more than most African visitors to Europe will experience from officialdom.

A factor in determining the response you receive from African officials will be your own attitude. If you walk into every official encounter with an aggressive, paranoid approach, you are quite likely to kindle the feeling held by many Africans that Europeans are arrogant and offhand in their dealings with other races. Instead, try to be friendly and patient, accept that the person to whom you are talking does not speak English as a first language and may thus have difficulty following everything you say. Treat people with respect rather than disdain, and they'll tend to treat you in the same way.

From a traveller's point of view, then, the simple truth about dealing with the law in Malawi is that so long as you don't break it, you're highly unlikely to fall foul of it or to have to worry about it. It should be emphasised, however, that it is highly illegal to possess or smoke marijuana (*chamba*), and that the government has recently cracked down on travellers who smoke the stuff by raiding several backpacker hostels and placing police informants to act as dealers. There are hostels in Malawi where marijuana is smoked fairly openly, but this doesn't affect the reality that travellers who are caught in the act or in possession risk at best paying a hefty 'fine' or being deported, at worst being prosecuted and jailed. Travellers who carry marijuana across international borders, no matter what their intention, are, legally speaking, drug smugglers, in Africa as elsewhere, and they will be treated as such if they are caught.

As is the case in many African countries, homosexuality is officially illegal in Malawi, but not something that local people are greatly aware of. It would take an act of overt exhibitionism for it ever to become an issue for travellers.

CURIOS

Malawi is known as one of the best places in southern Africa for curios, in terms of both price and quality, and the cheap surface mail from Malawi makes shipping out your purchases a viable prospect. Among the more popular items of sale are polished soapstone carvings, malachite jewellery, and a wide range of basketwork and pottery items. But Malawi is best known for its hardwood carvings, and for the carved wooden chairs which dominate the stalls in the larger cities. Just remember though, every purchase has contributed to the demise of a rare hardwood tree.

Though curios cannot be described as expensive anywhere in Malawi, they are generally cheapest away from Blantyre, Lilongwe and the more popular lakeshore resorts. You must expect to bargain over prices, and should also be aware that many curio sellers will be as happy to barter their wares against used clothing.

Two places that have been recommended as being particularly good value are the stalls at the Mangochi turn-off 3km from Liwonde town, which specialise in carvings, and the stalls 1km from Machinga towards Liwonde, which are good for chairs. There are also several good curio stalls in Salima, Nkopola and Nkhata Bay.

MEDIA AND COMMUNICATIONS
Post
International post in and out of Malawi is slow and unreliable: allow at least three weeks for mail to get through. Mail out of Malawi is very cheap, particularly surface mail, which makes it an excellent place from where to post curios.

A poste restante service is available in all large towns. Most travellers are likely to use Lilongwe or Blantyre for this purpose. Ask mail to be addressed as in the following example:

Philip Briggs
Poste Restante
Lilongwe
Malawi

Mail is filed in alphabetic pigeon holes under surnames. When you collect your mail, it's advisable to check under the initial of both your first name and surname, as misfiling of letters is commonplace. As a courtesy to other travellers, you might also want to pick out any letters which you notice have been misfiled, and to hand them to the person behind the counter. Cost is US$0.50.

A far better means of communication now is email, which is available at all the large international hotels, internet cafés and bureaux in large towns and at some backpackers' lodges and tourist resorts (see listings in the regional part of the guide).

For express courier and parcel service, DHL are well represented in Malawi.

Telephone
All telephone numbers in Malawi have eight digits and, presumably because there are so few phones in the country, there are no area codes. The international dialling code for Malawi is 265.

The mobile phone network in Malawi is operated by two companies – TNM carries the prefix digits 08 and Celtel uses 09. International roaming with your mobile phone from home is also possible.

Small it may be, but Malawi's telephone service is reasonably efficient by African standards, and lines are generally clear. Phone booths, some of which actually work, can be found outside most post offices.

Newspapers
Malawi has a free press, and a number of newspapers are available, most of which are printed in English, but, it must be said, are of little interest beyond their coverage of local politics and local sport.

The Times Bookshops in Blantyre, Lilongwe, Mzuzu and Zomba stock *The Weekly Telegraph, The Weekly Express* and *The Mail & Guardian* (the southern African edition of *The Weekly Guardian*), all of which sell for around US$3 in Malawi.

Television

There is an erratic state television service in Malawi. The televisions found in hotels and in private homes pick up satellite broadcasts from South Africa, including Sky-TV and CNN.

ELECTRICITY

Malawi uses the British three square-pin plug and a 240 volt supply, so take adapters and transformers if necessary.

COMMUNICATING WITH MALAWIANS

As many as 40 different Bantu languages are spoken in Malawi. Of these, Chichewa has become the *lingua franca* of the southern and central regions, a role which is usurped by Chitumbuka in the northern region.

The official language of Malawi is English. Most education takes place in the official language, and so a high proportion of urban Malawians speak fair English. Even in rural areas, it is most unusual to hit the sort of situation you might in some other African countries where nobody speaks a word of English. For this reason, unless you plan on spending a long time in Malawi, there is very little motivation to learn local languages. That said, it is polite to

MY GAP YEAR AT ST THERESA PRIVATE SCHOOL
Pete Bexton

I was sent to Malawi by a gap-year organisation called Project Trust, which specialises in 12-month placements. I was working as a volunteer teacher at St Theresa Primary School in Chiwembe, a township on the outskirts of Blantyre. The school was set up by Mrs Kotokwa, a local Malawian, in 1994. Initially she rented a single room in a decrepit government building, where she had three pupils in different classes and only two teachers – herself and one other. As can be imagined, this was a task in itself; however, after much dedication, she now owns her own land and buildings. Over 300 pupils attend the school and she has 20 trained teachers working alongside her. Although incomplete due to lack of funds, St Theresa is improving greatly because of the dedication and perseverance of both Mrs Kotokwa and the teachers.

Government schools in Malawi are free, but the standard of education is very poor and classes are grossly overcrowded. Classes may consist of up to 150 pupils, with a maximum of two teachers in charge. At present the school day lasts from 07:30 to 15:00, and consists of nine lessons, a morning break and a lunch break. St Theresa is a private school, so classes range from nursery to Standard 8, equivalent to an English primary school. Children's ages range from three years up to 16 or 17; this is because children have to re-sit classes if they fail. Occasionally a child will miss a year's schooling to help support his or her family. As with an English school, St Theresa's pupils study English, mathematics, French, religious education, general studies, science and drawing. Although the national language is know the basic greetings and to be able to respond to them, and it is always true that even the most clumsy attempt to speak a local language will go a long way to making friends in Africa.

Bantu languages

Chichewa is classified as a Bantu language, a linguistic group that had its origin in West Africa about 2,000 years ago, and which now includes practically every language spoken in sub-equatorial Africa. Bantu languages share a common pronunciation and grammar, and many have closely related vocabularies – if you speak one Bantu language, be it Swahili, Shona or Zulu, you will recognise many words that are similar or identical in Chichewa. For pronunciation and phrases, see *Language,* page 247.

Speaking English to Malawians

If you have ever attempted to speak a foreign language, you will probably have noticed that your skill at communicating is largely dependent on the imagination and empathy of the person you are speaking to. The moment some people realise you speak a few words of their language, they will speak to you as if you are fluent and make you feel thoroughly hopeless. Other

Chichewa, all subjects are taught in English. Since Malawi is such a poor country, and the school has very limited funds, the children have no bought toys. Sports equipment is non-existent and textbooks are old, incomplete and few and far between. However, the children are used to their lack of recourses and are able to make games using both balls and rope made out of plastic bags. Although their games are simple, they find great enjoyment in them, and they are very innovative when they need a new pastime.

In Malawi, the next stage of education after primary school is secondary school. To get to secondary school, the children must pass the General Certificate of Education (GCE) at the end of Standard 8. Children who do not pass the GCE have either to pay fees and go to a private school, or stop their education. Due to this there are a large number of children in Malawi that do not continue their education after about the age of 13.

My role at St Theresa was the same as any other teacher. I had a full timetable every day of the week, and I had my roster of doing break and lunch duties. This is one of the things that made my year even more enjoyable, as I was on the same level as all the other teachers, and was able to make friends with them as an equal. I was also able to give the teachers a Western perspective on teaching methods, and help with timetabling the school day. By working alongside the Malawians and developing close friendships with them, I hope they came to view white people as equal to themselves and not of higher intelligence.

It was a great privilege working alongside the Malawians, and I learnt more in this year than I ever could have hoped.

people will take care to speak slowly and to stick to common words, and as a result you feel like you're making real progress. The same sort of thing applies in reverse: when you speak English to somebody who knows it only as a second language, the ease of communication will to a large extent reflect your own ability to adapt your use of English to the situation.

The standard of English spoken in Malawi is much higher than in most African countries. Many educated Malawians speak English fluently and grammatically, and in such cases few adjustments are required on the part of the tourist. Nevertheless, the majority of Malawians who speak English have a relatively small vocabulary, use many words idiosyncratically, and tend to use phrasings and pronunciations which are obviously derived from Bantu grammar. Because so much English is spoken in Malawi, it is arguable that adjusting your use of English to reflect Malawian norms will prove to be a more important communication skill than would picking up a few phrases of Chichewa. If this seems fanciful, I can only say that after six African trips I have almost unconsciously (but more recently with some thought) acquired a kind of 'African English', and that I am regularly told by Africans how much easier they find it to understand me than they do most native English speakers.

The first and most obvious rule when speaking English to Malawians is to talk slowly and clearly. If you are not understood, there is little point in repeating the same phrase more loudly. Instead, look for less complex ways of conveying the same idea.

Listen to how Malawians pronounce words. Often, they will use Bantu vowel sounds even when speaking English (just as many English speakers use English vowel sounds when attempting to speak a Bantu language), and they may also carry across the Bantu practice of stressing the second last syllable. For instance, a word like 'important' may be pronounced more like 'eem-POT-int'. Another common habit is inserting vowel sounds between running consonants (for instance 'penpal' might be pronounced 'pin-EE-pel') or at the end of words (*basi* for 'bus'). It would be a little ridiculous to completely adjust your pronunciation along these lines, but it is helpful to bear this sort of thing in mind when attempting to decipher what somebody is saying to you, or when you are having difficulty being understood by somebody with limited English. And it is essential when pronouncing place names that you follow Bantu vowel sounds, or often you won't be understood.

Remember, too, that there is always a tendency to use the grammatical phrasing of your home tongue when you speak a second language. In most Bantu languages, the majority of enquiries are made by making a statement in an enquiring tone of voice. 'There is a room?' is more likely to be understood than 'Do you have a room?' 'This bus is going to Lilongwe?' is better than 'Do you know whether this bus is going to Lilongwe?'

Many English speakers are inclined to fluff straightforward queries to strangers with apologetic phrasing like 'I'm terribly sorry' or 'could you tell me'. Much of the time, in an African context, this sort of thing just obstructs communication. In a similar vein, colloquial phrases and terms such as 'mate' can only cause confusion: if you ask somebody for a 'Coke mate', they are unlikely to know what a cokemate is. Make your questions as direct as possible. Bear in mind, however, that politeness is most important in African cultures. Instead of asking long-winded questions, go through the greetings (in English or Chichewa) before you ask anything.

You will find that certain common English words are readily understood by Malawians, while other equally common words draw a complete blank. For instance, practically anybody will know what you mean by a resthouse, but they may well be confused if you ask where you can find accommodation. Another example of this is the phrase 'It is possible?', which for some reason has caught on almost everywhere in Africa. 'It is possible to find a bus?' is more likely to be understood than 'Do you know if there is a bus?' Likewise, 'Is not possible' is a more commonly used phrase than 'It is impossible'. This sort of thing can occur on an individual level as well as on a general one, so listen out for words which are favoured by somebody with whom you have a lengthy conversation.

MALAWI BY WHEELCHAIR (AND A 4WD)

Brian and Ruth Thomson

We entered Malawi via Mandimba. The border crossing was smooth, and the road to Mangochi very good, although Mangochi itself was a little run down. The bakery only had doughnuts but the supermarket had basics.

We stayed the first night in **Blantyre** at Doogles. We had to camp in the car park as you couldn't drive on to the campsite. Even if you could, there are steps into the bar and reception, and into the ablution block, which would make it quite difficult for a wheelchair. On the plus side, though, they have a happy hour twice a week, which is good value!

In **Limbe** we went to City Motors – a good place to get spares for the car. The ATMs shouldn't be relied on – we had to exchange money at Rennies. We then planned to stay in Zomba but the weather was awful so we decided to continue to **Senga Bay**. We had a great night in the Wheelhouse, where the bar presented no problems for Brian, and access to the ablutions block was easy as well.

Continuing north, the roads were good, and the road through to Kande Beach excellent – no more problems at the causeway. At **Kande Beach** we could drive right to the bar. We stayed in the crew rooms/chalets which were great for Brian, though this may not be possible for every traveller. The beach was almost non-existent due to the high level of the lake but we were assured that it would return. In October 2003 Kande are having a massive party to celebrate their tenth anniversary.

From here we drove to **Chitimba** and from there up to Livingstonia. It took us nearly an hour to get up, but the views were well worth the effort. A local company will drive you up – just enquire at Chitimba Beach Campsite. We stayed in one of their rooms without problem. Camping here would also have been straightforward and, although the sand would have made it hard with the wheelchair, there were plenty of people to help.

Finally, it was an easy drive to the border – only the last few kilometres before the border north of Karonga are potholes.

As Malawi is said to be one of the safest places to visit in Africa and the roads are so good, it is not a bad place for someone to start off their Africa experience. With a little help, the country is fine for a wheelchair user. Things are quite basic and showers tend to be cold but toilets very clean. People are very helpful and most speak good English – quite a treat after Mozambique to be understood again!

Brian Thomson was paralysed in an accident while doing routine maintenance on an overland truck in Kariba, Zimbabwe. A year later, in 2003, he returned to Africa on a six-month overland trip from Cape Town to Ethiopia to raise awareness of how 'able' one can be in a wheelchair and to highlight the cause of disabled people throughout the continent.

Health

Dr Jane Wilson-Howarth and Dr Felicity Nicholson

PREPARATIONS

Preparations to ensure a healthy trip to Malawi require checks on your immunisation status: it is wise to be up to date on tetanus (ten-yearly), polio (ten-yearly), diphtheria (ten-yearly), and for many parts of Africa immunisations against yellow fever, meningococcus, rabies, and hepatitis A are also needed. Yellow fever is not required for Malawi alone, but may be necessary if you are travelling through other African countries further north.

Hepatitis A vaccine (Havrix Monodose or Avaxim) comprises two injections given about a year apart. The course costs about £100, but protects for ten years. It is now felt that the vaccine can be used even close to the time of departure and has replaced the old fashioned gamma globulin. The newer **typhoid** vaccines (eg: Typhim Vi) last for three years and are about 85% effective. They should be encouraged unless the traveller is leaving within a few days for a trip of a week or less, when the vaccine would not be effective in time. **Meningitis** vaccine (containing strains ACW and Y) is also recommended, especially for trips of more than four weeks (see *Meningitis*). Immunisation against cholera is no longer required for Malawi. Vaccinations for **rabies** are advised for travellers visiting more remote areas (see *Rabies*). **Hepatitis B** vaccination should be considered for longer trips (two months or more) or for those working with children or in situations where contact with blood is likely. Three injections are needed for the best protection and can be given over a four-week period if time is short. Longer schedules give more sustained protection and are therefore preferred if time allows. A BCG vaccination against **tuberculosis** (TB) is also advised for trips of two months or more.

Ideally you should visit your own doctor or a specialist travel clinic (see pages 84–6) to discuss your requirements about eight weeks before you plan to travel.

Malaria prevention

There is no vaccine against malaria, but there are other ways to avoid it; since most of Malawi is very high risk for malaria, travellers must plan their malaria protection properly. Seek current advice on the best antimalarials to take. If mefloquine (Lariam) is suggested, start this two-and-a-half weeks (three doses) before departure to check that it suits you; stop it immediately if it seems to cause depression or anxiety, visual or hearing disturbances, severe headaches, fits or changes in heart rhythm. Side effects such as nightmares or

LONG-HAUL FLIGHTS
Felicity Nicholson

There is growing evidence, albeit circumstantial, that long-haul air travel increases the risk of developing deep vein thrombosis. This condition is potentially life threatening, but it should be stressed that the danger to the average traveller is slight.

Certain risk factors specific to air travel have been identified. These include immobility, compression of the veins at the back of the knee by the edge of the seat, the decreased air pressure and slightly reduced oxygen in the cabin, and dehydration. Consuming alcohol may exacerbate the situation by increasing fluid loss and encouraging immobility.

In theory everyone is at risk, but those at highest risk are shown below:

• Passengers on journeys of longer than eight hours duration
• People over 40
• People with heart disease
• People with cancer
• People with clotting disorders
• People who have had recent surgery, especially on the legs
• Women on the pill or other oestrogen therapy
• Women who are pregnant
• People who are very tall (over 6ft/1.8m) or short (under 5ft/1.5m)

A deep vein thrombosis (DVT) is a clot of blood that forms in the leg veins. Symptoms include swelling and pain in the calf or thigh. The skin may feel hot to touch and becomes discoloured (light blue-red). A DVT

dizziness are not medical reasons for stopping unless they are sufficiently debilitating or annoying. Anyone who is pregnant, who has suffered fits in the past, has been treated for depression or psychiatric problems, has diabetes controlled by oral therapy or who is epileptic (or who has suffered fits in the past) or has a close blood relative who is epileptic, should avoid mefloquine.

Malarone (proguanil and atovaquone) is a new drug that is almost as effective as mefloquine. It has the advantage of having few side effects and need only be continued for one week after returning. However, it is expensive and because of this tends to be reserved for shorter trips. Malarone may not be suitable for everybody (it has yet to receive a licence for children under 40kg in the UK) so advice should be taken from a doctor.

The antibiotic doxycycline (100mg daily) is a viable alternative when either mefloquine or Malarone are not considered suitable for whatever reason. Like Malarone it can be started one day before arrival. Unlike mefloquine, it may also be used in travellers with epilepsy, although certain anti-epileptic medication may make it less effective. Users must be warned about the possibility of allergic skin reactions developing in sunlight, which can occur in about 3% of people. The drug should be stopped if this happens. Women is not dangerous in itself, but if a clot breaks down then it may travel to the lungs (pulmonary embolus). Symptoms of a pulmonary embolus (PE) include chest pain, shortness of breath and coughing up small amounts of blood.

Symptoms of a DVT rarely occur during the flight, and typically occur within three days of arrival, although symptoms of a DVT or PE have been reported up to two weeks later.

Anyone who suspects that they have these symptoms should see a doctor immediately as anticoagulation (blood thinning) treatment can be given.

Prevention of DVT

General measures to reduce the risk of thrombosis are shown below. This advice also applies to long train or bus journeys.

- Whilst waiting to board the plane, try to walk around rather than sit.
- During the flight drink plenty of water (at least two small glasses every hour).
- Avoid excessive tea, coffee and alcohol.
- Perform leg-stretching exercises, such as pointing the toes up and down.
- Move around the cabin when practicable.

If you fit into the high-risk category (see above) ask your doctor if it is safe to travel. Additional protective measures such as graded compression stockings, aspirin or low molecular weight heparin can be given. No matter how tall you are, where possible request a seat with extra legroom.

using the oral contraceptive should use an additional method of protection for the first four weeks when using doxycycline. It is also unsuitable in pregnancy or for children under 12 years old.

Chloroquine and proguanil are no longer considered to be very effective for Malawi. However, they may still be recommended if no other regime is suitable.

All prophylactic agents should be taken with or after the evening meal, washed down with plenty of fluid and with the exception of Malarone (see above) continued for four weeks after leaving.

Travellers to remote parts would probably be wise to carry a course of treatment to cure malaria. Experts differ on the costs and benefits of self-treatment, but agree that it leads to over-treatment and to many people taking drugs they do not need; yet treatment may save your life. Discuss your trip with a specialist to determine your particular needs and risks, and be sure you understand when and how to take the cure. If you are somewhere remote in a malarial region you probably have to assume that any high fever (over 38oC) for more than a few hours is due to malaria (regardless of any other symptoms) and should seek treatment. Diagnosing malaria is not easy, which is why consulting a doctor is sensible: there are other dangerous causes of fever in Africa, which require different treatments. Presently quinine and doxycycline, or quinine and fansidar, are the favoured regimes, but check for up-to-date advice on the current recommended treatment. And remember, malaria may occur anything from seven days into the trip to up to one year after leaving Africa.

The risk of malaria above 1,800m above sea level is low. It is unwise to travel in malarial parts of Africa, which includes most of Malawi, whilst pregnant or with children: the risk of malaria in many parts is considerable and these travellers are likely to succumb rapidly to the disease.

In addition to antimalarial medicines, it is important to avoid mosquito bites between dusk and dawn. Pack a DEET-based insect repellent, such as Repel (roll-ons or sticks are the least messy preparations for travelling). You also need either a permethrin-impregnated bednet or a permethrin spray so that you can 'treat' bednets in hotels. Permethrin treatment makes even very tatty nets protective and prevents mosquitoes from biting through the impregnated net when you roll against it; it also deters other biters. Putting on long clothes at dusk means you can reduce the amount of repellent you need to put on your skin, but be aware that malaria mosquitoes hunt at ankle level and will bite through socks, so apply repellent under socks too. Travel clinics usually sell a good range of nets, treatment kits and repellents.

Protection from the sun

Give some thought to packing suncream. The incidence of skin cancer is rocketing as Caucasians are travelling more and spending more time exposing themselves to the sun. Keep out of the sun during the middle of the day and, if you must be exposed to the sun, build up gradually from 20 minutes per day. Be especially careful of sun reflected off water and wear a T-shirt and lots of waterproof SPF15 suncream when swimming; snorkelling often leads to scorched backs of the thighs so wear bermuda shorts. Sun exposure ages the skin and makes people prematurely wrinkly; cover up with long, loose clothes and wear a hat when you can. The glare and the dust can be hard on the eyes, too, so bring UV-protecting sunglasses and, perhaps, a soothing eyebath.

Travel clinics and health information

A full list of current travel clinic websites worldwide is available on www.istm.org/. For other journey preparation information, consult ftp://ftp.shoreland.com/pub/shorecg.rtf or www.tripprep.com.

UK

British Airways Travel Clinic and Immunisation Service There are now only three BA clinics, all in London: 156 Regent St, W1B 5LB (no appointments); 101 Cheapside, EC1V 6DT (tel: 020 7606 2977); 115 Buckingham Palace Rd, SW1W 9SJ (Victoria Station; tel: 020 7233 6661); see also www.britishairways.com/travelclinics. Also sell a variety of health-related goods.

Above Roan antelope, *Hippotragus equinus*, on the Nyika Plateau, one of the easiest places to see this beautiful antelope in Central Africa

Left The lesser striped swallow, *Hirundo abyssinicus*, is one of the most handsome swallows found in Malawi

Below Bushbuck, *Tragelaphus scriptus*, are found in most wooded habitats in Malawi

Above Malawi chair stall, Nkhata Bay
Below Reed baskets for sale, Nkopola

Fleet Street Travel Clinic 29 Fleet St, London EC4Y 1AA; tel: 020 7353 5678
Hospital for Tropical Diseases Travel Clinic Mortimer Market Centre, 2nd
Floor, Capper St (off Tottenham Ct Rd), London WC1E 6AU; tel: 020 7388 9600;
web: www.thhtd.org. Offers consultations and advice, and is able to provide all
necessary drugs and vaccines for travellers. Runs a healthline (09061 337733) for
country-specific information and health hazards. Also stocks nets, water purification
equipment and personal protection measures.
MASTA (Medical Advisory Service for Travellers Abroad) Keppel St, London WC1
7HT; tel: 09068 224100. This is a premium-line number, charged at 50p per minute.
MASTA pre-travel clinics Tel: 01276 685040. Call for the nearest; there are
currently 30 in Britain. Also sell malaria prophylaxis memory cards, treatment kits,
bednets, net treatment kits.
NHS travel website, www.fitfortravel.scot.nhs.uk, provides country-by-country
advice on immunisation and malaria, plus details of recent developments, and a list of
relevant health organisations.
Nomad Travel Pharmacy and Vaccination Centre 3–4 Wellington Terrace,
Turnpike Lane, London N8 0PX; tel: 020 8889 7014; email:
sales@nomadtravel.co.uk; web: www.nomadtravel.co.uk. As well as dispensing health
advice, Nomad stocks mosquito nets and other anti-bug devices, and an excellent
range of adventure travel gear.
Thames Medical 157 Waterloo Rd, London SE1 8US; tel: 020 7902 9000.
Competitively priced, one-stop travel health service. All profits go to their affiliated
company, InterHealth, which provides health care for overseas workers on Christian
projects.
Trailfinders Immunisation Centre 194 Kensington High St, London W8 7RG; tel:
020 7938 3999.
Travelpharm The Travelpharm website, www.travelpharm.com, offers up-to-date
guidance on travel-related health and has a range of medications available through
their online mini-pharmacy.

Irish Republic
Tropical Medical Bureau Grafton Street Medical Centre, Grafton Buildings, 34
Grafton St, Dublin 2; tel: 1 671 9200. Has a useful website specific to tropical
destinations: www.tmb.ie

USA
Centers for Disease Control 1600 Clifton Rd, Atlanta, GA 30333; tel: 877 FYI
TRIP; 800 311 3435; web: www.cdc.gov/travel. The central source of travel
information in the USA. Each summer they publish the invaluable *Health
Information for International Travel*, available from the Division of Quarantine at the
above address.
Connaught Laboratories PO Box 187, Swiftwater, PA 18370; tel: 800 822 2463.
They will send a free list of specialist tropical-medicine physicians in your state.
IAMAT (International Association for Medical Assistance to Travelers) 736 Center
St, Lewiston, NY 14092; tel: 716 754 4883. A non-profit organisation that provides
lists of English-speaking doctors abroad.

Canada

IAMAT (International Association for Medical Assistance to Travellers) Suite 1, 1287 St Clair Av W, Toronto, Ontario M6E 1B8; tel: 416 652 0137; web: www.sentex.net/~iamat
TMVC (Travel Doctors Group) Sulphur Springs Rd, Ancaster, Ontario; tel: 905 648 1112; web: www.tmvc.com.au

Australia, New Zealand, Thailand

TMVC Tel: 1300 65 88 44; web: www.tmvc.com.au. 20 clinics in Australia, New Zealand and Thailand, including:
Auckland Canterbury Arcade, 170 Queen Street, Auckland City; tel: 373 3531
Brisbane Dr Deborah Mills, Qantas Domestic Building, 6th floor, 247 Adelaide St, Brisbane, QLD 4000; tel: 7 3221 9066; fax: 7 3321 7076
Melbourne Dr Sonny Lau, 393 Little Bourke St, 2nd floor, Melbourne, VIC 3000; tel: 3 9602 5788; fax: 3 9670 8394
Sydney Dr Mandy Hu, Dymocks Building, 7th Floor, 428 George St, Sydney, NSW2000; tel: 2 221 7133; fax: 2 221 8401

South Africa

SAA-Netcare Travel Clinics PO Box 786692, Sandton 2146; fax: 011 883 6152; web: www.travelclinic.co.za or www.malaria.co.za. Clinics throughout South Africa.
TMVC (Travel Doctor Group) 113 DF Malan Drive, Roosevelt Park, Johannesburg; tel: 011 888 7488; web: www.tmvc.com.au. Consult the website for details of clinics in South Africa.

Switzerland

IAMAT (International Association for Medical Assistance to Travellers) 57 Voirets, 1212 Grand Lancy, Geneva; web: www.sentex.net/~iamat

Travel insurance

Don't think about travelling without a comprehensive medical travel insurance policy, one that will fly you home in an emergency. There are innumerable policies available, and many of the travel clinics listed above sell their own versions, so do shop around for the best deal for you.

Personal first-aid kit

The more I travel, the less I take. My minimal kit contains:

- A good drying antiseptic, eg: iodine or potassium permanganate (don't take antiseptic cream)
- A few small dressings (Band-Aids)
- Suncream
- Insect repellent; malaria tablets; impregnated bednet
- Aspirin or paracetamol
- Antifungal cream (eg: Canesten)
- Ciprofloxacin antibiotic, 500mg x 2 (or norfloxacin) for severe diarrhoea

MEDICAL FACILITIES IN MALAWI
Philip Briggs
Private clinics, hospitals and pharmacies can be found in most large towns, and doctors generally speak fluent English. Consultation fees and laboratory tests are remarkably inexpensive when compared to most Western countries', so if you do fall sick it would be absurd to let financial considerations dissuade you from seeking medical help. Commonly required medicines such as broad spectrum antibiotics and Flagyl are widely available and cheap throughout the region, as are malaria cures and prophylactics. Fansidar and quinine tablets are best bought in advance – in fact it's advisable to carry all malaria related tablets on you, and only rely on their availability locally if you need to restock your supplies.

If you are on any medication prior to departure, or you have specific needs relating to a known medical condition (for instance if you are allergic to bee stings or you are prone to attacks of asthma), then you are strongly advised to bring any related drugs and devices with you.

- Tinidazole (500mg X 8) for giardia or amoebic dysentery (see below for regime)
- Antibiotic eye drops, for sore, 'gritty', stuck-together eyes (conjunctivitis)
- A pair of fine pointed tweezers (to remove hairy caterpillar hairs, thorns, splinters, coral, etc)
- Condoms or femidoms
- Maybe a malaria treatment kit and thermometer

MAJOR HAZARDS
People new to exotic travel often worry about tropical diseases, but it is accidents that are most likely to carry you off. Road accidents are very common in many parts of Malawi, so be aware and do what you can to reduce risks: try to travel during daylight hours and refuse to be driven by a drunk. Listen to local advice about areas where violent crime is rife too.

COMMON MEDICAL PROBLEMS
Travellers' diarrhoea
Travelling in Malawi carries a fairly high risk of getting a dose of travellers' diarrhoea; perhaps half of all visitors will suffer and the newer you are to exotic travel, the more likely you will be to suffer. By taking precautions against travellers' diarrhoea you will also avoid typhoid, cholera, hepatitis, dysentery, worms, etc. Travellers' diarrhoea and the other faecal-oral diseases come from getting other peoples' faeces in your mouth. This most often happens from cooks not washing their hands after a trip to the toilet, but even if the restaurant cook does not understand basic hygiene you will be safe if your food

TREATING TRAVELLERS' DIARRHOEA

It is dehydration which makes you feel awful during a bout of diarrhoea and the most important part of treatment is drinking lots of clear fluids. Sachets of oral rehydration salts give the perfect biochemical mix to replace all that is pouring out of your bottom but other recipes taste nicer. Any dilute mixture of sugar and salt in water will do you good: try Coke or orange squash with a three-finger pinch of salt added to each glass (if you are salt-depleted you won't taste the salt). Otherwise make a solution of a four-finger scoop of sugar with a three-finger pinch of salt in a glass of water. Or add eight level teaspoons of sugar (18g) and one level teaspoon of salt (3g) to one litre (five cups) of safe water. A squeeze of lemon or orange juice improves the taste and adds potassium, which is also lost in diarrhoea. Drink two large glasses after every bowel action, and more if you are thirsty. These solutions are still absorbed well if you are vomiting, but you will need to take sips at a time. If you are not eating you need to drink three litres a day plus whatever amount is pouring into the toilet. If you feel like eating, take a bland, high carbohydrate diet. Heavy greasy foods will probably give you cramps.

If the diarrhoea is bad, or you are passing blood or slime, or you have a fever, you will probably need antibiotics in addition to fluid replacement. A single dose of ciprofloxacin (500mg) repeated after 12 hours may be appropriate. If the diarrhoea is greasy and bulky and is accompanied by sulphurous (eggy) burps, the likely cause is giardia. This is best treated with tinidazole (four x 500mg in one dose, repeated seven days later if symptoms persist).

has been properly cooked and arrives piping hot. The maxim to remind you what you can safely eat is:

PEEL IT, BOIL IT, COOK IT OR FORGET IT.

This means that fruit you have washed and peeled yourself, and hot foods, should be safe but raw foods, cold cooked foods, salads, fruit salads which have been prepared by others, ice-cream and ice are all risky. And foods kept lukewarm in hotel buffets are often dangerous. If you are struck, see box below for treatment.

Water sterilisation

It is much rarer to get sick from drinking contaminated water but it happens, so try to drink from safe sources.

Water should have been brought to the boil (even at altitude it only needs to be brought to the boil), or passed through a good bacteriological filter or purified with iodine; chlorine tablets (eg: Puritabs) are also adequate although theoretically less effective and they taste nastier. Mineral water has been found to be contaminated in Malawi but should be safer than contaminated tap water.

Malaria

Whether or not you are taking malaria tablets, it is important to protect yourself from mosquito bites (see box on page 90 and *Malaria prevention*, above), so keep your repellent stick or roll-on to hand at all times. Be aware that no prophylactic is 100% protective but those on prophylactics who are unlucky enough to catch malaria are less likely to get rapidly into serious trouble. It is easy and inexpensive to arrange a malaria blood test.

Dengue fever

This mosquito-borne disease may mimic malaria but there is no prophylactic medication available to deal with it. The mosquitoes that carry this virus bite during the daytime, so it is worth applying repellent if you see any mosquitoes around. Symptoms include strong headaches, rashes and excruciating joint and muscle pains and high fever. Dengue fever lasts only for a week or so and is not usually fatal. Complete rest and paracetamol are the usual treatment; plenty of fluids also help. Some patients are given an intravenous drip to keep them from dehydrating. It is especially important to protect yourself if you have had dengue fever before, since a second infection with a different strain can result in the potentially fatal dengue haemorrhagic fever.

Insect bites

It is crucial to avoid mosquito bites between dusk and dawn; as the sun is going down, don long clothes and apply repellent on any exposed flesh. This will protect you from malaria, elephantiasis and a range of nasty insect-borne viruses. Otherwise retire to an air-conditioned room or burn mosquito coils (which are widely available and cheap in Malawi) or sleep under a fan. Coils and fans reduce rather than eliminate bites. During the day it is wise to wear long, loose (preferably 100% cotton) clothes if you are pushing through scrubby country; this will keep ticks off and also tsetse and day-biting *Aedes* mosquitoes which may spread dengue and yellow fever. Tsetse flies hurt when they bite and are attracted to the colour blue; locals will advise on where they are a problem and where they transmit sleeping sickness.

Minute pestilential biting **blackflies** spread river blindness in some parts of Africa between 190 N and 170 S; the disease is caught close to fast-flowing rivers since flies breed there and the larvae live in rapids. The flies bite during the day but long trousers tucked into socks will help keep them off. Citronella-based natural repellents do not work against them.

Mosquitoes and many other insects are attracted to light. If you are camping, never put a lamp near the opening of your tent, or you will have a swarm of biters waiting to join you when you retire. In hotel rooms, be aware that the longer your light is on, the greater the number of insects will be sharing your accommodation.

MALARIA IN MALAWI
Philip Briggs

Along with road accidents, malaria poses the single biggest serious threat to the health of travellers in Malawi. The Anopheles mosquito which transmits the parasite is most abundant near marshes and still water, where it breeds, and the parasite is most prolific at low altitudes. Parts of Malawi lying at an altitude of 2,000m or higher (Zomba, Nyika and Mulanje plateaux) are regarded to be free of malaria. In mid-altitude locations such as Lilongwe, Blantyre and Mzuzu, malaria is largely but not entirely seasonal, with the highest risk of transmission occurring during the hot, wet summer months of November to April. The low-lying Lake Malawi hinterland and Shire Valley are high risk throughout the year, but the danger is greatest during the summer months. This localised breakdown might influence what foreigners working in Malawi do about malaria prevention, but since tourist activity in Malawi is focused around the lake, all travellers to Malawi must assume that they will be exposed to malaria and should take precautions throughout their trip (see pages 81–4 for advice on prophylactic drugs and pages 89–92 for avoiding bites).

Even those who take their malaria tablets meticulously and do everything possible to avoid mosquito bites may contract a strain of malaria that is resistant to prophylactic drugs. Untreated malaria is likely to be fatal, but even strains resistant to prophylaxis respond well to prompt treatment. Because of this, your immediate priority upon displaying possible malaria symptoms – which might include any combination of a headache, flu-like aches and pains, a rapid rise in temperature, a general sense of disorientation, and possibly even nausea and diarrhoea – is to establish whether you have malaria. The blood test for malaria takes ten minutes to produce a result and costs less than US$1 in Malawi. A positive result means that you have malaria. A negative result suggests that you don't have malaria, bearing in mind that the parasite doesn't always show up on a test, particularly when the level of infection is mild or is 'cloaked' by partially effective prophylactics. For this reason, even if you test negative, it would be wise to stay within reach of a laboratory until the symptoms clear up, and to test again after a day or two if they don't. It's worth noting that if you have a fever and the malaria test is negative, you may have typhoid, which should also receive immediate treatment. Where typhoid-testing is unavailable, a routine blood test can give a strong indication of this disease.

Tumbu flies or *putsi* are a problem where the climate is hot and humid. The adult fly lays her eggs on the soil or on drying laundry and when the eggs come in contact with human flesh (when you put on clothes or lie on a bed) they hatch and bury themselves under the skin. Here they form a crop of 'boils' which each hatches a grub after about eight days, when the

It is preferable not to attempt self-diagnosis or to start treatment for malaria before you have tested. There are, however, many places in Malawi where you will be unable to test for malaria, for instance at some of the more remote lakeshore resorts, and in national parks and montane areas. With malaria, it is normal enough to go from feeling healthy to having a high fever in the space of a few hours (and it is possible to die from falciparum malaria within 24 hours of the first symptoms). In such circumstances, assume that you have malaria and act accordingly – whatever risks are attached to taking an unnecessary cure are outweighed by the dangers of untreated malaria.

It is imperative to treat malaria promptly. The sooner you take a cure, the less likely you are to become critically ill, and the more ill you become the greater the chance you'll have difficulty holding down the tablets. There is some division about the best treatment for malaria, but the quinine/doxycycline regime (see page 81 for dosages) is safe and very effective. If these tablets are unavailable, your next best option is probably Fansidar, which is widely available in Malawi. One cure that you should avoid is Halfan which is dangerous, particularly if you are using Lariam as a prophylactic.

In severe cases of malaria, the victim will be unable to hold down medication, at which point they are likely to die unless they are hospitalised immediately and put on a drip. If you or a travelling companion start vomiting after taking your malaria medication, get to a hospital or clinic quickly, ideally a private one. Whatever concerns you might have about African hospitals, they are used to dealing with malaria, and the alternative to hospitalisation is far worse.

Malaria typically takes around two weeks to incubate (minimum seven days), but it can take much longer, so you should continue prophylaxis for the prescribed time after returning home. If you display possible malaria symptoms up to a year later, then get to a doctor immediately and ensure that they are aware you have been exposed to malaria.

Every so often I run into travellers who prefer to acquire resistance to malaria rather than take preventive tablets, or who witter on about homoeopathic cures for this killer disease. That's their prerogative, but they have no place expounding their radical views to others. Travellers to Africa cannot acquire any effective resistance to malaria, and those who don't make use of prophylactic drugs risk their lives in a manner that is both foolish and unnecessary.

inflammation will settle down. In putsi areas either dry your clothes and sheets within a screened house, or dry them in direct sunshine until they are crisp, or iron them.

Jiggers or **sandfleas** are another flesh-feaster. They latch on if you walk barefoot in contaminated places, and set up home under the skin of the foot,

QUICK TICK REMOVAL

African ticks are not the prolific disease transmitters they are in the Americas, but they may spread Lyme disease, tick-bite fever and a few rarities. Tick-bite fever is a non-serious, flu-like illness, but still worth avoiding. If you get the tick off whole and promptly the chances of disease transmission are reduced to a minimum. Manoeuvre your finger and thumb so that you can pinch the tick's mouthparts, as close to your skin as possible, and slowly and steadily pull away at right angles to your skin. This often hurts. Jerking or twisting will increase the chances of damaging the tick, which in turn increases the chances of disease transmission, as well as leaving the mouthparts behind. Once the tick is off, dowse the little wound with alcohol (local spirit, whisky or similar are excellent) or iodine. An area of spreading redness around the bite site, or a rash or fever coming on a few days or more after the bite, should stimulate a trip to a doctor.

usually at the side of a toenail where they cause a painful, boil-like swelling. They need picking out by a local expert; if the distended flea bursts during eviction the wound should be dowsed in spirit, alcohol or kerosene, otherwise more jiggers will infest you.

Bilharzia or schistosomiasis

With thanks to Dr Vaughan Southgate of the Natural History Museum, London
Bilharzia or schistosomiasis is a disease that commonly afflicts the rural poor of the tropics who repeatedly acquire more and more of these nasty little worm-lodgers. Infected travellers and expatriates generally suffer fewer problems because symptoms will encourage them to seek prompt treatment and they are also exposed to fewer parasites. However, it is still an unpleasant problem that is worth avoiding.

The parasites digest their way through your skin when you wade, bathe or even shower in infested fresh water. Unfortunately, many African lakes,including Lake Malawi, and also rivers and irrigation canals, carry a risk of bilharzia. In 1995, two-thirds of expatriates living in Malawi had evidence on blood testing of having bilharzia.

encountered bilharzia, and 75% of a group of people scuba-diving off Cape Maclear in Lake Malawi for only about a week acquired the disease.

The most risky shores will be close to places where infected people use water, wash clothes, etc. Winds disperse the cercariae, though, so they can be blown some distance, perhaps up to 200m from where they entered the water. Scuba-diving off a boat into deep offshore water, then, should be a low-risk activity, but showering in lake water or paddling along a reedy lake shore near a village is risky.

Although absence of early symptoms does not necessarily mean there is no infection, infected people usually notice symptoms two or more weeks after parasite-penetration. Travellers and expatriates will probably experience a fever and often a wheezy cough; local residents do not usually have symptoms. There is now a very good blood test which, if done six weeks or more after likely exposure, will determine whether you need treatment. Since bilharzia can be a nasty illness, avoidance is better than waiting to be cured and it is wise to avoid bathing in high risk areas.

Avoiding bilharzia

- If you are bathing, swimming, paddling or wading in freshwater which you think may carry a bilharzia risk, try get out of the water within ten minutes.
- Dry off thoroughly with a towel; rub vigorously.
- Avoid bathing or paddling on shores within 200m of villages or places where people use the water a great deal, especially reedy shores or where there is lots of water weed.
- If your bathing water comes from a risky source try to ensure that the water is taken from the lake in the early morning and stored snail-free, otherwise it should be filtered or Dettol or Cresol added.
- Bathing early in the morning is safer than bathing in the last half of the day.
- Covering yourself with DEET insect repellent before swimming will protect you.
- If you think that you have been exposed to bilharzia parasites, arrange a screening blood test (your GP can do this) MORE than six weeks after your last possible contact with suspect water.

Skin infections

Any mosquito bite or small nick in the skin gives an opportunity for bacteria to foil the body's usually excellent defences; it will surprise many travellers how quickly skin infections start in warm humid climates and it is essential to clean and cover even the slightest wound. Creams are not as effective as a good drying antiseptic such as dilute iodine, potassium permanganate (a few crystals in half a cup of water), or crystal (or gentian) violet. One of these should be available in most towns. If the wound starts to throb, or becomes red and the redness starts to spread, or the wound oozes, and especially if you develop a fever, antibiotics will probably be needed: flucloxacillin (250mg four times a day) or cloxacillin (500mg four times a day). For those allergic to penicillin, erythromycin (500mg twice a day) for five days should help. See a doctor if the symptoms do not start to improve in 48 hours.

Fungal infections also get a hold easily in hot moist climates so wear 100% cotton socks and underwear and shower frequently. An itchy rash in the groin or flaking between the toes is likely to be a fungal infection. This needs treatment with an antifungal cream such as Canesten (clotrimazole); if this is not available try Whitfield's ointment (compound benzoic acid ointment) or crystal violet (although this will turn you purple!).

Eye problems

Bacterial conjunctivitis (pink eye) is a common infection in Malawi; people who wear contact lenses are most open to this irritating problem. The eyes feel sore and gritty and they will often be stuck together in the mornings. They will need treatment with antibiotic drops or ointment. Lesser eye irritation should settle with bathing in salt water and keeping the eyes shaded. If an insect flies into your eye, extract it with great care, ensuring you do not crush or damage it otherwise you may get a nastily inflamed eye from toxins secreted by the creature.

Prickly heat

A fine pimply rash on the trunk is likely to be heat rash; cool showers, dabbing (not rubbing) dry, and talc will help. Treat the problem by slowing down to a

WILD ANIMALS

Philip Briggs

There are very few places in Malawi where you are likely to come into contact with potentially dangerous large mammals. Elephant and buffalo – the most dangerous of Africa's terrestrial herbivores – are restricted to wildlife reserves where you may only walk in the company of an armed guide.

The large mammal that you need most concern yourself with is the hippopotamus, which is reportedly responsible for more human deaths than any other African mammal. This is not because it is especially aggressive, but because its response to any disturbance while it is grazing is to head directly to the safety of the water, and it will trample anything that gets in its way. You should be cautious around any lake or large river unless you know for a fact that hippo are not present. Hippos are most likely to be out grazing towards dusk, in the early morning, and in overcast weather. The danger is getting between a hippo and the water (it would be most unlikely to attack you if it perceived a clear path to safety) so the risk is greater the closer you are to the shore. You should never walk in reed-beds unless you are certain that no hippo are present. On the other hand, you have little to fear on land by approaching a hippo that is already in the water.

Another animal you should watch out for near water is the crocodile, though only a very large croc is likely to attack a person, and then only if you are actually in the water or standing right on the shore. Anywhere near a town or village, you can be fairly sure that potential man-eaters will have been disposed of by their potential prey, so the risk is greatest in water away from human habitation. Crocodiles are responsible for hundreds of deaths in Africa every year. They are present in many parts of Lake Malawi, with Likoma Island having a particularly bad reputation.

It is also near water that otherwise placid terrestrial mammals are most likely to feel cornered and thus become aggressive. It is for this reason that bushbuck (or rather those bushbuck that live in tangled waterside relaxed schedule, wearing only loose, baggy, 100% cotton clothes and sleeping naked under a fan; if it's bad you may need to check into an air-conditioned hotel room for a while.

Meningitis

This is a particularly nasty disease as it can kill within hours of the first symptoms appearing. The telltale symptoms are a combination of a blinding headache (light sensitivity), a blotchy rash and a high fever. Immunisation protects against the most serious bacterial form of meningitis and the tetravalent vaccine ACWY is recommended for Malawi. Other forms of meningitis exist (usually viral) but there are no vaccines for these. Local papers normally report localised outbreaks. A severe headache and fever should make

vegetation as opposed to forest proper) have a reputation as the most dangerous African antelope. And any large animal with youngsters is likely to attack with little or no provocation.

There are campsites in Africa where vervet monkeys and baboons have become dangerous pests. I am not aware of any such place in Malawi, but it could happen. It is worth mentioning that feeding monkeys is highly irresponsible; not only does it encourage them to scavenge, but they may also become bold to the point where they are potentially dangerous, when they may have to be shot. If you join a guided tour where the driver or guide feeds baboons for your amusement, ask him not to. Finally, while vervet monkeys are too small to progress much beyond being a nuisance they can transmit rabies. Baboons are very dangerous and have often killed children and maimed adults with their vicious teeth. Do not tease or underestimate them. If primates are hanging around a campsite, and you wander off leaving fruit in your tent, don't expect it still to be standing when you return.

The dangers associated with large predators are often exaggerated. Most large predators will stay well clear of humans, and they are more likely to kill through accident or self-defence than design. Lions are arguably the one exception, but still it is very rare for a lion to attack a person without provocation and, in Malawi, lions are too thinly distributed to be a cause for concern. Leopards are more widespread but they are only likely to attack people if they are cornered. Spotted hyenas are common in Malawi, they are frequently associated with human settlements, and they are potentially very dangerous. Fortunately, they are also notoriously craven in their dealings with humans. A slight but real danger if you sleep in the bush without a tent is that a passing hyena might investigate a hairy object sticking out of a sleeping bag and you might be decapitated purely through predatorial curiosity. If you are in an area where large predators are still reasonably common, sleeping in a sealed tent practically guarantees your safety, so long as you don't do something daft like put meat in your tent.

you run to a doctor immediately. There are also other causes of headache and fever; one of which is typhoid, which occurs in travellers to Malawi. Seek medical help if you are ill for more than a few days.

Safe sex

Travel is a time when we may enjoy sexual adventures, especially when alcohol reduces inhibitions. Remember that the risks of sexually transmitted infection are high, whether you sleep with fellow travellers or locals. About 40% of HIV infections in British heterosexuals are acquired abroad. Use condoms or femidoms; spermicide pessaries help reduce the risk of transmission. If you notice any genital ulcers or discharge, get treatment promptly since these increase the risk of acquiring HIV.

Rabies

Rabies is carried by all mammals (beware the village dogs and small monkeys that are used to being fed in the parks) and is passed on to man through a bite, scratch or a lick of an open wound. You must always assume any animal is rabid (unless personally known to you) and seek medical help as soon as possible. In the interim, scrub the wound with soap and bottled/boiled water, then pour on a strong iodine or alcohol solution. This helps stop the rabies virus entering the body and will guard against wound infections, including tetanus.

If you intend to have contact with animals and/or are likely to be more than 24 hours away from medical help, then pre-exposure vaccination is advised. Ideally three doses should be taken over four weeks. Contrary to popular belief these vaccinations are relatively painless!

If you are exposed as described, treatment should be given as soon as possible, but it is never too late to seek help as the incubation period for rabies can be very long. Those who have not been immunised will need a full course of injections together with rabies immunoglobulin (RIG), but this product is expensive (around US$800) and may be hard to come by: another reason why pre-exposure vaccination should be encouraged in travellers who are planning to visit more remote areas!

Tell the doctor if you have had pre-exposure vaccine, as this will change the treatment you receive. And remember that, if you do contract rabies, mortality is 100% and death from rabies is probably one of the worst ways to go!

Snakes

Snakes rarely attack unless provoked, and bites in travellers are unusual. You are less likely to get bitten if you wear stout shoes and long trousers when in the bush. Most snakes are harmless and even venomous species will dispense venom in only about half of their bites. If bitten, then, you are unlikely to have received venom; keeping this fact in mind may help you to stay calm. Many so-called first-aid techniques do more harm than good: cutting into the wound is harmful; tourniquets are dangerous; suction and electrical inactivation devices do not work. The only treatment is antivenom. In case of a bite which you fear may have been from a venomous snake:

- Try to keep calm - it is likely that no venom has been dispensed.
- Prevent movement of the bitten limb by applying a splint.
- Keep the bitten limb BELOW heart height to slow the spread of any venom.
- If you have a crêpe bandage, bind up as much of the bitten limb as you can, but release the bandage every half hour.
- Evacuate to a hospital which has antivenom.

And remember:

NEVER give aspirin; you may offer paracetamol, which is safe.
NEVER cut or suck the wound.
DO NOT apply ice packs.
DO NOT apply potassium permanganate.

If the offending snake can be captured without risk of someone else being bitten, take this to show the doctor – but beware since even a decapitated head is able to bite.

FURTHER READING

Self-prescribing has its hazards so if you are going anywhere very remote consider taking a health book. For adults there is *Bugs, Bites & Bowels: the Cadogan Guide to Healthy Travel* by Jane Wilson-Howarth (3rd edn, 2002); if travelling with the family look at *Your Child's Health Abroad: A manual for travelling parents* by Jane Wilson-Howarth and Matthew Ellis, published by Bradt Publications in 1998.

Part Two

The Guide

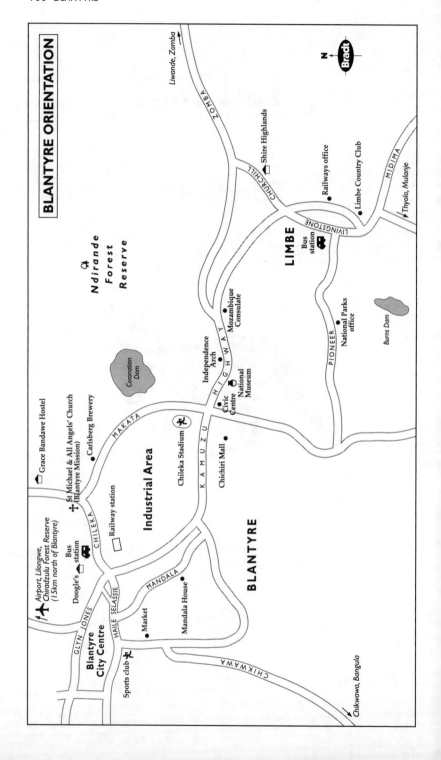

BLANTYRE ORIENTATION

Blantyre

Blantyre is Malawi's unofficial commercial capital, and the oldest European settlement in the country. The Blantyre Mission was founded in October 1876 by the Established Church of Scotland, and named after the small village in which David Livingstone was born. Under its first leader, Rev Duff Macdonald, the Blantyre Mission ruled over the surrounding hills with a despotic cruelty, flogging and killing suspected thieves and murderers without even the pretence of a trial. The behaviour of the early Blantyre missionaries caused a scandal in the British press, forcing many of them to retire, and Macdonald to be replaced by Rev Clement Scott in 1881.

The healthy, fertile climate around Blantyre proved attractive to European settlers, and the mission's strategic position served as an excellent communication centre for the traders who operated between Lake Malawi and the Zambezi Valley. Blantyre rapidly became the most important settlement in Malawi, a status it retains to this day, with a population of around 500,000, almost double that of the capital, Lilongwe.

Blantyre is more intrinsically attractive than Lilongwe, lying at an altitude of 1,038m in a valley ringed by low hills, the largest of which are Michuru (1,473m), Soche (1,533m) and Ndirende (1,612m). For all that, the city lacks any discernible character and cannot, by any stretch of the imagination, be thought of as a tourist attraction. But it remains the focal point of travel in southern Malawi, as well as the springboard for bus transport to Harare via Mozambique's Tete Corridor. Most visitors to Malawi spend a night or two in Blantyre at some point.

ORIENTATION

Blantyre's compact city centre is roughly triangular in shape, bounded by Glyn Jones Road to the north, Haile Selassie Road to the south, and Hanover Avenue to the west. The most important road is Victoria Avenue, which runs from north to south a block east of Hanover Avenue. Among the many institutions on Victoria Avenue are the tourist office, map sales office, two major supermarkets, the main branches of the Commercial and National banks, Avis Car Hire and the Times Bookshop. The Mount Soche Hotel, which lies opposite the junction of Victoria Avenue and Glyn Jones Road, is perhaps the best-known landmark in the city centre.

Immediately east of the city centre, Glyn Jones Road and Haile Selassie Road converge at a roundabout to become the Kamuzu Highway. About 200m east of this roundabout is the clocktower where Chileka Road branches from Kamuzu Highway to the northeast. The main bus station is 500m up Chileka Road; around it lies most of Blantyre's budget accommodation.

Kamuzu Highway connects Blantyre to the satellite town of Limbe, which lies 5km away from Blantyre and is administered by the same municipality. Although Limbe was originally a residential area and Blantyre a commercial and industrial area, Limbe now functions in most respects as a separate town, with its own main road, market and bus station. Regular minibuses connect Blantyre and Limbe via the Kamuzu Highway.

A 1:16,000 map of Blantyre and Limbe can be bought at any map sales office in Malawi.

CLIMATE

Blantyre has a pleasant, healthy climate. During the rainy season, which generally starts some time between October and December and ends in late April, temperatures are warm, the air tends to be rather humid, and rain can be expected most days, often in the form of short thunderstorms. From May to August, rain is unusual, the air is dry, and temperatures tend to be cool to moderate. The period from September to the start of the rains is the hottest season, with temperatures regularly soaring above 30°C. Humidity levels are low during this season, and the weather is frequently interrupted by heavy mists which can last for days.

GETTING THERE AND AWAY

Blantyre is the major transport hub in southern Malawi. Buses come and go regularly in every direction from the bus station on Chileka Road. Buses coming to Blantyre from the direction of Zomba or Mulanje stop in Limbe bus station before proceeding to Blantyre itself.

Travellers heading directly between Lilongwe and Blantyre will probably want to take advantage of the non-stop Coachline service between the cities. These coaches leave four times daily in either direction, at 07.00, 10.00, 13.00 and 17.00. The trip take three to four hours, and tickets cost roughly US$18 per person one way.

Buses leave Blantyre at around 06.00 every morning for Harare in Zimbabwe, passing through the Tete Corridor in northern Mozambique. The trip takes around 12 hours, depending on delays at the border posts. Ordinary buses cost roughly US$16 and leave from outside the main bus station, which is also where you can book tickets. Luxury express buses leave two or three times a week. Tickets cost US$25.

There are other international bus companies that operate out of Blantyre. Munorurama Bus Service leaves from the bus station in Chileka Road and runs luxury coaches to Harare (US$16), Beit Bridge (US$27) and Johannesburg (US$40). As they do not run every day, they offer free overnight accommodation if you have to wait.

Vaal Africa departs for Johannesburg at 09.00 on Saturdays, Sundays and Mondays from their depot behind the Caltex garage at the Lilongwe traffic circle on Glyn Jones Road and charges US$54 (web: www.vaalafrica.co.za). City to City buses leave for Johannesburg every day at 09.00 except Tuesdays and Fridays from the Petrodas garage at the clocktower circle and charges US$43.

Blantyre is also the centre of Malawi's limited and little-used rail network. The only route of interest for adventurous travellers is from Blantyre to Nayuchi on the eastern border, where it connects with the Mozambique rail service. It runs Mondays to Fridays, costs all of US$2.50 and entails a change at Nkaya, but it would probably be better starting in Liwonde. Not for the faint hearted.

WHERE TO STAY
Tourist class
The most upmarket hotel in Blantyre, the centrally-situated **Mount Soche Hotel** (PO Box 284, Blantyre; tel: 01 620588; fax: 01 620154; email: mountsoche@lemeridienmalawi.co.mw), is part of the Le Meridien Group. Several types of accommodation are available, ranging from a standard room at US$190/220 single/double to superior suites at US$330 double. All rates are inclusive of a buffet English breakfast, but exclude 10% service charge and 10% surtax. Facilities include satellite television in every room, a business centre, a large swimming pool, and 24-hour room service. Two excellent restaurants are attached to the hotel: the very swanky and highly regarded fifth-floor Michuru Restaurant, and the mid-range Gypsy Restaurant on the ground floor (see below).

More modern and just as comfortable is the newly rebuilt **Ryalls Hotel** (PO Box 21, Blantyre; tel: 01 620955; fax: 01 620201; email: ryalls@proteamalawi.com). Near to the Mount Soche Hotel on Hanover Avenue, Ryalls is part of the Protea Group and boasts the most up-to-date facilities including a full business centre, restaurant and bar. Rates before taxes are US$150/175 for single/double.

Slightly cheaper options which are still in the tourist class are the Protea Group's **Shire Highlands Hotel** (tel: 01 640055) on Churchill Road in Limbe costing US$90/100 for single/double, and **Tumbuka Lodge**, on the corner of Sharpe and Chilembwe roads in suburban Blantyre (tel/fax: 01 620487) at US$95/140 single/double. The Malawi Institute of Tourism operates the new **Alendo Hotel and Kachere Restaurant** at 15 Chilembwe Road where it trains staff to a high standard for the hospitality industry in Malawi. Rates in this neat, centrally situated little hotel are US$55/80 for self-contained single/double. All three of the above include breakfast and taxes.

Budget
The choice of affordable accommodation in Blantyre has improved but almost all budget travellers stay at **Doogle's Backpacker Lodge** (tel: 01 621128; email: doogles@africa-online.net). Situated about 100m from Blantyre's main

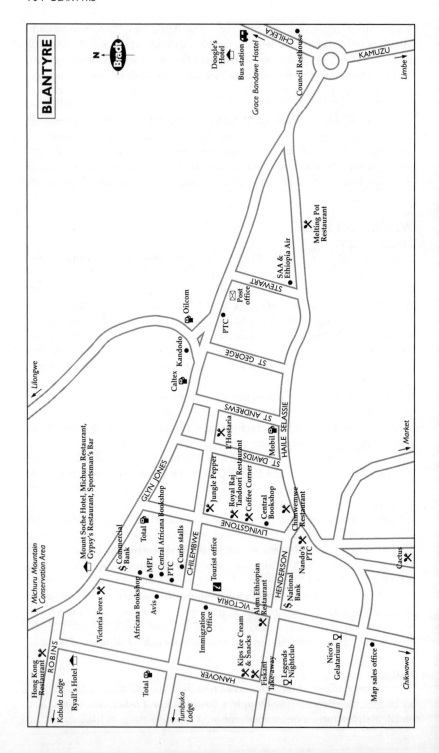

bus station, this large hostel offers camping for US$3 per person, dormitory accommodation for US$5.20 per person, and double bandas with bedding for US$10. Doogle's does good meals for around US$3–4, and facilities include a bar, swimming pool, good notice board, television lounge with video, hot showers, luggage storage and a large garden. Recently built self-contained garden suites are very comfortable at US$18 double and Doogle's has the best internet connection I found in all Malawi. Billy and Mark are always willing to assist, whether you want to spend a few hours tasting at the Carlsberg Brewery or a few weeks hiking the Mulange Massif.

Another recommended place to stay is **Kabula Lodge** (tel: 01 621216) in the quiet Blantyre suburb of the same name (follow signs past Mount Soche Hotel). Family run and popular with volunteer workers on extended stays, it offers a range of accommodation from US$7 for basic singles to US$20 for self-contained doubles and use of the well-equipped kitchens.

Aunty Vee's at 19 Henderson Street (tel: 01 623474) offers self-contained rooms at US$27/33 single/double. Budget rooms are also available at US$7 and the jovial Agnes can even be talked into allowing camping in the large grounds. **Wenela Lodge** (tel: 01 636754), behind Doogle's, is a quiet and neatly converted house, but its self-contained rooms are rather pricey at US$30/40 single/double.

The **Grace Bandawe Hostel** (tel: 01 634267) lies on Chileka Road opposite the old Blantyre Mission, about 500m out of town from the bus station. It has good rooms for US$20/25 single/double with shared bathroom or US$32 self-contained double suite. Clean dormitory accommodation is available for US$10 per person; an attractive feature of the dormitories is that they are partitioned into semi-private single and double rooms. Meals are served in the restaurant for around US$3 per plate. Grace Bandawe Hostel is very quiet and peaceful, but no alcohol is served because it is a religious institution, and it is quite a way from any other bars and restaurants.

The **Blantyre Council Resthouse**, a minute's walk from the bus station, has rooms for around US$8/double, but the rooms are very scruffy. In any case, the resthouse is almost always booked solid days in advance. It's easier to find a room at the **Limbe Council Resthouse**; prices are similar and the rooms are reputedly in better condition.

WHERE TO EAT

There are several relatively upmarket restaurants in Blantyre, most of which are open from 12.00 to 14.00 and around either 18.00 or 19.00 to 22.30. You can assume that most restaurants at the upper end of the price scale will add a 10% service charge and 10% tax to prices quoted on the menu.

Possibly the smartest place in Blantyre is the **Michuru Restaurant** on the fifth floor of the Mount Soche Hotel, where a wide selection of à la carte dishes cost US$12–15, more for prawns. On the ground floor of the same hotel, the relatively informal **Gypsy's Restaurant** serves à la carte meals in the US$8–12 range.

Deservedly one of the most popular restaurants in the city centre, **L'Hostaria** is set in an old house on Chilembwe Road, and it offers the winning combination of great meals and a relaxed, individualistic atmosphere. The pizzas here are really good, and reasonably priced at around US$5 each, while pasta and meat dishes fall into the US$6–10 range. You could also try the pizzas at **Jungle Pepper**, which come at a similar price but are geared more to the take-away market.

The **Raj Tandoori Restaurant** on Livingstone Road is the only Indian restaurant in the city centre, and very good it is too, with most meals likely to work out at around US$10 with rice and bread. Far more affordable is the perennially popular **Hong Kong Restaurant** on the intersection of Glyn Jones Road and Robins Road, where a massive plate of tasty Chinese food shouldn't set you back more than US$5 per head.

The **Melting Pot Restaurant** on Haile Selassie Road has a varied menu, with most dishes costing around US$7–8. The restaurants in the **Shire Highlands Hotel** and **Ryall's Hotel** are very good too.

Dropping in price, the **Alem Ethiopian Restaurant** on Victoria Avenue will come as a welcome surprise to those travellers who've already visited Ethiopia, while to others it will serve as an excellent place to try out one of Africa's most unusual cuisines. Run by a Tigrean woman, it serves a selection of Ethiopian dishes, most of which cost around US$6. Also well worth a try is **Nando's** on the corner of Henderson Street and Haile Selassie Road – this is a franchise of a popular South African fast-food chain which serves excellent Portuguese-style piri-piri chicken. A quarter chicken with chips here costs around US$3.

Kips Ice Cream & Snacks on Hanover Avenue serves ice-cream and a variety of inexpensive meals.

A popular daytime restaurant is **Chez Maky**, on the corner of Laws and Chilembwe roads (tel: 01 622124). Open 09.00 to 17.00, this laid-back venue serves light continental meals such as crêpes (US$1.50), quiches (US$4.50) and moussaka. With an art gallery and craft shop on the premises, one can while away the time with a cup of the best coffee in Malawi and home-made cake, listening to smooth jazz.

The hot new pub in 2002 was **Cactus**, down Slater Road. Owned by Doogle's (which also has a great pub), it has a Wild West theme and is very popular with expats and travellers. For nightlife, try Legends, in Cleopatra's Courtyard off Victoria Avenue. They even have monthly rave parties.

TOURIST INFORMATION
The **tourist office** (tel: 01 620300) on Victoria Avenue is reasonably helpful and stocks a good range of free pamphlets and books about Malawi.

Airlines
Major airlines represented in Blantyre include Air Malawi (Robin's Road; tel: 01 620811), British Airways (Victoria Avenue; tel: 01 624333) and South African Airways (Haile Selassie Road; tel: 01 620627/9).

Chileka International Airport (tel: 01 692274) lies 19km from the city centre. It is the oldest airport in Malawi, though these days it receives few international flights as compared with Kamuzu Airport outside Lilongwe.

Books and maps

The best general bookshop in Blantyre city centre is the **Central Bookshop** on Livingstone Avenue. This stocks a fair range of novels, as well as many books published in Malawi and a variety of imported field guides and travel guides.

Situated in the arcade behind the main PTC supermarket on Victoria Avenue, the **Central Africana Bookshop** stocks a good selection of current books about Malawi, as well as the country's best selection of obscure and out-of-print African titles. If you're looking for something specific in this line, you can contact them in advance at tel: 01 623227; fax: 01 622236; email: africana@iafrica.com.

There are branches of the **Times Bookshop** on Victoria Avenue, on Livingstone Avenue in Limbe, and in the foyers of the Mount Soche and Shire Highlands hotels. The range of books in these shops is nowhere as good as that in the Central Bookshop, but they do stock a selection of imported magazines and newspapers. The branches in the hotel foyers are open on Saturdays and Sundays, as well as during normal shopping hours.

There is a well stocked **Map Sales Office** in the Department of Surveys' office on the southern end of Victoria Avenue (tel: 01 623722).

Car hire

Avis Car Hire is the only internationally recognised car rental firm operating out of Blantyre. The main office is on Victoria Avenue opposite the PTC supermarket (tel: 01 623792). Other reputable car rental companies include Ceciliana (tel: 01 641219), Zoom (tel: 01 674889) and Soche Tours and Travel (see *Travel agencies and tour operators* below).

Foreign exchange

You can exchange money at any branch of the Commercial or National banks, or at one of the private forex bureaux in the city centre – when we were last in town the Victoria Bureau de Change diagonally opposite the Mount Soche Hotel was offering an excellent rate for both cash and travellers' cheques. Outside banking hours, most of the upmarket hotels will exchange money for hotel residents. Otherwise, it's normally possible to change US dollars or South African rands cash on the street around the junction of Glyn Jones Road and Victoria Avenue. This is reportedly not as safe as it used to be, and the street rate is not much better than others, so it's advisable to change only what you need to get you through until the banks next open.

Immigration

Visitors' passes and visas can be renewed at the Immigration Office on Victoria Avenue (tel: 01 623777).

Mozambique visas

Travellers heading to Mozambique or using the Tete Corridor to get to Zimbabwe can buy the appropriate visa at the Mozambique Consulate on Kamuzu Highway. Transit visas are issued on the same day at the kwacha equivalent of around US$11 or overnight at the equivalent of US$7. In order to take advantage of the same-day service, you must hand in your passport at the consulate before 08.30 for collection at 15.00. Any minibus between the city centre and Limbe can drop you near the consulate; ask for Masalima post office. It is also possible to arrange your transit visa through Doogle's, assuming that this is where you are staying. It may be worth noting that transit visas technically allow you to stay in Mozambique for *up to seven days from the date of issue* – proper tourist visas are considerably more expensive than transit visas and take three working days to be processed.

Supermarkets

The new Chichiri Mall at the traffic circle on Kamuzu Highway between Blantyre and Limbe has revolutionised shopping in this part of Malawi. With a huge, well-stocked Shoprite supermarket as its main tenant, the mall also boasts fashion shops, banks, a pharmacy, take-aways, a branch of Soche Tours and a Postnet agency for phone, internet, copying and DHL. Open until late and over weekends, this makes a welcome change from the smaller PTC and Kandodo supermarkets dotted around the city.

Travel agencies and tour operators

The three best-known tour operators running out of Blantyre are Soche Tours and Travel on Hanover Road (PO Box 2225, Blantyre; tel: 01 620777; fax: 01 620440; email: sochetours@malawi.net), AMI Travel on Victoria Avenue (PO Box 838, Blantyre; tel: 01 624733; fax: 01 621107) and Jambo Africa, which operates out of offices at the Tumbuka Lodge, on the corner of Chilembwe and Sharpe roads. They are linked to Chinguni Hills Camp in Liwonde National Park and can organise trips to any destination in Malawi (tel: 01 635356; fax: 01 633489; email: jamboafrica@africa-online.net; web: www.jamboafricatoursmalawi.com).

Internet

A number of internet offices and cafés are advertised in and around Blantyre, but some are pretty dodgy and I can only recommend the services at Doogle's, and Postnet at the Chichiri Mall.

Hospital

The new Mwaiwathu Hospital in Chileka Road, just above the bus station and Doogle's, offers a comprehensive medical service and is open all hours (tel: 01 622999; fax: 01 621190).

Industrial area

Situated to the northeast of Kumuzu Highway, the Ginnery Corner industrial area is the place to go looking for motor spares and repairs as well as having your gas cylinders filled at BOC Gases (tel: 01 671260).

THINGS TO DO
If you have a day free in Blantyre, you should certainly pop into the **National Museum**, which lies just off the Kamuzu Highway towards Limbe, and is open every day, except for Monday, between 10.00 and 16.00. The museum houses a range of traditional Malawian artefacts and musical instruments, as well as displays on Livingstone, the Livingstonia Mission and the early colonial era. Traditional dancing takes place in the grounds on Saturdays.

Also worth a look is **St Michael and All Angels' Church**, on Chileka Road between the bus station and Grace Bandawe Hostel. This is the second oldest building in Blantyre, built by Scottish missionaries between 1888 and 1891. The oldest building, erected in 1882, is Mandala House on Mackie Road, about 1km south of the city centre.

Many travellers go on the free day tour offered on Wednesday at 14.30 by **Carlsberg Brewery** (tel: 01 670222 or 620133), though it's doubtful whether the attraction lies so much in the brewing process as in the complimentary beer-swilling session at the end of the tour. It is best to arrange a tour a day in advance and to gather together a group of people at somewhere like Doogle's to split the taxi fare.

The **Paper Making Education Trust (PAMET)**, in Chilembwe Road close to Chez Maky, is a fascinating place where they hand-make paper and cardboard using elephant dung, grass, sisal, banana bark and recycled paper. Products such as photo albums and writing sets are available – great for souvenirs. Open for tours every afternoon, Mondays to Fridays (tel: 01 623895).

Limbe Town is vibrant and bustling and well worth exploring. From April to September tourists are welcome to visit the tobacco auctioning floors there (tel: 01 640377).

Michuru Mountain Conservation Area
The closest conservation area to Blantyre lies on Michuru Mountain about 8km northeast of the city centre. It protects a variety of habitats including plantation forest, indigenous woodland and open grassland. Mammals which occur naturally in Michuru include spotted hyena, leopard, serval, genet, bushpig, vervet monkey, baboon, bushbaby, bushbuck, grey duiker, klipspringer and reedbuck. Over 200 bird species have been recorded. Facilities include a basic campsite, and several day trails of between 2km and 5km in length. It is permitted to walk in the reserve at night, when a variety of nocturnal animals may be seen.

To get to Michuru, follow Glyn Jones Avenue west of the Mount Soche Hotel for roughly 200m, then turn left into Sharpe Road until, after about 100m, you hit a T-junction where you must turn right into Michuru Avenue. About 2km along Michuru Avenue the tarmac ends; a further 6km along the road you come to a turn-off marked by a green stone reading 'Michuru Conservation Area'. Continue along Michuru Road past this turn-off, and ignore the next two turn-offs (respectively marked 'CDC Farm' and 'Michuru Office'). The road which you need to turn into is marked 'Car Park and Nature Trails'.

If you don't have private transport, you could walk to Michuru and back as a day trip, but it's close on 10km each way, which won't leave you much time to explore the nature trails. A better idea perhaps is to get a taxi to the entrance gate and then try to hitch back. Alternatively, you could camp in the reserve. For further details about walking and camping in the conservation area, contact the Chief Forester's office on tel: 01 633887 or 01 661471. The Blantyre branch of the Wildlife Society of Malawi (PO Box 1429, Blantyre) funds six patrolmen, the hyena hide, trail slashing and minor road works. It has also undertaken the refurbishment of the educational centre and the toilet/ablution block.

Several of the other hills around Blantyre are protected in forest reserves, and they are popular for weekend walks with residents. With Mulanje and Zomba beckoning, these reserves are probably only of marginal interest to tourists, but if you feel like exploring, get hold of a copy of the booklet *Day Outings from Blantyre* (Wildlife Society of Malawi); it's available in most bookshops for a couple of dollars.

Chiradzulu Forest Reserve

Chiradzulu Mountain lies about 15km north of Blantyre. It supports the most accessible evergreen forest in the Blantyre area, though only a relatively small patch of 200ha remains, all of it above the 1,500m contour. The mountain is of particular interest to birdwatchers, as many unusual forest species are present, including a variety of robins, bulbuls, and the crowned eagle. It was at Chiradzulu in 1896 that the first specimen of the rare green-headed oriole was captured. Mammals that can be seen on the mountain include vervet and samango monkeys, baboon, spotted hyena, red duiker and bushbuck. The lower slopes of Chiradzulu, where they haven't been planted with exotic trees, are covered in thick *brachystegia* woodland.

The area around Chiradzulu Mountain has played a prominent role in the modern history of Malawi. It was near the base of Chiradzulu that Livingstone helped Bishop Mackenzie found the Church of Scotland's short-lived Mogomero Mission in 1861. The largest farm in the Chiradzulu area was later bought by one Mr Bruce, a stepson of Livingstone, and was managed by another member of the clan, William Livingstone. In 1915, William Livingstone was decapitated in front of his family during the rebellion initiated by Chiradzulu's most famous son, the Rev John Chilembwe.

Getting there and away

Chiradzulu Mountain can be visited either as a day trip from Blantyre or else from the small town of Chiradzulu, which is at the eastern base of the mountain. Chiradzulu Town lies about 20km from Limbe; you must first take the M3 towards Zomba, then, about 4km out of town, branch left on to the tarred S146. There are regular buses between Limbe bus station and Chiradzulu.

From Chiradzulu Town, the (unsignposted) turn-off to Chiradzulu Forest Reserve lies a few kilometres back towards Blantyre, about 1km south of the dam which lies immediately west of the S146. About 3km along the turn-off you enter a eucalyptus plantation, then about 1km further on you reach the edge of the forest. The indigenous forest is most easily explored along firebreaks, which separate it from the surrounding eucalyptus plantations.

The Providential Industrial Mission founded by John Chilembwe was forced to close after the above-mentioned incident, but re-opened ten years later, and it remains today an active mission with several points of historical interest dating to Chilembwe's time. If you are interested in visiting the mission, it lies near Mbombwe trading centre, roughly 5km east of the Limbe–Chiradzulu road, from where it can be reached via a signposted dirt road starting close to Chiradzulu Secondary School.

Where to stay

Chiradzulu Town is something of a backwater, with a stagnant, isolated atmosphere that is difficult to explain when you consider how close it is to Blantyre and the role it has played in Malawian history. If you have ambitions to spend the night in town, there is a very basic dollar-a-night hotel in the market, where an absence of facilities is compensated for by the friendliness of the family who own it. The hotel will boil up water for you to wash in, but unless you fancy a meal of *nsima* and boiled eggs, it might be worth bringing a bit of food along with you.

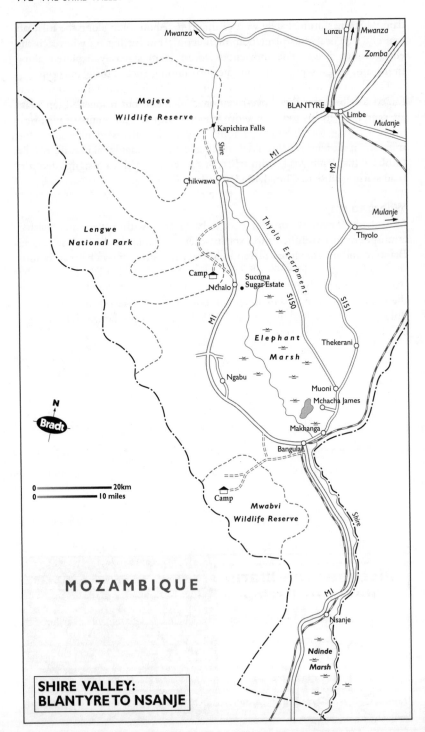

Mwanza

Lunzu Mwanza

Zomba

Majete
Wildlife Reserve

Kapichira Falls

BLANTYRE Limbe

Mulanje

Shire

M1

M2

Chikwawa

Thyolo Escarpment

Mulanje

Thyolo

Lengwe
National Park

Camp

Nchalo Sucoma
Sugar Estate

S150

S151

Elephant

Thekerani

Marsh

M1

Ngabu

Muoni

Mchacha James

Makhanga

Bangula

N

Bradt

0 ———— 20km
0 ———— 10 miles

Camp

Mwabvi
Wildlife Reserve

Shire

MOZAMBIQUE

M1

Nsanje

Ndinde
Marsh

SHIRE VALLEY:
BLANTYRE TO NSANJE

The Shire Valley

Southwest of Blantyre, the M1 snakes and slithers over the Thyolo Escarpment, offering fantastic views across the hills of Majete Wildlife Reserve and Mozambique, before it descends to the steamy lowlands of the Shire Valley. Despite a reasonably dense human population, the Shire Valley retains much of the atmosphere of wild, untrammelled Africa. In large part, this is due to the sluggish presence of the wide and lushly vegetated Shire River, still home to sizeable populations of hippopotamus and crocodile. But even among the people, the Shire Valley seems less influenced by the West than much of modern Africa – the subject of traditional witchcraft and sorcery came up in almost every conversation I had in the area.

The Shire Valley was the first part of Malawi to be visited by Europeans. In January 1859, Livingstone's Zambezi Expedition steamed up the Shire until its path was blocked by the cataracts that lie on what is now the southern border of Majete Wildlife Reserve. When Livingstone travelled up the Shire again in 1861, to help Bishop Mackenzie establish the first mission in Central Africa, much of the region was under the indirect control of Portuguese slavers. Worse still was to greet Livingstone on his final trip up the river in 1863 – the Shire had become, in the words of Dr Rowley, another member of the expedition, 'literally a river of death'. The banks were lined with dead and emaciated Africans; one member of the expedition calculated that a corpse floated past them every three hours.

The malaria that is hyperendemic to the Shire River claimed the lives of several members of Livingstone's expedition. In 1862, Bishop Mackenzie died on a now-sunken island at the confluence of the Ruo and Shire near Bangula. Two other clergymen, Rev Scudamore and Dr Dickinson, and the 25-year-old geologist Richard Thornton, all died in the Chikwawa area in 1863.

Today, the Shire Valley doesn't see a great deal of tourism, but it is not short of worthwhile attractions. Aside from the river itself, rich in atmosphere and historical connections, this area boasts two little-visited wildlife reserves, Majete and Mwabvi, as well as the Lengwe National Park. For backpackers, who may find the reserves difficult to reach without transport, there is the quite wonderful and highly accessible Elephant Marsh near Bangula.

CLIMATE

The Shire Valley is the lowest-lying part of Malawi, dropping to an altitude of 38m above sea level near Nsanje, and it is also one of the hottest. The most pleasant time to visit is around June and July, when the weather is reasonably cool and dry, and the wildlife reserves offer the best game viewing. Towards the end of the dry season and during the rains, the Shire Valley is uncomfortably hot and very humid.

The climate and altitude of the Shire Valley create ideal breeding conditions for mosquitoes. Many expatriates regard this area to be worse for malaria than even Lake Malawi, particularly during the hot rainy months between October and April, so make every effort to avoid being bitten by mosquitoes.

GETTING AROUND

The southern extension of the M1 starts at Blantyre and continues to the Mozambican border, past the towns of Chikwawa, Nchalo, Bangula and Nsanje. In theory, this road is surfaced in its entirety, but in practice it is quite badly pot-holed, especially south of Chikwawa, and several stretches have lost their surface entirely. For all that, you can travel its length in a saloon car, as well as most side roads which lead to other places of interest in the Shire Valley, though these may become impassable in anything less than a 4WD after heavy rain.

The M1 between Blantyre and Nsanje is served by buses. Services are not as regular as in some other parts of the country, but you should have no difficulty getting between any two points along the M1 using a combination of buses and *matola* rides. Without private transport, reaching the reserves to the west of the M1 is rather more problematic, and even if you could get to the entrance gates, it's unlikely you'd be allowed to enter on foot. The two major points of interest which are accessible to people using public transport are the Sucoma Sugar Estate and the fascinating Elephant Marsh.

CHIKWAWA

Chikwawa is a reasonably large but rather nondescript town lying on the west bank of the Shire a couple of kilometres from the M1 towards Majete Wildlife Reserve. The area immediately around Chikwawa is of interest mainly to bird enthusiasts. About 1km out of town, in September, a nesting colony of carmine bee-eaters can be reached by following the dirt road opposite the police station to the west bank of the Shire River. On the M1, about 3km south of the turn-off to Chikwawa, the Kasinthula fish ponds are noted for waterbirds, particularly the large numbers of migrant waders which are attracted to the area between July and December. There are several resthouses in Chikwawa.

MAJETE WILDLIFE RESERVE

Majete Wildlife Reserve protects a 691km² area of hilly *brachystegia* woodland sloping down to the western bank of the Shire River and, except for a small stretch of road along the Shire, the reserve is not developed for tourism. In the early 1990s, the herd of approximately 200 elephants was poached to probable extinction in a matter of three months, but one can still hope to spot kudu, baboon, vervet monkeys, bushbabies, hippo, crocodile and even anteaters. However, the real attraction of Majete is not its wildlife, but the Shire River, especially the impressive Kapichira Falls near the park entrance, and the birds in the riparian forest fringing the river banks. A hydro-electric scheme at Kapichira has recently disrupted things somewhat.

Getting there and away
Majete lies about 20km from Chikwawa along a rough dirt road. The turn-off to Majete is signposted from Chikwawa. If you're heading to the Safari Camp, the turn-off is signposted a few kilometres before Majete's entrance gate.

Where to stay
There is no longer any accommodation within the reserve, but you can stay at **Majete Safari Camp**, a private establishment about 5km outside the entrance gate. Abandoned by its original owners, it is now competently run by the local villagers. Camping costs US$3 and chalets with beds, toilets and hot water US$6 per person. All food must be brought in and can be prepared there by the friendly Mr Jones and his assistants. The position of the camp, overlooking the rapids where Livingstone's path up the Shire was blocked, is both beautiful and rather poignant. Birdwatching from the camp is good; the small island which faces the camp is reportedly the only known breeding site in Malawi of the rock pratincole. The Kapichira Falls and the solitary grave of Richard Thornton are both within easy walking of the camp.

LENGWE NATIONAL PARK
This 887km² national park lies along the Mozambican border west of the Shire River. Only the eastern extension of the park has been developed for tourism, but within this small area there is a good network of roads, as well as several viewing hides and an inexpensive camp and campsite.

Though relatively arid, with an annual rainfall figure of well under 1,000mm, Lengwe is densely vegetated. There is lush riparian woodland along some of the watercourses, and the remainder of the park is covered in wooded savannah and dense thickets interspersed with some impressive stands of baobab and palm trees. Tourist traffic is low (I saw no other vehicles while I was in the park), and dense vegetation lends the winding roads a secluded air.

The variety of large mammals present in Lengwe isn't great, but game viewing is nonetheless good. The park supports the most northerly population of the beautiful nyala antelope, rare elsewhere but common here. Lengwe is also a good place to see samango monkeys; a troop lives in the woodland around the main hide. Other mammals you should see are impala, bushbuck, warthog, vervet monkey and baboons, and with a bit of luck buffalo and greater kudu. The only large predators in the reserve are spotted hyena and leopard. Among the more interesting birds that I saw were racquet-tailed roller, Boehm's bee-eater and yellow-spotted nicator.

Entrance to the park costs US$5 per person per 24 hours. A useful booklet and map can be bought at the gate for a nominal fee.

Getting there and away

The turn-off to Lengwe is on the M1 a few kilometres north of Nchalo. From the turn-off, it's a 6km drive through a sugar plantation to the gate. Without transport, you could certainly walk to the gate, though it's not obvious what you'd do once you got there – you are not allowed to enter the park without a vehicle.

Where to stay

The rest camp lies about 1km from the entrance gate. It consists of four chalets, each with two double rooms, a shared lounge/dining room, and a fridge. There is a small grocery shop in the camp, but unless you fancy dining on soap and washing powder, you are advised to bring all the food you need with you. The bar has cold beers and sodas. A double room in a chalet costs US$18. You can pitch a tent at the adjoining campsite for US$3 per person.

NCHALO

The small town straddling the M1 south of Lengwe is, in practice, little more than an extension of the massive Sucoma Sugar Estate, the entrance to which lies in the town centre. There is no compelling reason for travellers to stay in Nchalo, though there are a few resthouses should the need arise. There is also a PTC supermarket and a good market if you're stocking up for a visit to Lengwe or elsewhere.

There is certainly a case for popping into **Sucoma Sugar Estate**, especially if you have a car. The place to head for is the Sports Club, which lies on the bank of the Shire about 6km from the estate's entrance gate. The club has pleasant self-contained rooms for US$10 per person, and also serves meals and drinks. From the grounds you will normally see hippos and a good variety of birds. You could also ask about taking the club's motorboat out on to the river, where you can expect to see plenty of hippos, crocs and birds. Provided that the boat is not being used for other purposes, there shouldn't be a problem and you'll probably only be asked to cover fuel costs. A small game park on the estate is the only place in Malawi where you can see giraffe – entrance fee is US$1.

Day visitors to the club should be prepared to pay a nominal fee for temporary membership (no more than US$1). That said, the atmosphere is very friendly: provided that you're polite and look neat, I doubt that anybody will feel strongly motivated to question your presence. Accommodation is best booked in advance; tel: 01 428200 for details.

About 12km south of Nchalo, near the township of Ngabu, the comfortable **Ngabu Inn** has self-contained double rooms for US$10 as well as a campsite, restaurant and bar.

BANGULA

Bangula lies on the Mozambican border near the confluence of the Ruo and Shire rivers. It is the obvious base for visits to the Elephant Marsh (though travellers without their own transport might be better staying the night at Makhanga). The best place to stay in Bangula is the **Council Resthouse**, which has large, self-contained doubles for US$2 and rooms using communal showers for US$1. There are also several private resthouses. Meals are served at **Jehova's Restaurant** (next to the PTC supermarket), but don't let the voluminous and tantalising menu painted on the wall raise your hopes too much – a fairly standard plate of chicken and rice is about all that was on offer when I was there.

MWABVI WILDLIFE RESERVE
This small, little-known and infrequently visited reserve lies in the far south of Malawi near the Mozambican border. The rugged terrain supports a mixture of *brachystegia*, mopane and acacia woodland. Poaching has had a drastic effect on animal numbers; the black rhinoceros is almost certainly extinct, and game viewing is generally poor, in part due to the dense vegetation. Among the large mammals still to be found in Mwabvi are greater kudu, sable antelope, bushbuck, nyala, baboon, vervet monkey, leopard and possibly lion. The thickets protect several bird species more normally associated with coastal habitats, for instance Rudd's apalis, Woodward's batis and grey sunbird.

Getting there and away
Coming from Blantyre, the turn-off to Mwabvi lies on the M1 just before Bangula, roughly 5km after you cross the bridge over the Thangadzi River. Turn right into this earth road and follow it until you reach the ADMARC market and a tsetse control barrier, where an indistinct and unsignposted track, hidden among houses, leads to the right. This track leads to the entrance gate of the reserve, where you must sign in. The camp is 10km from the entrance gate: take the right fork about 1km past the gate, then about 6km further take the left fork at a baobab tree bearing the signpost 'Game reserve – no shooting'.

Ideally, you want to visit the reserve in a 4WD, though a saloon with high clearance should make it through in the dry season. Mwabvi is not a practical destination without your own transport.

Where to stay
Camping is the only form of accommodation at Mwabvi and you will have to take all your own provisions, including water from the main gate. The game scout at the camp is normally happy to accompany visitors on walks to the Ndipitakuti Gorge and a nearby sandstone pillar.

ELEPHANT MARSH
This 65km long by 19km wide permanent marsh forms the eastern floodplain of the Shire River. It's a lush, beautiful area with a rich sense of place; the water is thick with blue-flowered hyacinth and white lilies, and the surrounding area is studded with massive baobab trees and tall palms.

Elephant Marsh was named by Livingstone, who, on his first expedition up the Shire, recorded seeing a herd of around 800 elephants coming to drink. The elephants were shot out by the turn of the century, but, although it is not protected in any way, the marsh remains a nature sanctuary of note. It supports Malawi's largest population of crocodiles, as well as a substantial number of hippos and smaller mammals such as otters. Of most interest, however, are the birds attracted to the marsh – they are spectacular both in number and in variety, whether or not you have a specific interest in birds.

The best way to explore Elephant Marsh is by boat. Boat trips can be organised in Mchacha James, a small village on the edge of the marsh about 15km from Bangula.

Getting there and away

To reach Mchacha James from Bangula, you need first to get to Makhanga village, which lies about 10km east of the M1 along a road forking out of Bangula town centre 100m or so south of the railway crossing. There is a fair amount of *matola* transport to Makhanga, though in wet years, when the marsh practically laps the Bangula–Makhanga road, the abundant birdlife is a good inducement to walk.

Mchacha James lies on the edge of the marsh about an hour's walk from Makhanga. To get there, follow the main road out of Makhanga towards Muona. Precisely 2km past the signpost in Makhanga reading 'Ministry of Culture and Education', an unsignposted turn-off to the left of the Muona Road leads to the village. There are several left forks in this area – if you're unsure which one to take, follow the Muona road until you notice an idiosyncratic double-storey building (signposted 'Pentecostal Holiness Church') to your left, then turn back towards Makhanga and take the first turn-off, now to your right and only 100m from the church.

From the turn-off, you'll wander through a sprawling village for about 4km before you reach a mosque. There's no real danger of getting lost provided you stick to the widest track, but there are plenty of people around if you need to ask directions – 'James' is the key word. The boat owners live near the mosque so just ask around: chances are they'll find you before you find them.

Please note that if using your own vehicle, it is impossible to use this route until the bridge across the Shire River to the east of Bangula is rebuilt, but if using public transport, you can cross by boat. An alternative dry-season route is down the S151 from Thyolo.

Boat trips

At Mchacha James, docked along with the dugouts used by local fishermen, is a pair of relatively sturdy rowing boats owned by two brothers who are happy to punt visitors around the marsh for a fee. The rate for boat hire will depend on how long you want to go out for, and also on your negotiating skills: a two-hour trip should cost between US$5 and US$10 per boat.

Gliding silently along the water, surrounded by lush vegetation and with birds in every direction, is sheer visual bliss; for me it was an unquestionable highlight of my time in Malawi. The punting brothers form an amusing double act, repeating and finishing each other's sentences like Thomson and Thompson on safari. More to the point, both brothers are highly articulate and knowledgeable about every aspect of the marsh, and they are excellent bird guides, likely to generate enthusiasm in the most aviphobic of passengers. To whet the appetite of bird enthusiasts, we saw around 30 species in two hours, including fish eagle, purple and goliath heron, glossy ibis, openbill and yellow-billed stork, malachite kingfisher and – two birds which rank highly on many South African birders' most wanted list – the cryptically marked pygmy goose and tern-like African skimmer.

If you don't have a private vehicle, it's probably wise to spend the night before you explore the marsh in Makhanga. It is possible to visit Mchacha James as a day trip from Bangula, but the marsh is ideally explored in the early morning, so it's best to overnight as nearby as possible. It would also make sense, provided that you arrive in Makhanga early enough, to do a reconnaissance trip to Mchacha James and make arrangements for a boat the afternoon before you intend to go out on the marsh.

Where to stay
There is at least one resthouse in Makhanga: the **Tiyesembo Resthouse**, with single rooms for US$1 and doubles with a fan for US$2. There is no running water, and it doesn't appear to serve meals so bring some food with you from Bangula. On the plus side, the bar has a fridge filled with cold sodas and beers.

If you have a vehicle, it's more tempting to stay at one of the resthouses in Bangula (see *Bangula*, pages 116–17). As far as I am aware, there is no accommodation in Mchacha James itself, though if you have a tent you could presumably ask around for somewhere to camp free.

BACKROADS NORTH OF ELEPHANT MARSH
From Mchacha James, the S151 continues in a northerly direction to Muona Mission, where it forks along two little-used routes, both of which are often unusable during the rainy season, but which might repay exploration at other times of the year.

The S150 continues from Muona along the east bank of the marsh below the Thyolo Escarpment. This road is generally flooded after rains, as the marsh expands, but it should be passable during the dry season, and it can offer excellent birding as it sticks close to the marsh's edge.

The S151 climbs the Thyolo Escarpment north of Muona, eventually emerging at Thyolo Town. The main attraction of this road is the dramatic views back to the Shire Valley during the ascent. In a 4WD you can normally use the S151 at any time of year. If you have a saloon car, then you should enquire about the current condition before you set off.

There is no public transport along either route, and private vehicles are few and far between, so hitching could prove very difficult.

Thyolo and Mulanje

The M2 south of Limbe winds to Thyolo through a highland area quite different in character to any other part of Malawi. This is tea-growing country, strikingly reminiscent of the Kericho district of western Kenya: breezy, rolling hills swathed in orderly rows of tea bushes and still supporting the occasional remnant patch of indigenous forest in valleys and along watercourses.

As you cross the plantation-covered hills around Thyolo, you can hardly fail to be aware of the staggeringly proportioned granite outcrop that dominates the eastern skyline. This is the Mulanje Massif, the highest mountain in Central Africa, rising almost 2km above the surrounding Phalombe Plain to an altitude of 3,002m.

Tourism to this part of Malawi is inevitably, and rightly, centred around Mulanje, which arguably offers the finest hiking in the country, and is renowned by mountaineers for its exceptional rock-climbing. Thyolo, too, is worth a stop, as a base from which to explore the biologically rich mahogany forest on the upper slopes of Thyolo Mountain.

CLIMATE

This is a region of stark climatic contrasts. Thyolo and its surrounds have a pleasingly moderate highland climate, but temperatures climb as you descend to the Luchenza River and Phalombe Plain. Weather conditions on top of Mulanje are relatively cool, and night-time temperatures can be downright chilly, especially between June and August.

GETTING AROUND

There are two routes between Blantyre and Mulanje: the tarred M2 through Thyolo and, to its north, the unsurfaced M4. There are six buses daily in each direction along the M2 between Blantyre and Mulanje Town. The journey takes around four hours, less if you catch an express bus. Buses connecting Blantyre to Mulanje via the M4 don't take significantly longer than those using the M2, but the trip is unpleasantly dusty. You can also travel along the M2 using *matola* rides, starting by picking up a vehicle to Thyolo at Limbe bus station.

Some buses from Blantyre terminate at Mulanje Town, but many others continue along the western and northern base of the Mulanje Massif through

Phalombe to Migowi. Other buses continue through Mulanje Town to Muloza on the Mozambican border.

THYOLO

Thyolo – pronounced *Cholo* – is the tea capital of Malawi, and one of the oldest towns in the country. The leafy administrative centre consists of a cluster of colonial-era government offices built around a rather pointless traffic circle, and it is separated from the busy market and bus station by a tea field. About 1km back towards Limbe lies a string of smarter shops, among them a PTC supermarket.

As with most Malawian towns, there is nothing much to do in Thyolo, though if you're not in a rush and heading to Mulanje, it's a pleasant enough place to hang about. If you're looking for the chance to limber up your legs before making an assault on Mulanje, the countryside around Thyolo is riddled with dirt roads which make for great rambling, with the attractive option of exploring the nearby Thyolo Mountain Forest Reserve and Satemwa Tea Estate.

Getting there and away

All buses along the M2 between Blantyre and Mulanje stop at Thyolo. Note, however, that some buses between Blantyre and Mulanje use the dirt M4 and thus don't go anywhere near Thyolo – check which route the bus is using. Far quicker than buses are the minibuses and other *matola* vehicles which run directly between Limbe's bus station and Thyolo.

Where to stay and eat

Of the usual selection of places, the **Tione Motel** is far better than its faded exterior suggests. Clean doubles using communal facilities cost US$1.50 and large, self-contained doubles with hot water cost US$3. The Tione Motel has a busy bar and a fair restaurant. It's about five minutes' walk from the bus station – anybody will direct you.

You can camp at the **Thyolo Club** (tel: 01 473259) for US$3 per person, inclusive of day membership.

THYOLO FOREST RESERVE

Unfortunately, as in so many other parts of the world, this forest reserve on the slopes of the 1,462m Thyolo Mountain has been invaded by peasant farmers. In spite of the valiant efforts of the owners of the Satemwa Tea Estate, what was once one of Malawi's best-preserved mahogany forests is being chopped up for forest-in-a-bag (charcoal) and turned into marginal little patches of farmland.

To see the pristine remains of the forest and birds such as the green-headed oriole, white-winged apalis, Thyolo alethe, little green bulbul and moustached green tinker barbet, your only chance is to visit the adjoining Satemwa Tea Estate.

Getting there and away

To get to the forest reserve you have to pass through the Satemwa Tea Estate, which requires prior arrangement (see below for contact details). Look for their well-signposted turn-off about 4km out on the Limbe side of Thyolo. The security guard at the gate will direct you to the estate office.

Where to stay

There are now two accommodation options near Thyolo Mountain, both of which lie within the Satemwa Tea Estate. **Chawani Bungalow** has four bedrooms, each sleeping two people. It is set on the slopes of Thyolo Mountain, within easy walking distance of the forested upper slopes, and on a clear day it offers a great view across to Mulanje. The whole bungalow costs US$70, which may be prohibitive to independent travellers, but would be excellent value for a group. The **Satemwa Guesthouse** is a colonial-era plantation house with three bedrooms each sleeping two people. The whole bungalow costs US$65, again great value for a group. Both bungalows are fully furnished and have a chef/houseman available to do the cooking and cleaning.

Dairy products such as milk and cheese can be bought on the estate, while a wide range of foodstuffs is avaliable at the PTC 7km from the estate in Thyolo. In addition to walking, fishing and birdwatching, the estate offers tours of the tea plantation, which is one of the oldest in the country, established in 1895. For those without a vehicle, transport to the bungalows can be arranged at the estate office, which lies a mere 500m from the main Limbe–Thyolo road.

The management recommends you make a reservation, especially at weekends. To book or make further enquiries, contact Satemwa Tea Estate; tel: 01 473356; fax: 01 473368; email: 113213.233@compuserve.com.

MULANJE

This attractive and spacious small town, set amid tea estates at the southern base of the Mulanje Massif, is visited by most people who plan to hike on Malawi's highest mountain. Mulanje is split into two discrete parts. Coming from the direction of Blantyre, you arrive first at the commercial centre, called Chitakali, where there is a PTC supermarket, a well-stocked vegetable market, a few basic resthouses, and also the turn-off to Likhubula Forestry Station (the most popular base for climbing Mulanje). Mulanje itself lies about 2km past Chitakali, and it is reached by following the flame-tree-lined avenue which bisects Chitakali Tea Estate. Mulanje Town is where most of the administrative buildings can be found, as well as a few smarter motels.

Getting there and away

Several buses run between Blantyre and Mulanje every day, including two express buses. You can also do the trip in hops, using *matola* vehicles from Limbe to Thyolo, then to Luchenza, and finally to Mulanje. It is easy to hitch a lift between Chitakali and Mulanje Boma.

Where to stay

If you want to stay near the junction to Likhubula, there are a few cheap resthouses to choose from in Chitakali. The **Chididi Motel** looks about

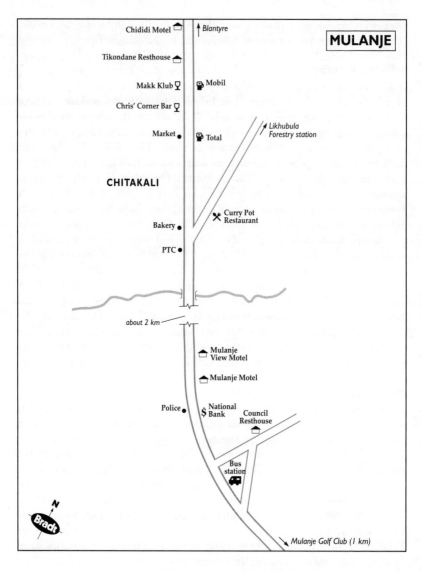

the best of an indifferent bunch, offering clean bright rooms with three-quarter beds for US$1.40.

In Mulanje itself, the **Council Resthouse** has scruffy rooms using communal showers for US$0.80 as well as good self-contained doubles at a very reasonable US$1.60. The **Mulanje Motel** is much smarter and still not particularly expensive at US$2/4 for a large single/double using communal showers. Smarter yet, but still very affordable, the **Mulanje View Motel** charges US$3/5 for a single/double using communal hot showers, and US$10 for a self-contained double. All rates include a good breakfast.

You can camp at the **Mulanje Golf Club**, which lies about 1km out of

town towards the Mozambican border, for US$6 per person inclusive of day
membership and use of facilities such as the bar, restaurant, television room
and snooker table.

Where to eat

Both the **Mulanje View Motel** and **Mulanje Hotel** have good restaurants
with meals for around US$2. In Chitakali, the **Curry Pot Restaurant** is the
best bet for a meal. The owner, Jasmine, dishes up the best samosas and curries
in Malawi at very reasonable prices.

If you're heading to the Mulanje Massif, you can stock up at the PTC or
Kandodo supermarket in Chitakali, which stock frozen sausages, fresh bread
and the usual tinned goods. The market in Chitakali has as good a range of
vegetables as any in Malawi.

MULANJE MASSIF

Mulanje is a vast, isolated granite massif rising sharply and dramatically above
the Phalombe Plain southeast of Blantyre. The massif covers an area of
650km², and largely comprises a plateau of rolling grassland averaging around
2,000m in altitude. This plateau is incised by several thickly wooded ravines,
while rising above it are 20 peaks that reach an altitude of over 2,500m. One
of these, Sapitwa Peak, is at 3,002m the highest point in Central Africa.

Mulanje is composed of hard metamorphic rock such as granite and syenite.
The rock which forms the massif is roughly 130 million years old and it has
gradually been exposed as the softer rocks around it have been eroded. In this
respect, Mulanje is very similar to the granite koppies that are such a
characteristic feature of the Central African landscape. The difference is
simply one of scale – Mulanje is a very, very big koppie.

Several different vegetation types cover Mulanje. The lower slopes of the
massif, where they have not been planted with exotic pines and eucalyptus, are
covered in closed-canopy *brachystegia* woodland. The main vegetation type of
the plateau is not dissimilar in appearance to the alpine moorland found on
East Africa's larger mountains: a combination of heathers, heaths and grasses.
The moorland is notable for supporting a wide array of wild flowers, including
various helichrysums, irises, lobelias and aloes, a large number of which are
endemic to the mountain.

Evergreen woodland and forest is largely restricted to ravines and
watercourses. The most notable forest tree on Mulanje is the endemic
Mulanje cedar (*Widdringtonia whytei*), a magnificent timber tree which can
reach a height of over 40m. Mulanje's cedars have been depleted in the last
century due to timber felling, but several impressive stands remain, the most
accessible of which lies in the saddle southeast of the Chambe Basin and
includes many trees that are thought to be over 300 years old.

Mulanje's fauna is less diverse than is its flora. In the open highlands, the
only mammal species seen with any regularity are klipspringer, rock hyrax, red
rock hare and vole. In the woodlands of the lower slopes and in forested areas,
there is a good chance of seeing vervet and (in the Chambe basin) samango

monkeys. Red duiker, bushbuck, leopard, bushpig and porcupine are also present in wooded habitats.

The selection of birds recorded on the grasslands of the plateau is not great; species of interest include Shelly's and Hildebrandt's francolin, wailing cisticola, a variety of swifts and swallows (the localised blue swallow is present from October to March), and raptors such as auger buzzard, black eagle, lanner and peregrine falcon and rock kestrel. Of more interest are the birds found in the forest and woodland, including a variety of bulbuls, robins, thrushes, flycatchers, bush shrikes and warblers.

With easy access from Blantyre, well-organised and inexpensive facilities, and some of the most dramatic scenery in the country, it is not surprising that Mulanje is Malawi's premier hiking and rock-climbing destination, popular with tourists and expatriates alike. There are several routes from the base to the plateau, but the only ones that are used with much regularity are the Skyline Path to the Chambe Basin and the Lichenya Path to the Lichenya Plateau. Both of these routes start at Likhubula Forestry Station, which lies at the eastern base of the mountain about 10km from Mulanje Town.

In addition to there being inexpensive accommodation at Likhubula Forestry Station, there are seven huts on the plateau, connected to each other by well-

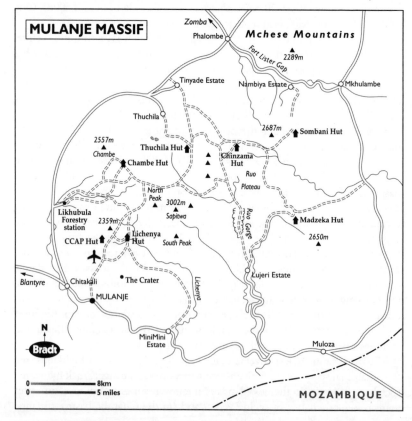

marked trails ranging from three to six hours' walking duration. With 20 peaks to explore, Mulanje has enough walking and climbing potential to keep anybody busy for at least a month. Frank Eastwood's comprehensive *Guide to the Mulanje Massif* (see below) covers almost every possible walking and climbing route.

Many of the streams on Mulanje are stocked with trout. Fishing is allowed with a permit, which can be obtained from the Forestry Office.

Further information
Frank Eastwood's 150-page *Guide to the Mulanje Massif* (Lorton Communications) is the definitive guide to the mountain. Even a casual rambler would have to be crazy to visit Mulanje without this book, and it is absolutely essential for people undertaking lengthy hikes or who intend climbing rock faces. The guide includes not only a wealth of background information but also detailed descriptions and times for all hiking routes and rock climbs, and maps of the more popular routes including the Skyline and Lichenya paths. *Guide to the Mulanje Massif* is widely available in Blantyre (try the tourist office if you can't find it in a bookshop) and costs around US$3.

The map sales office in Blantyre sells an excellent 1:40,000 contour map of the Mulanje Massif for US$1.50. It was first published in 1995, and shows all footpaths and huts on the plateau.

Rock climbers and hikers planning to use unusual routes are advised to contact the Mountain Club of Malawi in Blantyre.

Getting there and away
Likhubula village lies about 10km from Chitakali along the Phalombe road. From Chitakali, one bus heads out to Phalombe every day, stopping at Likhubula village, and it's easy enough to find a *matola* ride. It is also a very attractive walk. Likhubula Forestry Station is about 1km from the village; the turn-off is signposted around 50m after you cross a bridge over the Likhubula River.

Where to stay
Likhubula
There is only one basic dollar-a-night resthouse in Likhubula village, as well as a bottle store and a sprawling, but poorly stocked, market. More attractive accommodation can be found in the compound of Likhubula Forestry Station, about 1km from the village. Best value is the **CCAP Resthouse**, which consists of a group of chalets, each with six beds, a shower, a toilet, a kitchen with a hotplate and basic utensils, and a dining room. The chalets cost US$4 per person, dorms US$2.50 and camping US$1.50.

There is also the attractive old forestry resthouse which has been privatised and renovated as the Likhubula Forest Lodge. Bedding and towels are provided and a well equipped kitchen is at your disposal. Rates range from US$12 for a simple single to US$20 per person in an en-suite double room. Camping costs US$1.50 and for a similar amount per day they will look after your car while you're hiking.

It's worth spending some time at the forestry station: the setting is superb and there are some interesting rock pools and waterfalls to be visited. The rock pools are practically in the forest station, while the waterfall lies about 45 minutes' walk from the station and is difficult to find without a guide.

On Mulanje

On the mountain itself there are seven huts, six of which are run by the Forestry Department and one by the CCAP. All huts cost US$2 per person. Firewood and water are provided at all the huts, but you must bring your own food, and bedding is provided only at the CCAP Hut. The six forestry huts can be booked at Likhubula Forestry Station: availability is not normally a problem. Camping is permitted on the mountain, but only around the huts. Staff at the huts cut firewood and light cooking fires. Some pots and pans are available, but take your own candles.

The most frequently used forestry huts are **Chambe Hut** and **Lichenya Hut**, both of which lie on the eastern side of the massif, within a day's walk of Likhubula Forestry Station. Chambe Hut lies in the Chambe Basin at an altitude of 1,860m, about three to four hours' walk from Likhubula along the Skyline Path. The hut contains six hard bunks and floor space for an additional ten people. The old Lichenya Hut, on the Lichenya Plateau at an altitude of 1,840m and about five hours' walk from Likhubu Forest Station, burnt down a few years ago, but has since been rebuilt and is now even bigger and better.

The church-run **CCAP Hut** is also on the Lichenya Plateau, about 2km from Lichenya Hut, and at the higher altitude of 1,995m. A bed at the CCAP Hut costs the same as one at the forestry huts, and bedding is provided. Beds can be booked at the CCAP Resthouse in Likhubula.

The other four forestry huts are only likely to be used by hikers who spend several days on the mountain, or who ascend by one of the more obscure routes.

Thuchila Hut lies on the north of the massif at an altitude of 2,000m near the edge of the Thuchila Plateau, about five hours' walk from Chambe Hut. There are excellent views of the peaks from Thuchila Hut, and it is the best base from which to climb Sapitwa Peak. The hut sleeps up to 16 people, but watch out for rats.

Chinzama Hut lies on the north of the plateau, at an altitude of 2,150m in the Ruo Basin, about three hours' walk east of Thuchila Hut. It sleeps up to 12 people. Also at the north of the plateau, three hours' walk east of Chinzama, **Sombani Hut** lies at an altitude of 2,080m and sleeps eight people.

In the southwest of the massif, **Madzeka Hut** is around four hours' walk from either Chinzama or Sombani hut. It lies at an altitude of 1,820m and sleeps up to 12 people.

Hiking practicalities

Organising a hike up Mulanje is a straightforward procedure. The most normal base for doing this is Likhubula Forestry Station, where you can book mountain huts and arrange porters and guides as required. Guides are not strictly necessary, especially if you have a map and a copy of *Guide to Mulanje Massif*, but their services are inexpensive so you might consider hiring one. A porter is strongly recommended, at least for your first day – the ascent of Mulanje is *very* steep. Expenses are minimal: entrance fee is US$1, huts only cost US$2 per person per night, and even a guide or porter shouldn't set you back more than US$7 or so per day. Camping is US$1 per day.

It is worth paring down your luggage to the bare minimum before tackling Mulanje; spare gear can be left at the forestry station or at Doogle's in Blantyre. What you do need is a sleeping bag or thick blanket, and plenty of warm clothing for the chilly highland nights. You must also bring all the food you will need. The ideal place to stock up is in Blantyre, but there is a PTC supermarket in Chitakali opposite the turn-off to Likhubula and, a few hundred metres away, a well-stocked vegetable market.

A week or so would be required to do a full circuit of the huts, and you could spend considerably longer than a week on Mulanje if you so chose, but most visitors settle for two or three days, a day each for the ascent and descent, and one day for exploring part of the plateau. The most popular options are either to loop, using the Chambe Path one way and the Lichenya Path the other way, with a night each at Chambe and Lichenya huts; or else to ascend and descend along the same route, so that you can spend your free day on the mountain without being hindered by a heavy pack. If you aren't carrying bedding, the best hut to use is the CCAP Hut on Lichenya Plateau; the nearby Sunset Viewpoint is well worth a visit.

Mulanje can be climbed at any time of year. The dry, cool months from April to September are generally regarded as the best for hiking, though there is a danger of treacherous mists (called *chiperone*) enveloping the massif between May and July. If you are caught in *chiperone* conditions, you must stay put, as walking is very dangerous, even along marked trails. During the rainy season (November to early April), many paths become slippery and some may be temporarily impassable due to flooding. The Skyline Path to Chambe is safe at all times of year as it only crosses one river, and there is a bridge.

Mulanje is not high enough for serious altitude-related illness to be a cause for concern, though people arriving directly from sea level may feel some mild effects at higher altitudes.

Women hiking alone should be careful. They, and anyone else for that matter, should consider hooking up with the Mountain Club of Malawi, who visit Mulanje, or other mountains, almost every weekend. They have a wealth of local knowledge which can save you money and trouble and enhance the whole Mulange experience. Contact Ben on tel: 621520 or email: benlewis@malawi.net.

Another option is to contact Tiyende Pamodzi Scouts at PO Box 716, Zomba, tel: 01 527307 or through Land and Lake Safaris, and they will tailor a hike or trek for you.

If you're in the area around mid-June, ask about the Porters' Race organised by the Mountain Club. The Mulanje porters race up and down 21km of mountain for prizes, including a bicycle.

PHALOMBE AND MIGOWI

From Likhubula, a road arcs around the northeastern face of Mulanje to the small towns of Phalombe and Migowi. There is a fair amount of public transport as far as Migowi, in the form of the occasional bus and more regular *matola* rides.

Phalombe is the site of a rather impressive Catholic Mission, where there are a couple of basic resthouses. The major attraction is the nearby Fort Lister Pass which separates Mulanje from its smaller, more northerly neighbour Mount Mchese. Fort Lister was built by Britain in 1893 to help close off the slave route between Lake Malawi and the Mozambique coast, and it was abandoned in 1902. Within the ruined fortifications lies the grave of Gilbert Stevenson, a cousin of the author Robert Louis Stevenson. Fort Lister lies 10km east of Phalombe, about 500m south of the road through the pass.

There is nothing about Migowi that invites superlatives – it's just another pleasant, friendly and totally nondescript Malawian town, no more and no less. It is, however, a potential springboard for a couple of *very* off-the-beaten-track explorations. First up is a back route across little-used dirt roads to Chiradzulu Mountain and Blantyre. When I tried to catch a lift this way, the presence of a few hopeful locals heading in the same direction suggested that vehicles do roll past from time to time, but I had no luck and eventually returned to Mulanje Boma the way I had come. A second possibility is to continue northwards via Kalinde and Nambazo to the remote, marshy southern shore of Lake Chilwa. As with the Chiradzulu route, I don't think this is one to be approached if you are in a hurry. If you get stuck in Migowi, there are several basic resthouses to choose from.

Zomba and Surrounds

This is a lovely part of Malawi, a relatively low-lying plateau interrupted by a number of large mountains, most notably the vast Zomba Mountain above the town of the same name. The most popular tourist attraction in the region is undoubtedly Zomba Mountain, a hikers' paradise with plentiful birds and small mammals, as well as wonderful views across to Mulanje and Mozambique. Also growing in popularity, especially since Mvuu Camp was privatised and thoroughly refurbished, is Liwonde National Park, one of the most atmospheric reserves in Africa, dominated by the palm-fringed, crocodile- and hippo-infested waters of the Shire River. The Zomba area also has at least one excellent off-the-beaten-track option: the little-known but thoroughly worthwhile Lake Chilwa.

CLIMATE
Zomba and Lake Chilwa have relatively temperate climates, though the open nature of the lakeshore means it is very exposed in the midday heat. Liwonde and the Shire River are hot and humid.

GETTING AROUND
Zomba and Liwonde lie on the most popular route between Blantyre and Lilongwe. If you are driving, it's a well-surfaced road, and if you're not, there are plenty of buses connecting both towns to Lilongwe, Blantyre and points in between. Hitching is also reasonably easy.

Lake Chilwa, the least visited of the region's attractions, is straightforward to reach on public transport – there are a couple of *matolas* daily between Zomba Town and Kachulu on the shore of Lake Chilwa. Liwonde National Park is best entered by boat from Liwonde Town – a relatively expensive option, but worth every cent. The Zomba Plateau is within walking distance of Zomba Town, but it's a steep hike, and most people either take a taxi to the top or hitch.

ZOMBA
The capital of Malawi until 1975, and seat of parliament until 1994, Zomba is probably the most immediately appealing of Malawi's larger towns. Admittedly,

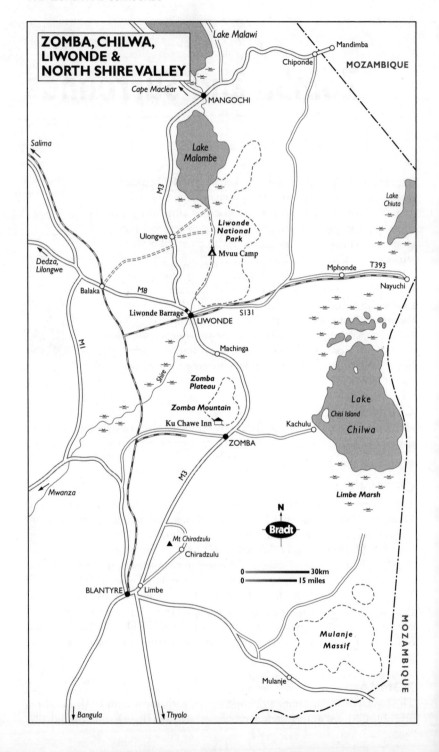

**ZOMBA, CHILWA,
LIWONDE &
NORTH SHIRE VALLEY**

this isn't saying much, but Zomba does have in its favour a wonderful setting at the base of Zomba Mountain, and a distinct atmosphere, determined by its leafy avenues and the cluster of fading colonial buildings between the main road and the wooded foot slopes of the mountain. One of the most interesting old buildings in Zomba is the State House, which dates from 1901.

The Zomba area was explored in early 1859 by Livingstone's Zambezi Expedition. Livingstone and John Kirk climbed Zomba Mountain, reaching its summit near the site of the modern Ku Chawe Inn. Livingstone is also credited as the first European to reach Lake Chilwa (in fact, the lake, like many of Livingstone's 'discoveries' in Malawi, was probably already known to Portuguese traders).

In 1859, the Manganja agriculturists of Zomba were suffering greatly at the hands of Yao slave raiders. The Zambezi Expedition became indirectly involved in the Yao–Maganja war when, in August 1861, Bishop Mackenzie, together with a handful of British soldiers and over 1,000 Manganja warriors, marched from Mogomero Mission on to the slopes of Zomba Mountain and razed several Yao slaving villages.

Livingstone had been impressed by the fertility of the Zomba area, and so it was the obvious choice of the Church of Scotland as the site of their first mission in the Shire Highlands. However, the ferocity of the local slave trade and the large number of wild animals living in the area forced them instead to start the mission further south, at what is now Blantyre. The modern town of Zomba was founded in the 1890s by Sir Harry Johnston as the capital of the British Central African Protectorate.

Zomba today exudes a rustic peacefulness belying its sometimes bloody past. A small town in comparison with Lilongwe or Blantyre, Zomba nevertheless boasts a vegetable market as good as any in the country, a lovely golf course and park, a major university, and several interesting buildings of Indian and British design. For all that, you can exhaust Zomba's charms in a few hours, and few travellers would bother to stop there at all were it not the gateway to Zomba Mountain, one of the most popular rambling and hiking areas in Malawi.

The Safari Forex Bureau near the bus station offers very good rates for US dollars cash and travellers' cheques.

Getting there and away

All express and country buses between Blantyre and points north (Monkey Bay, Lilongwe and Mzuzu) stop at Zomba. There are also regular minibuses between Zomba and Limbe.

Where to stay

There is no tourist-class accommodation in town, though the **Government Resthouse**, set in the former residence of Sir Harry Johnston some distance from the town centre, does come pretty close, with good self-contained rooms for around US$45/60 single/double. Most upmarket tourists prefer to stay at the Ku Chawe Inn on Zomba Plateau, which is within easy reach of town, assuming that you have a vehicle.

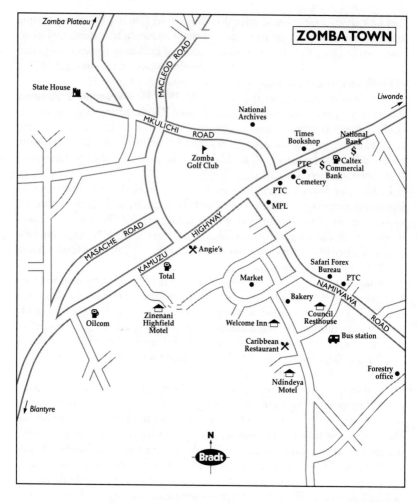

The **Council Resthouse** opposite the bus station used to be quite popular with travellers, but most people avoid it these days – if the persistent reports of theft from the rooms don't put you off, then a lungful of the odour emanating from the communal showers and toilets probably will. The best thing that can be said for this place is that it's very cheap at US$0.80 for a bed in a dormitory, US$1.60/2 for an ordinary single/double in the main building, or US$3.20 for a self-contained double in a discrete and rather less whiffy wing.

Surprisingly, there aren't too many private resthouses near the bus station. The **Welcome Inn** is a standard dollar-a-night dump, which at least doesn't smell.

The **Ndindeya Motel** offers considerably more appealing rooms at US$3/6 for an ordinary single/double and US$7/10 for a self-contained single/double, with breakfast an extra US$1 or so per person. We've heard a couple of reports of theft from the rooms here, and would advise you against leaving any valuables in your room while you are out.

The **Zinenani Highfield Motel** is a newer place, five to ten minutes' walk from the bus station through the market. It looks to be the best value in its range at US$2.60 for an ordinary single or US$4.60 for a self-contained double – the rooms are fairly clean, there's a restaurant and bar attached, and we've heard no reports of theft.

Where to eat
The clubhouse at the **Golf Course** serves excellent meals at surprisingly reasonable prices (nothing much over US$3). It also does great filter coffee; as much as you can drink for a few kwacha.

The restaurant at the **Ndindeya Motel** serves good meals (tasty chicken or beef stew with rice or chips) for around US$1.50. Directly opposite the motel, the **Caribbean Restaurant** does good fried *chambo* or chicken with fresh vegetables and chips, rice or boiled potatoes. You'll have to negotiate a price with the manager, which can become rather irksome, though all will be forgiven when the food arrives. **Angie's Take-Away** serves burgers, curries, fried *chambo* and similar dishes for around US$2.

The PTC and Kandodo supermarkets are well stocked by Malawian standards, and the Kandodo stocks freshly-baked pastries and bread. The market in Zomba is not, as is sometimes claimed, one of the largest in Africa, but it does stock a better-than-average selection of fresh fruit and vegetables.

ZOMBA PLATEAU
Zomba Mountain rises immediately to the northeast of Zomba Town. It is one of the most popular areas in Malawi for walking and hiking. The extensive plateau, protected in Malawi's oldest forest reserve (gazetted in 1913), is covered largely in plantation, but it still contains significant patches of indigenous riverine and montane forest, as well as areas of tangled scrub and *brachystegia* woodland. The plateau is circled by motorable roads, and is crossed by innumerable footpaths.

Although Zomba is noted mostly for its scenery and birds, a good variety of large mammals is present, albeit in small numbers. Leopards are the most common large predator, though hyenas and even lions are still seen from time to time. Antelope species include bushbuck, klipspringer and red duiker. Vervet monkeys and baboons are reasonably common, and samango monkeys are occasionally seen in indigenous forests, particularly around Chingwe's Hole.

Getting there and away
The 13km road from Zomba Town to the top of the plateau used to split about halfway up into a separate up-road and down-road but is now two-way traffic to the top. The Ku Chawe Inn, forestry campsite and other private cottages are all clustered near the edge of the escarpment at the end of the road. To get to them, follow the road signposted for Ku Chawe Inn from the centre of Zomba town opposite the Kandodo supermarket. The road is tarred the whole way.

There is no public transport to the top of the mountain. If you are in a hurry, the best thing to do is organise a private taxi at Zomba bus station. This

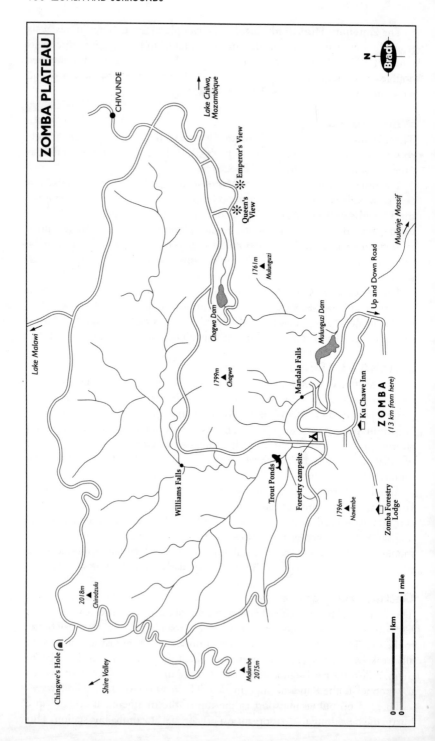

ZOMBA PLATEAU

will cost around US$8, possibly a little less if you bargain. I decided to hitch, and I caught a free lift even before I'd selected a good hitching spot. Perhaps I was lucky, as I saw no vehicles when I walked down a couple of days later. Still, with an early start, you shouldn't have a problem getting a lift, particularly at weekends. The alternative is to walk, which is perfectly feasible, though steep going towards the end.

The other option heading down is the so-called 'Potato Path' which is signposted from near the Ku Chawe Inn and takes about an hour to walk when dry – but is dangerously slippery and steep in wet conditions.

If you want to stay at the newly privatised Zomba Forestry Lodge, you need to get about halfway up the old up-road, just before it becomes a single lane road. The turn-off to the resthouse is clearly signposted. It's about 4km from the turn-off to the resthouse.

If you're walking up, and want to go as light as possible, you can leave luggage at the Council Resthouse in Zomba for a nominal fee.

Where to stay

The **Ku Chawe Inn** has been the flagship hotel in the Le Meridien chain since it re-opened following extensive renovations. The hotel is set in attractive grounds boasting a commanding position right on the edge of the escarpment, and the views across to Lake Chilwa are wonderful. Standard rooms cost US$121/200 single/double while superior rooms cost US$131/228 and deluxe rooms US$149/263, all inclusive of a full English breakfast but not taxes. All rooms are self-contained with running hot water and television; standard rooms have two single beds and an electric heater, while the more expensive rooms have double beds and log fires. The restaurant is excellent, with most dishes costing around US$8. Bookings can be made either by contacting the hotel directly at PO Box 71, Zomba (tel: 01 514237; fax: 01 514230) or else through the Le Meridien head office in the Mount Soche Hotel in Blantyre.

There are several **private cottages** behind the Ku Chawe Inn. Most of these are booked out as a unit and though you'd be taking a bit of a chance if you arrived without a booking, the odds are probably in favour of you finding a vacant cottage, except at weekends and on public holidays. Rates are variable but generally around US$5 per person, though if you just pitch up you can probably negotiate with the caretaker of any empty cottage. All the cottages have electricity, hot water, fridges and fully equipped kitchens. The CCAP cottage is one of the best, and you can check availability beforehand at the CCAP headquarters opposite the police station in Zomba Town. Other cottages include Phalombe Cottage and Mandala Cottage. If these are all full, it's normally possible to organise a room for around US$5 per person at the riding stables, which are about 1km from Ku Chawe Inn.

One of the most beautiful huts on the plateau is Montfort Cottage, the property of a nunnery in Zomba Town. Travellers are welcome to stay there, but they must make prior arrangements to collect the keys from the nunnery. Tel: 01 522565 to make a reservation.

The Department of Forestry **campsite** is about 1km from Ku Chawe Inn. It's a beautiful spot, surrounded by trees, and has a hot shower.

Zomba Forestry Lodge is in the forest reserve about halfway up the mountain (see directions on page 137). It consists of four self-contained rooms, costing US$15 per person, and facilities include hot water, a solar fridge and a firewood cooker. Recently privatised and renovated, this comfortable lodge is now run by Land and Lake Safaris (PO Box 2140, Lilongwe; tel: 01 757120; fax: 01 754560; email: landlake@malawi.net). Bedding and towels are provided and, although it is self-catering, friendly staff are on hand to prepare and serve your meals.

Although Chitinji Camp is only about 6km from Ku Chawe Inn (follow the signs), it is straight up the mountain via a forestry road and only suitable for 4WDs or hikers. At 1,830m, you'd be pretty chilly up there camping (US$2.50 per person), and would be warmer in the solid little stone house with hot showers and flush toilets (US$5.50 per person).

Another pleasant alternative is the Kuchawe Trout Farm. The guesthouse sleeps four in two bedrooms, sharing a lounge and kitchen, and costs US$7 per person. Camping is US$3 and sport fishing is offered in the nearby stream.

Where to eat

The only place to eat is at the Ku Chawe Inn, where à la carte meals cost around US$8. If you're not prepared to pay that sort of price, bring all the food you need from Zomba Town. Remarkably, Himalayan raspberries are grown on the plateau; you can buy a generous portion from the vendors outside Ku Chawe for around US$1.

Things to do

The Zomba Plateau is mostly of interest to ramblers and hikers, though its major points of interest can be seen from a vehicle by following the road that encircles the plateau. Horseback excursions can be arranged through the riding stables 1km from the Ku Chawe Inn.

Mulunguzi Dam

A short nature trail runs from the campsite past Mulunguzi Dam and along the forested banks of the Mulunguzi River and the Mandala Falls. This is a good area to see mammals (most commonly bushbuck and vervet monkey). Birds which are likely to be seen include black saw-wing swallow, mountain wagtail, Bertram's weaver, Livingstone's turaco and white-tailed crested flycatcher.

Chingwe's Hole

This natural hole lies about two hours' walk from the Ku Chawe Inn and can be reached by car. Chingwe's Hole is rumoured to reach the base of the Rift Valley, though recent explorations suggest it may only be 20m deep. A 3km circular nature trail leads from the hole past some excellent viewpoints (views to Lake Malombe) and into a patch of montane forest where blue monkeys are seen with regularity, and a variety of forest birds (starred robin, Schalow's turaco, a variety of bulbuls and warblers, as well as the very localised Thyolo alethe) are present.

There is a tradition that chiefs in the old days threw their enemies into 'bottomless' Chingwe's Hole, and a persistent rumour that Banda's regime revived this tradition.

Further information
An extensive network of signposted roads and footpaths means that the walking opportunities on the Zomba Plateau are practically limitless. The relief model of the plateau in the Forestry compound is useful for getting your bearings. Dedicated walkers are pointed to the excellent 36-page booklet *Zomba Mountain: A Walker's Guide* by Martyn and Kittie Cundy, which can be bought at most bookshops in Blantyre for around US$2. The book covers 15 walking routes, and includes several maps.

LAKE CHILWA
Chilwa, the southernmost of Malawi's major lakes, couldn't contrast more in atmosphere with Lake Malawi. Surrounded by flat plains and isolated hills, Chilwa's shallow, slimy, reed-lined waters extend over 650km^2, though they are subject to great fluctuations in water level. Only a century ago, Chilwa extended close to the bases of Mulanje and Zomba (both of which are now around 30km from the lake's shore), while in 1968, a severe local drought caused the lake to dry up altogether. There is no outlet to Lake Chilwa, and its size is almost totally dependent on the run-off from Zomba and Mulanje. Lake Chilwa has recently been designated a Ramsar Wetland of international importance and is receiving funding for its preservation. Water levels are up again and the lake now produces 20% of Malawi's fish requirements. With a number of boats offering transport and the best aquatic-bird viewing in Malawi, Lake Chilwa is well worth a visit.

There is a definite atmosphere about Chilwa, remote and perhaps slightly malevolent, though at dusk, with only Mulanje and Zomba mountains punctuating the open horizon, the pink and orange-tinged sky is the picture of serenity. The well-vegetated and in parts rather marshy shore is a birdwatchers' paradise, supporting a great variety of herons, waders and other shorebirds (glossy ibis were particularly common when I visited).

The best access to the lake is at a fishing village called Kachulu, which lies on the western shore, roughly 30km by road from Zomba Town. It's a lovely spot, and Kachulu is the sort of small, friendly workaday African village that too few visitors to Africa ever get to experience.

Getting there and away
Buses no longer run to Kuchulu, but minibuses and *matolas* leave when full from Zomba or the turn-off just north of Zomba – cost about US$1.

An interesting and challenging travel route would be to hop aboard one of the large motorised boats that service the villages on and around the lake from

Kachulu and get off on the Mozambique side at Sombe. I was told it would cost only US$2.

Where to stay

There are two basic resthouses in Kachulu, both of which have single rooms for around US$1. The private resthouse seems better than the Council Resthouse; the long-drop toilets are reasonably clean, and the obliging staff will boil up hot water for an open-air shower. If you have thoughts of exploring the lake beyond Kachulu, you'll probably need a tent.

Where to eat

There are a few restaurants in Kachulu, but you would be well advised to bring your own food from Zomba. If you're stuck, you'll probably be able to find some bread and tomatoes or bananas at one of the kiosks in the distinctly underwhelming market. If you want to explore beyond Kachulu, you should definitely aim to be self sufficient in food.

Things to do

Kachulu and the nearby lakeshore are certainly worth a couple of hours' investigation, particularly if you're interested in birds. You can also organise a boat across to Chisi Island, which consists of a couple of semi-submerged hills. There are some huge flocks of birds on Chisi's shore, while the baobab-studded hills are reputedly home to monkeys and hyenas. There are several small villages on Chisi and it could well be a rewarding place for self-sufficient campers to pitch a tent for a day or two. It's easy to organise a boat across to Chisi: the ride takes about 30 minutes each way. Bear in mind that dense reedbeds pose a navigational hazard to inexperienced rowers, so don't hire a boat without a local fisherman to take you around.

More ambitiously, boat-taxis connect Kachulu to several other points on the lake. They leave when full and charge US$0.50 to cross to the main island.

The northern part of Lake Chilwa is very marshy, particularly during the rains, and it is rated as one of the best birdwatching areas in Malawi, with large flocks everywhere, notably greater and lesser flamingoes, pelicans and the localised black egret. With your own vehicle, you could explore the area by driving along the D221 east of Liwonde Town, then (at Nsarama) turning left on to the earth T393 to Mphonde village, 8km from the Mozambican border. The best time to visit Mphonde is between September and December. As far as I am aware there is no public transport to Mphonde, but you could check it out in Liwonde.

If you do explore Lake Chilwa beyond Kachulu, it would be useful to have the appropriate 1:50,000 or 1:250,000 maps (the detail on the latter is pretty good) – and do write to tell me about it for the next edition of this book.

Wilfred J Plumbe has written to recommend the University of Malawi's *Lake Chilwa Co-ordinated Research Project: decline and recovery of a lake*, edited by Margaret Kalk, to interested readers – though it was published in 1970 and is probably now out-of-print. A new publication that will be of interest to some readers is the annotated bird checklist for Lake Chilwa sold (among other places) at the Wildlife Society Office in Blantyre and the Ku Chawe Inn on the Zomba Plateau.

LIWONDE

The town of Liwonde lies on the Shire River, about 50km south of its outlet from Lake Malombe. Like many Malawian towns, Liwonde is divided into two parts. The nominal town centre, which lies just off the main tar road between Zomba and Mangochi, about 1km from the river, has a selection of shops – including a PTC supermarket – a hospital and a large and well-organised market.

More scruffy, but of interest to tourists, is the satellite town (sometimes referred to as Liwonde Barrage) which straddles the main road on the west side of the bridge across the river. Liwonde Barrage is the main access point to Liwonde National Park, but even if you have no intention of visiting the park, it's worth stopping for the Shire River. It is a vision of tropical Africa: low-wooded hills in the background, fishermen punting past in traditional dugouts, hippos grunting and snorting, and thick reed beds rustling with birdlife.

Getting there and away

Liwonde lies just south of the junction where the M8/M1 to Lilongwe via Dedza diverges from the M3 between Blantyre and Monkey Bay. It is thus a major route focus, with regular buses in every direction stopping to pick up passengers. Most buses don't actually go into town, but stop at Liwonde Barrage and (country buses only) at the turn-off to the town centre. The best place to disembark is at the barrage. Liwonde is also the best place to board the train to Nayuchi on the Mozambican border. It departs at 06.00, Mondays to Fridays, and costs US$1.

Where to stay

Warthog's Wallow (PO Box 166, Chilema; tel/fax: 01 532409) lies in attractive grounds on the south bank of the river. The neglected facilities are in disrepair, but include a swimming pool and a riverfront platform where you can enjoy a cold drink while watching the hippos frolic. A self-contained room with fan, net and hot water costs US$24/40 single/double inclusive of breakfast and a three-course dinner. Self-catering accommodation is available at US$11/16 single/double.

Next door to Warthog's Wallow, the **Manpower Shireside Lodge**, aside from having an appalling name, is a bit of a dump at US$6/12 for a functional self-contained single/double.

Actually at Liwonde Barrage, and newly renovated, the **Sun Village Lodge** is a decent place with self-contained executive rooms for US$45 double. There are several cheaper places along the turn-off: the **Liwonde Holiday Resort** seems rather ambitiously named (it's no more than an ordinary resthouse) but it is reasonable value at US$1/2 single/double. There are also a few resthouses in Liwonde town centre, if you prefer to stay there, or down near the station.

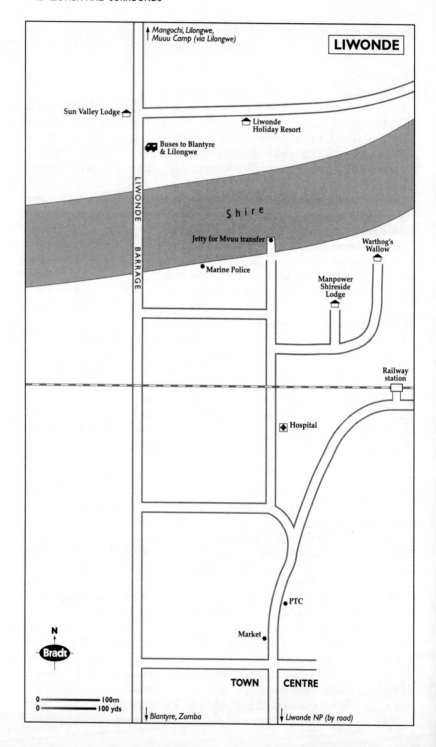

LIWONDE

↑ Mangochi, Lilongwe,
↑ Muuu Camp (via Lilongwe)

Sun Valley Lodge ⌂

⌂ Liwonde
Holiday Resort

🚌 Buses to Blantyre
& Lilongwe

LIWONDE BARRAGE

S h i r e

Jetty for Mvuu transfer ●

Warthog's
Wallow ⌂

● Marine Police

Manpower
Shireside
Lodge ⌂

Railway
station

⊞ Hospital

● PTC

Market ●

N

Bradt

0 ━━━ 100m
0 ━━━ 100 yds

TOWN   CENTRE

↓ Blantyre, Zomba

↓ Liwonde NP (by road)

LIWONDE NATIONAL PARK

The one national park in Malawi that truly lives up to expectations of a 'bush' reserve, Liwonde is neither particularly large by African standards, nor does it offer a game viewing experience comparable to somewhere like the Serengeti or Kruger Park. What makes Liwonde special is the atmosphere: dominated in almost every sense by the sluggish Shire River and its wildly lush fringing vegetation, it is a setting that evokes every romantic notion of untrammelled Africa. When we sat at Mvuu Camp at dusk, gazing over the river, our ears filled with the chirruping of frogs and grunting of hippos, we found it difficult to think of a scene anywhere in our travels that seemed so quintessentially African. Taken on its own merits, which in essence are aesthetic, I would rate Liwonde as one of the truly great African game reserves.

The game viewing at Liwonde doesn't quite match the atmosphere – the relatively small size of the park and dense human population in surrounding areas means poaching is an ongoing concern – but there is plenty of wildlife to be seen. An estimated 900 elephants are resident in the park, and it is quite normal to see three or four herds coming to drink at the river in the course of a day. Even more impressive is the hippo population. Some 4,000 hippos live along the 40km stretch of the Shire River which runs through the reserve (more than one every 20m!), surely one of the densest hippo populations on the African continent. Crocodiles, too, are ridiculously common – and, in many cases, quite terrifyingly large. Other common species include the exquisite and localised sable antelope (estimated population 600), as well as waterbuck, impala, bushbuck and warthog. Liwonde is also excellent for birding, both in terms of numbers seen (my own list was around 100 species, and a recent ornithological tour counted over 250 in two days!) and in terms of rarities.

Two lions have returned to the park and are spotted fairly regularly around Mvuu, and you may hear hyenas at night, but leopards were last seen in 1998. It is hoped that if the numbers of prey can be increased, then predators might return in larger numbers from the less populated parts of Mozambique. A successful wildlife introduction project that must be applauded is that of the J & B Circle. Since 1992, this group of 12 wildlife enthusiasts, with sponsorship from the famous whisky group, has worked to reintroduce the extinct black rhino to Liwonde National Park. With support from the South African National Parks Board, the first pair of black rhinos was airlifted from South Africa to a specially fenced and guarded sanctuary within the park. Since then, more have been brought in and they have started breeding. Buffalo, eland, hartebeest, roan antelope and zebra have also been established. It's great to be able to report on an African wildlife success story.

A national park entrance fee of US$5 per person per day is levied at the entrance gate plus US$2 per car per day (even if left parked opposite Mvuu Camp).

Getting there and away

Most people who take their own vehicle to Liwonde use a side road connecting the M3 between Liwonde Barrage and Mangochi to the west bank

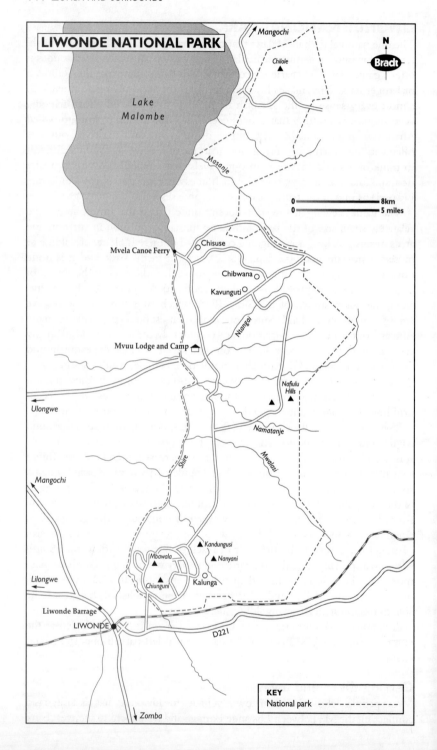

LIWONDE NATIONAL PARK

N

Bradt

↗ Mangochi

Chilole ▲

Lake
Malombe

Masanje

0 ——————— 8km
0 ——————— 5 miles

Mvela Canoe Ferry ○ Chisuse

Chibwana ○
Kavunguti ○

Ntangai

Mvuu Lodge and Camp

Nafiulu
Hills ▲
▲

← Ulongwe

Namatanje

Shire

Mwalesi

← Mangochi

▲ Kandungusi
Mbawala ▲ Nanyani ▲
← Lilongwe
Chiunguni ● ○ Kalunga

Liwonde Barrage
LIWONDE ● D221

↓ Zomba

KEY
National park ------------

of the river opposite Mvuu Camp. This turn-off is signposted from the village of Ulongwe. After 14km, it reaches the entrance gate from where it's another 1km to the river. There is a flag you can raise in order for the staff at Mvuu take a boat across to fetch you. This is the easiest way to drive to Mvuu, but it has one major disadvantage in that you'll effectively be without a vehicle at Mvuu, and so will need to do all your drives in camp vehicles. If you prefer to have your own vehicle, you should use the main entrance to the national park, which is signposted from the D221 about 3km from Liwonde Town. The distance from the entrance gate to Mvuu is 30km, and although internal roads are sometimes closed during the rainy season, you should normally get through to the camp in a 4WD at any time of year (ask Central African Wilderness Safaris for current advice).

A more attractive way of entering Liwonde National Park is to take a boat along the Shire River from Liwonde Barrage. If you plan on staying at Mvuu, a boat transfer can be organised in advance through the management, at a cost of US$20 per person. For day trips, Waterline, a service based at the jetty at the Liwonde Barrage, does boat safaris along the river at a cost of US$90 for up to four people. Bookings through Land and Lake Safaris, Lilongwe.

For backpackers, the cheapest way to get to Mvuu is to use a bicycle-taxi from Ulongwe to the west bank of the river, and then raise the flag to be fetched by a boat from Mvuu. The cost of these bicycle-taxis is negotiable, but expect to pay around US$4 each way. If you like, you can normally arrange for the person who cycles you there to come back to meet you when you plan to leave.

Central African Wilderness Safaris can arrange road transfers to Mvuu from anywhere in Malawi. There is also an airstrip in the reserve, should you be in a position to charter a flight.

Where to stay

Mvuu Lodge and Camp is an outstanding set-up that caters to everybody from self-catering backpackers to upmarket tourists. Perfectly sited on the east bank of the Shire about 25km north of the barrage, Mvuu lies in a group of immense baobab trees, facing a dense papyrus bed and a borassus palm forest. Hippos wander through the camp at night, while elephants regularly come to drink on the bank opposite, and both the river and surrounding bush are alive with birds. Accommodation is very comfortable, and the food is excellent.

Accommodation at the main camp is in luxurious standing tents or self-contained chalets. The standing tents cost US$50/70 single/double (bed only) or US$165/280 for a full-board package inclusive of two game activities daily. There is an attached campsite, charging US$8 per person, making the camp reasonably affordable to budget travellers with their own tent. Campers can eat in the restaurant, which charges US$8 for breakfast, US$10 for lunch and US$15 for dinner, but a self-catering kitchen is available for those bringing their own food. A freezer and cooking utensils are supplied, and a cook can be arranged by request.

About 200m from the camp, and run as a separate entity, Mvuu Lodge is a wonderful exclusive bush camp consisting of five double tents with private balconies overlooking a small, marshy pool on the bank of the river. Mvuu Lodge holds its own with the best luxury tented camps in southern Africa, blending a high level of comfort and tasteful decor with a wonderful bush atmosphere, and – even allowing for taste – we rate it to be comfortably the best lodge or hotel in Malawi. The raised communal deck offers excellent mammal and birdwatching (hippos sometimes graze metres away at night, a blessing if you happen to be a noisy eater!) and there is a telescope and a library of field guides to amuse yourself with. There is also a swimming pool reserved for the use of lodge guests. Accommodation costs US$230 per person full board, inclusive of all activities, and with private rangers allocated to the lodge.

Mvuu Camp and Lodge are owned and managed by Central African Wilderness Safaris, PO Box 489, Lilongwe; tel: 01 771153; fax: 01 771397; email: info@wilderness.malawi.net.

In an admirable attempt to help the local community in benefiting directly from tourism, Central African Wildlife Safaris have assisted them in developing the **Ligwangwa-Njobvu Cultural Lodge**. Two new and neatly furnished huts have been constructed 6km from Mvuu where guests pay US$25 per person to overnight in an African village. Food and drinks served are local specialities, as are the singing and dancing. Book through Central African Wildlife Safaris – all proceeds go to the villagers.

Chinguni Hills Camp lies in a beautiful setting in the south of the park and offers affordable rooms, which are probably more suited to younger travellers and backpackers. Still being developed and expanded at the time of writing, it would be best to contact them on tel: 01 838159; email: chinguni@africa-online.net or through Jambo Africa (see Blantyre listings).

Things to do

The Mvuu Lodge and Camp itself is a rewarding place to explore, and you can see an amazing amount of wildlife from it. Hippos and crocodiles are a permanent presence on the river, as is a large variety of waterbirds, while elephants come down to drink most days and gigantic monitor lizards can be seen basking on the riverbank. The woodland around the camp offers some great birding, with a good chance of picking up several Liwonde specials, including brown-breasted barbet, Lilian's lovebird, Livingstone's flycatcher, collared palm thrush, eastern bearded scrub robin, fish eagle and Boehm's bee-eater. The localised bat hawk can be seen near the river on most evenings. People staying at the lodge are likely to see a greater variety of animals coming to drink at the pool: bushbuck and impala are regular visitors, leopards are seen on occasion, and the birdlife is outstanding.

Visitors with private transport have a fair number of dirt roads to explore. Of particular interest are the road following the Shire River north from Mvuu to where it exits Lake Malombe, and the circuit of roads around Chiunguni Hill, which offers excellent views as well as good game viewing. The staff at Mvuu can give you current advice about where to see game.

Mvuu Camp offers a variety of game-viewing activities, including boat safaris and game drives at US$18 per person and walking safaris at US$10 per person. All activities are led by trained guides, whom we found to be very knowledgeable and sharp at identification without ever adopting a lecturing style. The cost of activities is included in full-board packages, but must be paid for by campers and those who take bed-only accommodation.

Early morning game walks offer the wonderful experience of exploring the African bush on foot. You're not likely to see a great number of mammals on these walks (warthog, impala and hippo are most likely to be encountered near the camp), but this is compensated for by the prolific birds.

Launch trips along the Shire River leave Mvuu every morning after breakfast. Close encounters with hippos are guaranteed, you can be confident of seeing elephants, waterbuck, impala, crocodile and vervet monkeys, and there is a fair chance of seeing sable antelope from the boat. Birds are everywhere: among the more common species are fish eagle, jacana, white-bellied cormorant (these breed along the river profusely in the dry season), darter, long-toed plover, African skimmer, and a variety of kingfishers and herons. The vegetation, too, is splendid: thick stands of borassus and wild date palms, ghostly baobab trees, yellow fever trees and dense beds of papyrus.

The night boat safaris from Mvuu were a first for us, and are a must for serious birders as they offer an excellent chance of spotting Pel's fishing owl in action, as well as the nocturnal white-backed night heron. We were amazed at how closely the boat was able to approach roosting birds: we crept up on several giant and malachite kingfishers (the latter nothing short of dazzling in the spotlight), as well as huddled flocks of colourful little bee-eater and Boehm's bee-eater.

Morning game drives can be arranged on request, but it is more usual to do a drive which starts at dusk, extending into the first hours of night. Night drives are your best chance of seeing predators such as leopard, spotted hyena, civet and genet. Other animals which are commonly observed on night drives are bushbaby, sable antelope and, of course, hippos.

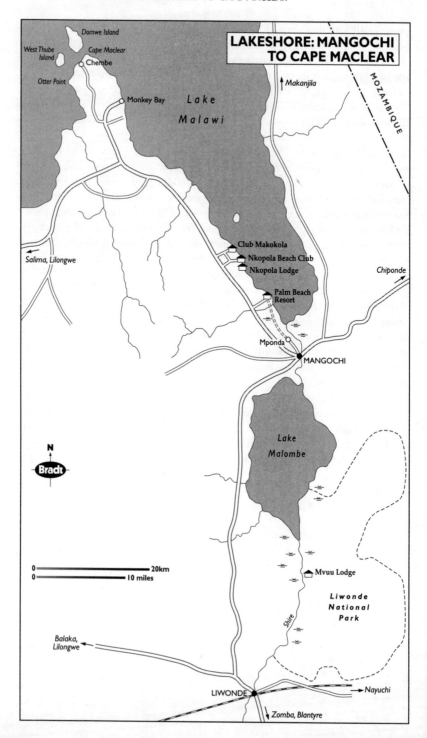

The Lakeshore from Mangochi to Cape Maclear

The southern shore of Lake Malawi is well developed for tourism. All but one of the major tourist-class hotels on the lake lie on the stretch of shore between Mangochi and Cape Maclear, and Cape Maclear itself is far and away the most popular backpackers' haunt anywhere in the country.

The largest town in the region, Mangochi, doesn't actually lie on Lake Malawi but on the west bank of the Shire River a short way south of Lake Malawi and north of Lake Malombe. Nevertheless, Mangochi is best grouped with the southern lakeshore – not least because its main source of tourist traffic comes from travellers who have arrived at Cape Maclear to discover that Mangochi is the nearest place where you can change foreign currency into local money.

CLIMATE
Hot and sticky.

GETTING AROUND
There is plenty of public transport along the surfaced road connecting Monkey Bay to Mangochi and to Liwonde, Zomba and Blantyre. This road is also good for hitching.

Most of the resorts along the southern lakeshore are within 2km of the tarred road, and so they are easy to walk to. The exception is Cape Maclear itself. There is no public transport along the 18km road between Monkey Bay and Cape Maclear, so you will either have to hitch or else wait for a *matola* ride: you'd be unlucky to wait more than an hour or two.

If you are heading to this part of the lakeshore from somewhere further north, be aware that road transport is not quite so straightforward due to the exceptionally poor state of the dirt road that connects the main Salima–Balaka road and main Monkey Bay–Blantyre road. Most private vehicles driving from Lilongwe to Monkey Bay or Nkopola follow the N1 south through Dedza and Ntcheu, then cut through Liwonde back north to the Mangochi area. Should you decide to brave the 'short cut', turn east at Golomoti.

There are no longer any buses connecting Salima and Monkey Bay using the road mentioned above, so many backpackers bus along the same route suggested for drivers. If you want to try the direct route, public transport is limited to a few crowded pick-up trucks daily. To catch one of these coming from Salima, ask to be dropped off at Golomoti rather than at the turn-off that is signposted for Monkey Bay about 1km south of Mua – the latter might look to be the main road on some maps, but has been impassable for a long time due to a washed-out bridge. You shouldn't wait more than an hour for a vehicle to leave, and should expect the trip to the junction with the Monkey Bay road to take at least three hours.

There are two other ways of travelling between this area and points further north. The first is by one of the lake steamers which connect Monkey Bay to Nkhotakota, Likoma or Nkhata Bay (see page 215 for itinerary details). The other is to organise a private boat between Cape Maclear and Salima, a trip which takes about three hours (by comparison with the full day you'll require to travel between these places by road) and costs around US$12 per person for a minimum of ten people.

MANGOCHI

Mangochi was previously known as Fort Johnston, after Sir Harry Johnston, the first Consul General of Nyasaland. Fort Johnston was one of the earliest colonial settlements in Malawi, established on the east bank of the Shire River in 1891 to help restrict the Yao slave trade. In 1897, the fort was relocated to the site of the modern town, on the west bank of the river. Fort Johnston was declared a township in 1899, and throughout the colonial era it remained a river port and naval centre of some importance. Shortly after Malawi's independence, it was renamed Mangochi.

Mangochi is one of the few Malawian towns with an identifiable character. The wide avenues, lined with jacarandas, borassus palms and thick fruit trees, are a reminder of Fort Johnston's former importance, while the crumbling buildings that line the Shire waterfront testify to a recent decline in fortunes. The overall impression, sad to say, is that of a colonial outpost going to seed. Walking around the old part of Mangochi, with its tangible Muslim influences (dating to the slaving era), faded whitewashed buildings, and sticky tropical atmosphere, I was reminded of some of the more run-down towns on the Swahili coast of East Africa.

In a country so lacking in towns with any sense of place whatsoever, it is tempting to recommend Mangochi as a worthwhile stop. But perhaps I'm clutching at straws. Sightseeing is limited to a few less than riveting national monuments: a war cemetery; a waterfront clocktower, built in 1903 in memory of Queen Victoria and since dedicated to the 143 people who drowned when the MV *Viphya* sank on Lake Malawi in 1946; and, nearby, the cannon from HMS *Gwendolyn* which sank the German *Hermann Von Wessman* at Liuli in 1914. Possibly of more interest is the Lake Malawi Museum depicting the lake's history (US$1).

On a more practical note, Mangochi is a reasonable place to stock up on goods if you're heading on to camp at Liwonde or along the Lake Malawi shore. There is a good selection of shops including a PTC supermarket and

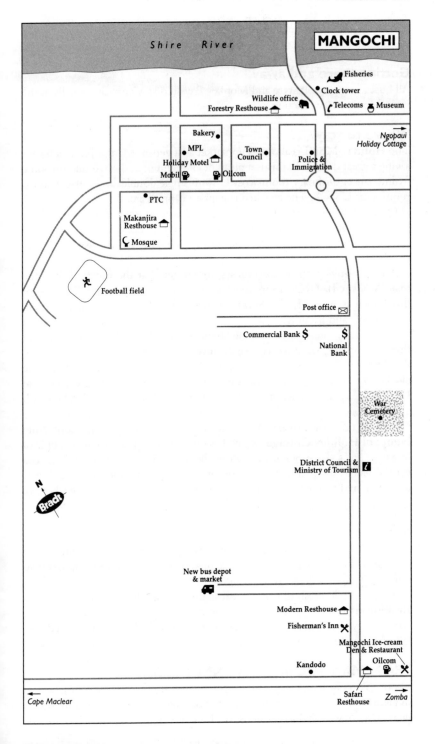

bakery. Mangochi is the closest place to Cape Maclear where you can change money at a bank.

Getting there and away

All buses between Blantyre and Monkey Bay stop at Mangochi, usually at the main Monkey Bay junction.

Where to stay

The **Holiday Motel** is about as upmarket as it gets in Mangochi, which isn't saying a great deal. Still, this is a pleasant enough hotel, though due for some maintenance. Ordinary rooms cost US$4/5 single/double, and self-contained rooms cost US$6/8. The attached restaurant is pretty good.

Quite a few cheaper resthouses are dotted around town. Probably the best bet is the **Makanjira Resthouse** behind the PTC supermarket, where self-contained doubles cost US$5. The nearby **Jabalani Resthouse** also looks worth a try.

A few relatively scruffy resthouses are clustered at the junction with the main Monkey Bay road, 15 minutes' walk from the town centre. The best of this bunch is probably the **Safari Resthouse**, a bit run-down, but clean, comfortable and friendly.

There is no forest worth talking about within Mangochi town limits, but there *is* a rather good **Forestry Resthouse**, not signposted but easy to find in the Department of Forestry compound on the waterfront north of the clocktower. The rooms here are up to the usual standard and great value at US$1.80 per person. Facilities include a lounge and an equipped kitchen with a fridge.

Travellers with private transport might be interested in contacting **Ngopani Holiday Cottage**, which lies on a private farm close to a couple of forest reserves about 80km by road to the northeast of Mangochi. This is a very isolated spot, and great value at US$3 per person. For bookings, directions and further details, tel: 01 651799 (day) or 01 584567 (after hours), or fax: 01 651646.

Where to eat

The restaurant in the **Holiday Motel** does reasonable food for around US$2 per plate – the standard chicken stew, chips and the like, but much tastier than normal.

A far more interesting place to eat is the **Mangochi Ice-Cream Den & Restaurant** near the junction with the main Monkey Bay road. This place serves everything from curries and steaks to burgers and fish, with most dishes falling in the US$2–3 price bracket, as well as good ice-cream sundaes.

FROM MANGOCHI TO MONKEY BAY

About 10km north of Mangochi, the Shire River flows from the southern heel of Lake Malawi. This far southern part of the lake consists of a roughly 15km-wide sliver of water which extends for about 50km up to Monkey Bay and the

Cape Maclear peninsula. The Southern Lakeshore, as this stretch of shore is often called, caters primarily for upmarket visitors, boasting two of the lake's smartest hotels, Club Makokola and Nkopola Lodge, as well as a variety of smaller and cheaper resorts. Working from south to north:

Palm Beach Resort (tel: 01 594564) lies 12km from Mangochi and about 2km north of the Shire River outlet. The large grounds are very attractive and dotted with tall palm trees, but the resort as a whole seems slightly lacking in character. Accommodation is in self-contained chalets, costing US$26/37 bed and breakfast. There is a bar and a good restaurant where meals cost around US$4. The resort lies about 1km from the main road and can be reached via a signposted turn-off.

In the small fishing village of Nkopola, which is situated on an attractive baobab-studded stretch of lakeshore about 10km north of Palm Beach Resort and 1km from the main Mangochi Road, lies Sunbird's **Nkopola Lodge**. This is a most attractively laid-out upmarket hotel with a wonderful position at the base of a rocky and thickly wooded hill. The birdlife here is fantastic (though I wouldn't get overexcited about the walk-in aviary), and vervet monkeys inhabit the grounds. Other attractions are the large swimming pool, excellent watersports facilities, and the string of good curio stalls lining the road outside the lodge grounds. The food here is also very good, in particular the lunchtime buffet barbecue held at the swimming pool, and there is satellite television in the bar. Standard rooms cost US$77/106 single/double, while superior rooms cost US$96/125 single/double, inclusive of a good breakfast. Bookings can be made at PO Box 14, Mangochi, Malawi, tel: 584444; fax: 584694 or email: nkopola@sdnp.org.mw.

Adjacent to Nkopola Lodge, and with a similarly attractive position, **Nkopola Beach Club** is a more family orientated place, also run by Le Meridien. Chalets cost US$60 for up to three people, caravan sites cost US$12, standing tents US$30 double. Residents rates' are roughly half of this. The only other accommodation in Nkopola is **Martin's Beach Hotel**, which has large, self-contained rooms with hot showers, flush toilets, netting and fans for US$8/12 single/double – good value, indisputably, though the bland location lets it down a bit.

The recently renovated **Sun 'n' Sand Holiday Resort** (tel: 594550; fax: 594723 or email: sunnsand@malawi.net) offers a conference centre, large swimming pool, selection of sports and even a small supermarket. Rates range from US$23/29 single/double in standard rooms to US$34/59 single/double in self-contained suites, breakfast included.

About 2km north of Nkopola, **Club Makokola** (or Club Mak as it's known locally) is without doubt the best known of Malawi's lakeshore hotels, and the extensive renovations that have taken place over the last couple of years have done much to improve it. A neatly kept nine-hole golf course and a good selection of watersports make this a favourite holiday destination for families, especially as Air Malawi flies into the airstrip there. At US$80/130, this is also the most affordable of Malawi's top lakeshore hotels, and the watersports facilities at the adjacent Rift Lake Charters are the best on the lake. Bookings for Club Mak can be made at PO Box 59, Mangochi; tel: 01 594244; fax: 01 594417; email: clubmak@malawi.net. All of the above lakeshore hotels can organise excursions to Kama Croc, a nearby crocodile farm, and a cashew nut estate. Every year, around mid-July, the Lake Malawi International Yachting Marathon takes place. A challenging and sometimes dangerous race, it starts at Club Makokola and runs in stages, overnighting en route at Livingstonia Beach Resort, Sani Beach Resort, Dwanga, Likoma Island, Chinteche Inn and finishing up at Nkata Bay. Entry fees are US$200 per person and US$100 per yacht and includes accommodation, catering and transport. Email: murray_kj@hotmail.com, zina@africa-online.net or any Malawi-based tour operator. They tell me it's one long party!

MONKEY BAY

Monkey Bay is mostly of interest to travellers as the southern terminus of the lake ferry and as the springboard for visits to Malawi's 'Backpackers' Mecca', the ever popular Cape Maclear. Unfortunately, most of the lakeshore immediately around Monkey Bay is government property. Many travellers end up in Monkey Bay, as it is the end of the road as far as buses are concerned, but very few do anything more than head straight on to Cape Maclear. Quite a few travellers are caught by the fact there is no bank in Monkey Bay, nor is there a black market. If you don't have enough local currency, the nearest place where you can change money is Mangochi.

Getting there and away

Note that pick-up trucks connecting Monkey Bay and the village of Chembe on Cape Maclear habitually try to overcharge travellers. To give you some idea, the 'correct' price for this trip when we were here in July 2002 was US$1.

Where to stay and eat

If you arrive in Monkey Bay late in the day, there are a few basic resthouses. There is also a reasonably well-stocked PTC supermarket in town. Fuel is available at a Mobil station.

CAPE MACLEAR

Cape Maclear is one of the most important travellers' congregation points in Malawi. At its peak in the early 1990s, it was described as Africa's answer to Kathmandu or Marrakech, a place to which travellers would flock in their hundreds to enjoy a *chamba* and Carlsberg-enhanced atmosphere that for most people was thoroughly irresistible.

Cape Maclear may be past its prime, but it remains the main backpacker focus on the southern lakeshore, and its tremendous natural assets are undiminished – the beautiful beach is set on a peninsula ringed by forested hills, faced by several small islands, and noted for spectacular sunsets and wonderful snorkelling. In the first edition of this guide we wrote that 'Cape

Maclear has its detractors, and it is tempting to number myself amongst them. I won't deny that I enjoyed myself there, but it all seemed a bit much at times. In the days when backpackers' hostels were few and far between in Africa, Cape Maclear offered a welcome respite from the more enervating and exhausting aspects of African travel. In the current travel climate, with backpackers' hostels springing up all over southern Africa, Cape Maclear threatens to become just another stop on an increasingly culturally insular mass travel circuit. After a couple of days there, I was relieved to leave and to return to Malawi.' Many of the above points remain valid, but we enjoyed Cape Maclear a great deal more this time – there are still a lot of backpackers around, but not to the extent that you feel like you could be on a beach in Australia rather than in Africa.

It is worth stressing that the main reason why Cape Maclear has dropped in popularity in recent years is a corresponding increase in crime. So far as I can ascertain, however, much of this crime was the work of a couple of gangs, and the recent installation of a police station in Chembe village appears to have ended most of the criminal activity. We didn't feel at all threatened on our most recent visit to Cape Maclear, and our enquiries suggested that whatever problem once existed is now under control – whether permanently or temporarily remains to be seen. The message? Cape Maclear remains a very special place, and well worth visiting – just be alert!

Cape Maclear was the first site of Dr Robert Laws' Livingstonia Mission, established on October 17 1875 and abandoned a few years later due to the high incidence of malaria in the area. Several of the missionaries at Cape Maclear died of malaria; their graves can be seen near the entrance to the Golden Sands Rest Camp. While based at Cape Maclear, Laws became the first European to circumnavigate the lake, which he discovered to be 100km longer than Livingstone had estimated.

Lake Malawi National Park

Lake Malawi National Park, proclaimed in 1980, encompasses most of Cape Maclear and the surrounding lake waters as well as nine offshore islands. This national park is the most important freshwater fish sanctuary in Africa, if not in the world, protecting a diversity of species second to none. Scuba diving and snorkelling are popular activities in the park, offering the opportunity to see a diversity of colourful *mbuna* cichlids, a game-viewing experience the equal of anything Malawi has to offer on land. Several fishing villages remain unprotected enclaves within the park; the largest, Chembe, has a population of roughly 5,000, and is the main focus of tourism in the area, with several low-key resthouses and restaurants, a scuba-diving centre, and a variety of watersport and snorkelling equipment for hire.

Getting there and away

The turn-off to Cape Maclear is signposted from the main road to Mangochi about 4km south of Monkey Bay. There is no public transport along the 18km stretch of road that connects the turn-off to Cape Maclear, but it's easy enough

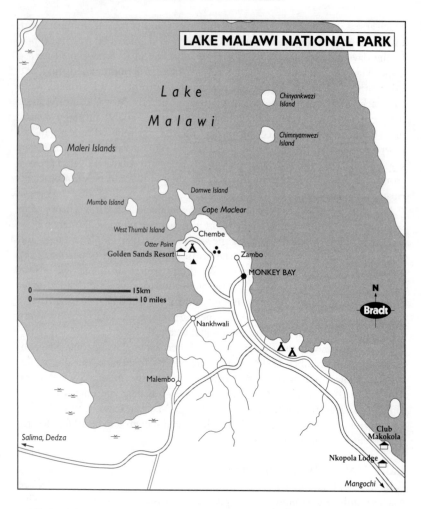

to find a lift, and a vehicle does the run to Monkey Bay two or three times most days. For hitching purposes, the best place to wait is at the turn-off, though *matola* vehicles generally depart from Monkey Bay itself, so they may be full when they pass the turn-off.

Where to stay

Cape Maclear's prolonged popularity owes much to **Steven's Resthouse** in Chembe Village. One of the best-known local hotels in Malawi, this place has been operating for as long as I've been travelling in Africa, and throughout this time it has enjoyed a reputation for its friendly, traveller-orientated atmosphere. Sad to report, then, that most people feel Steven's has gone downhill in recent years, and that its popularity leans heavily on its reputation. Steven's offers a variety of accommodation: rooms using communal showers cost US$1/1.50 single/double, while self-contained rooms cost US$3/4.50 double/triple. An affordable restaurant and waterfront bar are attached to the resthouse and camping costs US$0.60 per person.

The last few years have seen a number of new campsites and resthouses springing up in Chembe and usually the newest one is the best, as they seem to deteriorate fast. The newest and best backpackers' spot in 2002 was **Fat Monkeys**, offering 12 basic but comfortable rooms with shared facilities at US$5.50 double. Camping is US$1 per person and a lively bar and restaurant serves meals for around US$3.50. Set away from the main village, it has a private beach and good security.

There are several cheaper places to stay on the beach, all a bit run-down and within 500m of Steven's. **Emanuel's**, on the edge of the village towards Lake Malawi National Park, has rooms with mattresses for around US$1 per person as well as cheap camping. In the opposite direction, **The Gap** has even more basic rooms (grass mats only) for US$0.80 per person, and it also allows camping.

The **Macheje Lodge** (previously the Top Quiet Resthouse) is set back from the beach behind Steven's and offers US$2 doubles. Much better-looking is **Chirwa Lodge**, with dorms costing US$1.70 and doubles for US$3.40.

In Lake Malawi National Park, about 2km past Steven's, the **Golden Sands Rest Camp** has self-contained chalets and bungalows for US$1 per person, and a campsite for US$0.60 per person (to which must be added an entrance fee of US$5 per person per 24 hours). Golden Sands is by far the most peaceful place to stay at Cape Maclear, and it has a great position on the beach below Otter Point.

The most upmarket place to stay on Cape Maclear is **Chembe Lodge**, an excellent tented camp with an attractive situation about 2km east of the main cluster of accommodation (the turn-off is signposted along the main road between Monkey Bay and Cape Maclear). The standing tents cost US$25 per person, or you can pitch your own tent for US$5 per person. Facilities include a generator, flush toilets and hot showers, as well as a bar, a restaurant serving good food, and various watersports activities. Advance bookings are best made through the central office in South Africa; tel: +27 11 706 1210; fax: +27 11 463 3001.

A company called **Kayak Africa** (on the beach between Steven's and Emanuel's) organises popular outings to their tented camp on one of the islands off Cape Maclear, from where excellent kayaking, snorkelling and diving are possible. Three-night island breakaways are offered at their luxury camp on Domwe Island for US$360, including all meals and watersports. For the traveller on a tighter budget, self-catering kayak safaris are available at US$50 per person, per day (tel: +27 21 689 8123; fax: +27 21 689 2149; email: letsgo@kayakafrica.co.za).

Where to eat

The options for eating out in Cape Maclear are rather limited and your best bet is probably to have your meals where you're staying, as all of the resthouses offer food at around US$3.50 per plate. There is, however, one good place to go where you can rub shoulders with the locals, eat lots of tasty food and down a few 'Greens' at half of what it will cost you elsewhere. **Thomas' Bar and Restaurant**, between Kayak Africa and Emanuel's, charges US$1.50 for fish and chips and beers cost only US$0.40. It's no wonder they have a sign in the bar which reads 'Drinking is a talent, Prove it here'. But right below it is another – 'Pay before you Drink'. **Fatsani Grocery and Tea Room**, in the centre of the small village, sells basic commodities (lots of soap) and some food, but don't risk the tea room – it's used as a storeroom for sacks of dried fish.

A popular way of eating out in Cape Maclear is to organise a **beach barbecue** through one of the children who hang around Steven's and the other resthouses. This will generally cost around US$3 per person, for which you get a generous portion of fish (normally *kampanga*), rice and tomato sauce. The atmosphere on the beach at night is great and there is little danger of going to bed hungry. It is customary to pay half the fee upfront, so that food can be bought, and while I have heard of children vanishing with the money, the system normally seems to work well.

Things to do

For many people, activity at Cape Maclear consists of spending the days hanging out on the beach, interspersed with the occasional aimless wander around the village. Armed with a cold Carlsberg, doing nothing is certainly an attractive enough prospect in the beautiful surrounds.

One of the most popular activities are day trips to nearby West Thumbi Island; these can be arranged through any of the children who hang out around Steven's for a very reasonable US$10 per head, inclusive of a fish barbecue, snorkelling equipment and transport by boat. The cichlid community around Mitande Point on West Thumbi is regarded as one of the most diverse in the lake.

There is also excellent snorkelling at Otter Point, in Lake Malawi National Park about 2km from Steven's. The clear water here is teeming with cichlids of all colours: blue, orange and yellow. On land you should see rock hyrax, baboons, a variety of lizards, and if you're lucky even a klipspringer or grysbok. Spotted necked otters are common in the area. Entrance to the national park costs US$5 per person. You can hire snorkelling equipment in the village.

The Scuba Shack next to Steven's Resthouse offers excellent diving courses with good modern equipment. A four-day Open Water course costs US$195, while a Dive Master course, including accommodation, is US$380. Casual dives centre around an interesting old wreck and cost US$20.

Danforth Yachting, between Steven's and Otter Point, charters a fully equipped and crewed 38ft ocean-going catamaran, which sleeps eight guests. Daysails are US$60 per person and overnighters cost US$120. Longer sails, diving and other watersports are also offered (email: danforth@malawi.net; website: www.danforthyachting.com).

Further information
A Guide to the Fishes of Lake Malawi National Park by Lewis, Reinthall and Trendall (Worldwide Fund for Nature) includes excellent background information on the cichlids and other fish of Lake Malawi. Fish that are likely to be seen within the national park are illustrated, and their distribution and status is given. The book also gives details of the birds and mammals of the park, and it includes a pull-out waterproof map with notes to underwater trails in the more popular diving areas.

Dedza and Surrounds

This chapter covers Dedza, a sizeable town lying along the M1 south of Lilongwe, as well as some of the forest reserves that surround it. The Dedza area is not often visited by tourists, and it lacks the obvious attractions of somewhere like Cape Maclear; nevertheless, its mountains and forests have much to offer keen walkers and birdwatchers, and it will be attractive to people who have the urge to explore a part of Malawi that is both accessible and beautiful, yet which might go weeks on end without seeing a tourist.

There are several forest reserves around Dedza. The three covered in this chapter – Dedza Mountain, Chongoni and Mua-Livulezi – are selected on the basis of accessibility. Dedza Mountain can be explored on foot as a day trip from Dedza Town. Chongoni requires a little more exertion to reach on foot, but once you are there, you can take several days to look around, staying at the forestry resthouse that lies within the reserve. If you want to visit some of the less accessible reserves, the booklet *Day Outings from Lilongwe* is your best source of printed information. It may also be worth speaking to the Forestry Office in Dedza: my experience is that they are very willing to offer advice to visitors, and they may well agree to let you camp in some forest reserves. The Forestry Office is on the outskirts of Dedza Town; tel: 01 220275.

Before you head to this area, you'd do well to get hold of the 1:50,000 map of Dedza (sheet 1434A4) for Dedza Mountain and Chongoni Forest Reserve, supplemented by the 1:50,000 map of Golomoti (sheet 1434B3) for Mua-Livulezi. These can be bought at the map sales offices in either Lilongwe or Blantyre. If they're not available, the Monkey Bay map (sheet 7) in the Malawi 1:250,000 series is also very useful.

CLIMATE

The Dedza area has a pleasant highland climate, warm by day and cool by night. Temperatures are higher in Mua-Livulezi than in the other reserves, as it is at a much lower altitude.

GETTING AROUND

Dedza lies on the M1 between Lilongwe and Blantyre. This road is not as popular with tourists as the lakeshore route via Salima, Monkey Bay and

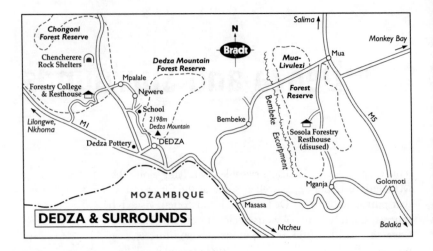

DEDZA & SURROUNDS

Zomba, but it is the quickest route between Malawi's two largest cities, and thus carries a relatively heavy volume of traffic. In a private vehicle, the drive from Lilongwe to Dedza shouldn't take much more than an hour. All buses that travel between Lilongwe and Blantyre on the M1 stop at Dedza, express buses included. The bus journey from Lilongwe to Dedza takes less than two hours.

If you are visiting Dedza en route between the two main cities, it's worth knowing that the M1 is one of the most hitchable roads in Malawi: you'd be unlucky to wait more than an hour for a lift. Hitching directly out of Lilongwe is tricky as most of the traffic is local, so it's best to get yourself to Nathanje, a small town on the M1 about 30km south of Lilongwe. Minibuses and other *matola* vehicles to Nathanje leave regularly from in front of the bus station in Lilongwe. In the unlikely event that you get stuck in Nathanje, there are a couple of basic resthouses to choose from.

If you're heading between Dedza and Blantyre, the main town you'll pass through on the M1 is Ntcheu. All you need to know about Ntcheu is that it is on the Mozambican border, it's thoroughly dull and scruffy, and it has several resthouses, a good PTC supermarket, and a bank. You're unlikely to get stuck in Ntcheu unless you want to.

DEDZA

Dedza lies 84km south of Lilongwe at the southern foot of the 2,198m high Dedza Mountain, and in the centre of an area noted for its striking granite outcrops and plentiful forests. Dedza is an unremarkable town, but it is very agreeable, with a comfortable highland climate and attractive setting. It is mostly of interest to travellers as the base from which to visit Dedza Mountain and the little-visited Chongoni and Mua-Livulezi forest reserves.

Getting there and away

All buses between Lilongwe and Blantyre stop at Dedza.

Where to stay and eat

Of several basic resthouses, the **CTC Mini-Motel** is about the best, with clean doubles for US$2. It also has an above average restaurant. The **Rainbow Resthouse** is also acceptable, though relatively overpriced at US$3/4 single/double – especially as there are only bucket showers. Much better value is **Golden Dish Catering**, which has self-contained doubles for US$2.50. It also does the best meals in town for around US$1.50.

The ex-Goverment Resthouse, attractively positioned overlooking the golf course at the base of the mountain, is now owned by the **Golf Club**, but it still offers accommodation of a relatively high standard. Large, pleasant rooms with basins cost US$5/7 single/double. There are communal hot baths, and a restaurant and bar.

It's well worth walking the 2km out of town for a lazy afternoon tea under a thatched gazebo at the **Dedza Pottery Coffee Shop**. This excellent and rather unexpected place serves filter coffee, lemonade, quiches, scones, fresh bread with jam, and a variety of other home-made goodies you won't come across too often in Malawi. The coffee shop is not, by Malawian standards, cheap, but nor is it so expensive you'll regret the treat. You may also want to look in at the adjacent pottery shop for a useful and colourful memento of Malawi (tel: 01 223069).

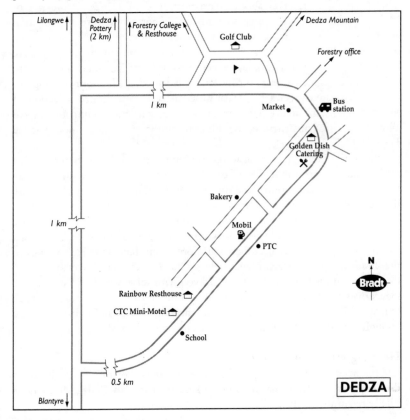

There is a reasonably well-stocked PTC supermarket in Dedza. The market is also pretty good, and you can buy fresh bread at the bakery marked on the map.

Dedza Mountain Forest Reserve

Dedza Mountain lies immediately north of Dedza Town. The mountain is largely covered in plantation forest, but there are still remnant patches of evergreen and riverine forest on the upper slopes, supporting typical forest animals such as samango monkey, bushpig, baboon and even leopard. The indigenous forest is also notable for birds and epiphytic orchids, while more open areas are rich in wild flowers after the rains.

The mountain can be climbed as a day trip from behind the Golf Club Resthouse using any of several converging and diverging routes. You first need to climb for about 2km towards the post office transmission tower (clearly visible from town), from where it's about 3km to the peak. With the 1:50,000 map, you shouldn't get lost, but if you're uncertain ask at the Forestry Office in Dedza for directions.

CHONGONI FOREST RESERVE

This large forest reserve, about 10km northwest of Dedza, is the site of Malawi's main Forestry College. Chongoni supports a mixture of plantation and *brachystegia* woodland, as well as small patches of evergreen forest on some of the hills which dot the area. The most common mammals in the reserve are baboons, grey duiker and klipspringer. Leopard and samango monkey are present in evergreen forest. Birdwatching is varied, with a similar range of *brachystegia*-related species to Dzalanyama, as well as a limited selection of forest species. The many paths and roads through and around the reserve allow for days of unstructured rambling using the excellent resthouse at the Forestry College as a base.

One of the more interesting walks in Chongoni is to Chencherere Hill, a steep granite outcrop about 5km from the Forestry College. The simplest way to reach the hill is to follow the dirt road to Linthipe north for about 4km, then to turn left at the fork signposted for Chencherere Rock Shelters. There are reportedly five rock shelters on the hill, all of which house prehistoric rock paintings, but I only found two and if either of them had any rock paintings they were obscured beneath more recent half-witted scrawlings of the 'Fred was here' variety. Nevertheless, Chencherere is well worth visiting: the stiff scramble to the top will reward you with some wonderful panoramic views over the forest to the surrounding hills. I also had sightings of rock hyraxes and baboons. From the top of the hill, it's apparent that there are enough potential walks in this area to keep you busy for days.

Getting there and away

Chongoni can be reached by any of several routes. For motorists, the most direct approach is from the M1. For walkers, the route via Dedza Mountain is highly recommended.

From the M1

The simplest route to the Forestry College, and the one that involves the least walking, is to take a bus or hitch along the M1 between Dedza and Lilongwe until you reach the signposted turn-off roughly 10km north of Dedza. According to the signpost, it's 6km from the turn-off to the college along a motorable dirt road.

Via Dedza Pottery

A longer but equally straightforward route, again open to both motorists and walkers, is to head from the bus station in Dedza Town back towards the M1 for about 1.5km until you see a turn-off signposted for Dedza Pottery. Follow the turn-off, past Dedza Pottery and a large saw mill. After about 10km, you will see the turn-off to the Forestry College signposted to your left. The resthouse is about 1.5km along this turn-off.

Via Dedza Mountain

If you're walking out to the college, you may prefer to use the more interesting and scenic cross-country route via Dedza Mountain Forest Reserve. This route starts behind the golf course: follow the road in front of the Golf Club's Resthouse (see Dedza Town map, page 163) northeast for about 1km, where you must take a right fork, then, after another 500m or so, a left fork. There are some striking granite outcrops to your left along this stretch of road, and the vegetation immediately around you is quite open.

After the second fork, you pass through plantation forest for about 2km before skirting a group of buildings to the left. Keep to the road for another 1km, then take a left fork downhill, across a small wooden bridge, and into Dedza Secondary School. Shortly after you enter the school compound, a fork to the right takes you across a concrete bridge and then through the main school buildings, from where it's about 1km along a rough road to a T-junction and a cluster of buildings including a Chibuku bar. Anybody at the bar will be able to show you the footpath that leads north to Ngwere village (about 1km) then eastward to Mpalale village (a further 2km). From Mpalale, it's about 500m to the dirt road between Dedza Pottery and Chongoni. Turn left into the main road and you'll reach the signposted turn-off to Forestry College after about 200m.

If you use this route, it will help if you have a map, though you can't really go wrong by asking for directions (ask for the secondary school, then Ngwere, then Mpalale). The total distance using this route is about 12km.

Where to stay

The **Chongoni Forestry Resthouse** lies in the college grounds, in a patch of *brachystegia* woodland at the base of the impressive granite dome of Chiwawa Hill. The rooms at the resthouse are excellent value for money. Standard doubles cost US$3 per person, while self-contained doubles complete with hot bath, heater, dressing table and mirror cost US$4 per person. You can camp in the resthouse compound for US$1.50 per person. Facilities include a well-equipped kitchen, a communal dining room and lounge, and a bar serving cold beers and sodas. You must bring all the food you need with you.

The resthouse often goes for weeks without visitors, but it does occasionally fill up with forestry people, so before you head all the way out it's advisable to check availability with the Forestry Office in Dedza Town; tel: 01 220275.

MUA-LIVULEZI FOREST RESERVE

This sizeable forest reserve, which lies at an altitude of around 800m below the Bembeke Escarpment, protects medium-altitude *brachystegia* and bamboo woodland rather than the plantation and evergreen forest more typically found at higher altitudes. Little information about the fauna of the reserve is available, but my own observations suggest it offers good birding, and the predominantly indigenous vegetation may still support a few mammals, most probably vervet monkey, duiker, leopard and hyena.

A combination of lovely scenery, pristine woodland, and the sense of being well off any beaten tourist track makes the Mua-Livulezi a highly attractive and relaxing area to explore over a couple of days, and the reserve is of particular interest if you want to cross between the M1 near Dedza and the southern shore of Lake Malawi. Unfortunately, the recent closure of the Sosola Resthouse has removed the most obvious base for such exploration. I have included the information on this place on the basis that the resthouse may yet re-open, and until such time self-sufficient campers could probably get permission to camp near the site of the resthouse (ask for permission at the Forestry Office in Dedza), or at one of the homesteads near the reserve boundary, or in the village of Mganja.

Getting there and away

Even if you have no intention of exploring the forest reserve, it's worth taking the winding road that descends from Masasa (on the M1, 10km south of Dedza Town) to Golomoti near Lake Malawi, as it is one of the most scenic roads in the country. There is no public transport as such along this road, but it's easy enough to pick up a *matola* ride in Masasa, particularly if you arrive before midday.

To get to Mua-Livelezi, you want to stop at Mganja, a sizeable village about halfway between Masasa and Golomoti. Any *matola* heading between Masasa and Golomoti will drop you here. There is nowhere to stay in Mganja – a shame, as it's a pleasant and attractively situated place – but it's difficult to imagine you'd have any problems finding somewhere to pitch a tent, or any reason to worry greatly about security if you did camp.

Unless you have your own transport, the odds are you'll have to walk the 10–15km between Mganja and Sosola – no great hardship as the scenery is lovely and the road surprisingly flat given the hilly surrounds. From Mganja, you need to head out on the road signposted for Mua. This is an attractive walk, with the Bembeke Escarpment rising to the west, and small rural homesteads every few hundred metres. Ask permission, and you could almost certainly camp at one of these homesteads for a small sum. After about 5km, you enter the forest reserve (you'll be in no doubt when you cross the boundary as cultivation immediately gives way to thick *brachystegia* woodland) and a further 500m or so down the road, you veer sharply to the left to cross a concrete bridge over the clear, babbling Namkokwe River. This is a nice place for a dip, and (although I can give no guarantees) it is probably too rocky and fast flowing for bilharzia to be a realistic cause for concern.

About 2km past the Namkokwe River you'll cross a second small bridge, and then about 2km further on you cross a third. Around 50m after the third bridge, turn into the rough, unsignposted one-vehicle-wide track to your left and follow this through mixed plantation and bamboo woodland for about 3km. About 500m before the resthouse, there used to be a stone bridge and a group of semi-derelict buildings, but I understand the bridge has now collapsed.

From Sosola, instead of returning to Mganja, you could continue on to Mua on the M5. The Mua Mission is an interesting place, with a good museum (see page 187). To do this, retrace your steps for the 3km back to the turn-off, but then instead of turning left towards Mganja, turn right. The distance to Mua is similar to that to Mganja, and with an early start, omitting the path to the abandoned resthouse, you could hike between Mganja and Mua in a day. This is an excellent route for cyclists, with stunning scenery the whole way.

Where to stay

The rustic and isolated **Sosola Forestry Resthouse** was officially closed in 1997. I have no idea whether it will be re-opened, but you should be allowed to camp in the grounds. Before heading this way, speak to the Forestry Office in Dedza for current details. If it does ever re-open, Sosola is an utterly charming retreat, with a creaky wooden balcony offering views across to Lake Malawi, and an attractive garden cleared from dense bamboo stands and dotted with flame trees.

NKHOMA MOUNTAIN

Reaching a height of 1,784m, this *brachystegia*-covered mountain lies to the east of the main road between Lilongwe and Dedza, and it offers some rewarding walking as well as great views over the surounding plains. The mission near the base of the mountain offers accommodation, and access is straightforward whether you are driving, cycling or dependent on public transport, making this another yet excellent off-the-beaten-track excursion in the Dedza area.

The turn-off to Nkhoma lies on the M1, 35km south of Lilongwe, and from there it is 16km to the mission grounds. On Saturday, which is market day in Nkhoma Town, there is direct transport between Nkhoma and Dedza. On other days, there is a least one bus daily between Lilongwe and Nkhoma. There is an inexpensive and clean resthouse in the mission grounds, and more basic local accommodation can be found in town, near to the market. You could also ask at the mission about the rustic hut that lies halfway up the mountain. The ascent from the mission to the rocky summit is quite steep (550m over 2km), and the staff will be able to point you along the right path.

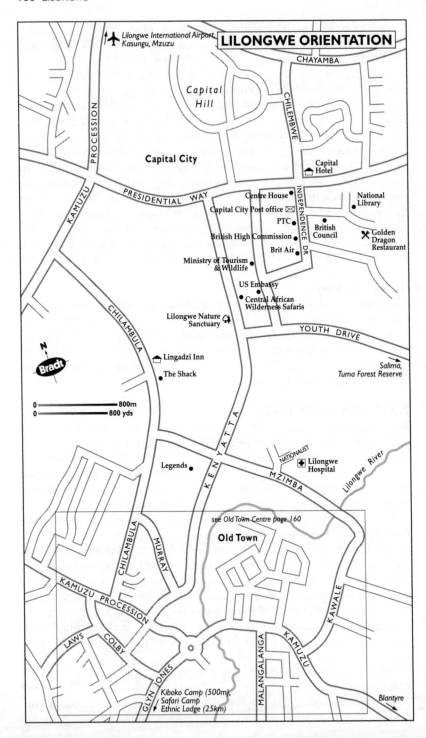

LILONGWE ORIENTATION

Lilongwe International Airport
Kasungu, Mzuzu

CHAYAMBA

Capital Hill

CHILEMBWE

Capital City

PROCESSION

KAMUZU

PRESIDENTIAL WAY

Capital Hotel

Centre House
Capital City Post office ⊠

National Library

PTC

INDEPENDENCE DR

British Council

Golden Dragon Restaurant

British High Commission

Brit Air

Ministry of Tourism & Wildlife

US Embassy

Central African Wilderness Safaris

CHILAMBULA

Lilongwe Nature Sanctuary

YOUTH DRIVE

N

Bradt

Lingadzi Inn

The Shack

Salima, Tuma Forest Reserve

0 ――――― 800m
0 ――――― 800 yds

KENYATTA

NATIONALIST

Lilongwe Hospital

Lilongwe River

Legends

MZIMBA

see Old Town Centre page 160

Old Town

CHILAMBULA

MURRAY

KAWALE

KAMUZU PROCESSION

LAWS

COLBY

GLYN JONES

MALANGALANGA

KAMUZU

Kiboko Camp (500m), Safari Camp Ethnic Lodge (25km)

Blantyre

Lilongwe

Lilongwe is the blandest of African capitals. Arriving, as most visitors do, in the so-called 'old town', what you'll see is indistinguishable from any number of small southern African towns. And you're in for a major disappointment if you head up to the new town – Capital City – expecting something more ostentatious. The Capital City sprawls unconvincingly over a lightly wooded hill; what many maps show as the city centre amounts to little more than a couple of shopping malls and a few restaurants and government buildings melting into leafy suburbia.

Bland though it may be, Lilongwe is one of the most equable capitals in Africa: the climate is comfortable, getting in and out of town is simplicity itself, cheap accommodation is abundant and conveniently situated, shops and markets are well stocked, and the city is almost entirely free of the sort of tourist-targeted crime that makes so many other African cities a potentially treacherous initiation for visitors.

Lilongwe was founded in 1906 on the banks of the Lilongwe River, initially as a settlement for Asian traders, though its pleasant climate rapidly attracted European business. In 1909, the fledgling township's future status was assured when it became the terminus of the first road connecting Malawi to Zambia. By the 1930s, Lilongwe boasted a hotel, a hospital, a European sports club, and a mosque and Muslim Sports Club built by the thriving Asian business community. In 1947, Lilongwe was accorded full township status. By the time of Malawi's independence, Lilongwe was, with a population of around 20,000, second only in size to Blantyre, and its central position made it the obvious choice to replace the colonial capital of Zomba. Lilongwe was formally made the capital of Malawi in 1975, since when its population has easily doubled.

Lilongwe holds little that is likely to be of interest to most tourists. Capital City is worth a look, and the old town is a pleasant place to stroll around, particularly the market and the nearby Asian quarter. The only genuine tourist attraction is the underrated and little-visited Lilongwe Nature Sanctuary which lies between the old town and Capital City. But, in all honesty, it is tempting to recommend that tourists who have no specific reason to visit Lilongwe bypass the city altogether.

CLIMATE

Lilongwe lies on a plateau west of the Rift Valley at a medium altitude of 1,067m. Daytime temperatures are moderate to warm, and most of the annual average rainfall of around 750mm falls between November and April.

ORIENTATION

The old town – to all intents and purposes Lilongwe as it was prior to the Capital City being built in 1975 – is the main business and shopping area, and it's where you'll find most of the hotels and any government offices that are likely to be of interest to tourists. The main business road through the old town is Kamuzu Procession, and the most important intersection is that with Kenyatta Avenue (the road that leads to Lilongwe Nature Sanctuary and Capital City). Along Kamuzu Procession, within 200m of this intersection, are, from north to south, the Lilongwe Hotel, the main post office, the large Nico Centre, the tourist office, and the Times Bookshop. There is a minibus rank where you can pick up transport to Capital City on Kenyatta Avenue about 100m from the intersection in front of the Shoprite Centre.

About 100m south of the post office, Kamuzu Procession forms a large roundabout with Glyn Jones Road to the west and a small unnamed road straight ahead. The Sports Club lies on this corner, and the map sales office lies at the end of the unnamed road. From the roundabout, Kamuzu Procession continues across a bridge over the Lilongwe River to the west, where it climbs through the old Indian trading quarter. About 500m past the bridge, a traffic light marks the intersection with Malaganga Road, which is where you'll find the bus station, market, Council Resthouse and the majority of cheap private resthouses.

Capital City lies 5km from the old town along Kenyatta Avenue. The two parts of town are separated by the *brachystegia* woodland of Lilongwe Nature Sanctuary. Aside from housing most of the embassies and airline offices, as well as the British Council, there are few urgent reasons why tourists might want to visit Capital City.

Lilongwe International Airport lies 26km north of the city centre on the M1 to Kasungu.

GETTING THERE AND AWAY

Getting in and out of Lilongwe couldn't be more straightforward. All buses and minibuses to Lilongwe terminate at the large bus station in the old town. Buses to most destinations in Malawi leave from the same bus station throughout the morning through to mid-afternoon, so there is no reason for rushed early starts. The Shire bus line also has a depot opposite Shoprite.

Most buses between Lilongwe and points further north along the M1 stop at Lilongwe International Airport, and during daylight hours there is no reason to concern yourself about travelling to town by bus. Taxis between the city centre and the airport cost a fixed fare of US$12.

GETTING AROUND

During daylight hours, minibuses run back and forth pretty much non-stop between the old town and Capital City. The best place to pick these up in the old town is near the main bus station, on the opposite side of the Caltex Garage to the Council Resthouse and also from in front of the Shoprite Centre. The fare is cheap and tourists are not normally overcharged.

There are plenty of taxi cabs in Lilongwe, and fares are cheap by international standards. Main taxi ranks in the old town are opposite the bus station (directly in front of the Council Resthouse), in front of the post office, and in the grounds of the Lilongwe Hotel. In the Capital City, you'll find taxis in the grounds of the Capital Hotel. Taxis are also available at the airport.

WHERE TO STAY
Upmarket

There are only two tourist-class hotels in Lilongwe. The **Capital Hotel** (PO Box 30018, Capital City, Lilongwe; tel: 01 773388; fax: 01 771273; email: capital@lemeridienmalawi.co.mw) is the more upmarket of these, very much geared towards businessmen, and conveniently located on Capital Hill within easy walking distance of the centre of the capital. Facilities include a large swimming pool, satellite television in all rooms, a business centre, representative offices of several airlines and a Times Bookshop in the foyer. There is a highly regarded upmarket restaurant in the hotel, as well as a good snack bar. A wide selection of rooms is available, ranging from standard rooms at US$159/208 single/double through to deluxe suites at US$246/317 single/double.

The **Lilongwe Hotel** (PO Box 44, Lilongwe; tel: 01 756333; fax: 01 756580; email: llh@sdnp.org.mw) is a well-known and conveniently central landmark in the old town, a location that is probably more attractive to most tourists than the relatively bland Capital City. Built in the colonial era, this hotel is more atmospheric than its counterpart in the new city centre, with flowering gardens and an attractive swimming pool area. Large, comfortable rooms with satellite television cost US$129/160 single/double and suites cost US$172/205.

Bookings for both of these hotels can be made through Le Meridien's Central Reservation Office at the Mount Soche Hotel in Blantyre.

Midrange

Attractively situated between the old and new towns, **Lingadzi Inn** (PO Box 30367, Capital City, Lilongwe; tel: 01 720644) is an adequate and moderately priced hotel, the sort of place budget travellers might want to book into should they be flying into Lilongwe late in the day. The best features of this hotel are the neat, pretty grounds. Oddly enough, this is perhaps the only hotel or lodge in Malawi where you can be pretty certain of hearing hyenas at night, since it borders the Lilongwe Nature Sanctuary. Rooms cost US$90/126 single/double and as with other Le Meridien hotels can be booked in advance through the Central Reservations Office at the Mount Soche Hotel in Blantyre.

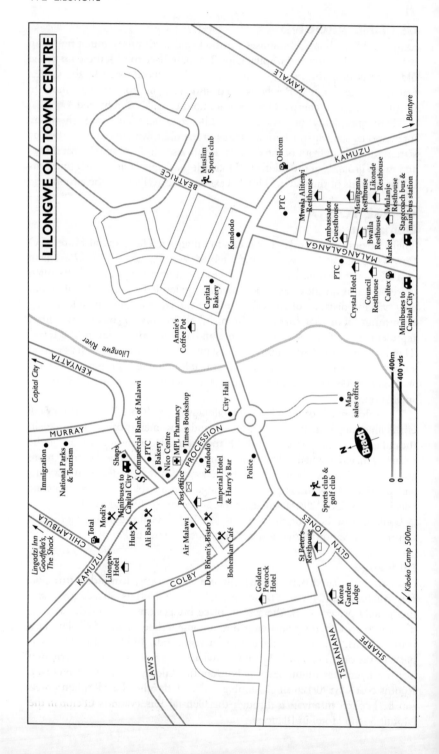

LILONGWE OLD TOWN CENTRE

Similar in style and standard is the **Capital City Motel** (PO Box 30454; tel: 01 783231; fax: 01 784624), which lies about 3km from Capital City along Youth Drive and offers adequate rooms from around US$30/40 single/double using communal showers and US$45/65 self-contained single/double. Facilities include a pleasant bar and restaurant, and satellite television in every room. There is live jazz music here every Sunday from 14.00.

Two establishments have recently been refurbished in the old town. The **Imperial Hotel** (email: imperial@malawi.net), an old 1940s-style place, is just above the post office and offers smart, affordable and central accommodation, ranging between US$25/40 for economy rooms and US$50/80 for en suite single/double. A long balcony overlooks the street below, and the vibey bar beckons downstairs. The **Korean Garden Lodge** (ex Ivy's) (tel: 01 753467; fax: 01 756612; email: kgl@malawi.net; web: www.kglodge.net) is set in quiet gardens behind St Peter's Resthouse. With good security for yourself and vehicle, it charges US$15/20 single/double to share a bathroom, and US$32/39 for self-contained single/doubles.

A number of private guesthouses have opened in Lilongwe in recent years. One of the newest is **Hueglin's Guesthouse** (tel: 01 782364), owned and managed by Central African Wilderness Safaris. Situated off Blantyre Street, to the north of the Capital City, this guesthouse has six double rooms, three of which are self-contained, and the charges are US$60/100 B&B single/double for a room using communal bathroom, and US$95/140 B&B for a self-contained single/double. Also recommended, the German-run **Wendel's Bed & Breakfast** (tel: 01 770237; fax: 01 771771; email: wendels@malawi.net; web: www.wendels.com) lies close to the city centre.

Budget

Run by a well-travelled Dutch couple, **Kiboko Camp** has become the most popular backpacker haunt in Lilongwe, and also offers safaris within Malawi and to Luangwa National Park in Zambia (see page 180). Camping costs US$3 per person, with separate sites for overland trucks and for independent travellers, while dormitories cost US$5 per person and chalets are US$12 per person. Facilities include a bar and a barbecue area. Kiboko Camp lies on Likuni roundabout, which is on Glyn Jones Road about 1km past the golf club. If you are coming from the main bus station, the best way to get to Kiboko is to pick up a minibus heading to Likuni and ask to be dropped at the roundabout. Coming out of town, Kiboko Camp is the property with a high reed fence and hedge on the far left side of the roundabout. Contact details are Private Bag 295, Lilongwe; tel: 01 828384; fax: 01 754978; email: kiboko@malawi.net. (Email and internet access for guests.)

More central, and also catering specifically for backpackers, are the rooms at the back of **Annie's Coffee Pot**. These are a four-bed dormitory costing US$3 per person, two private rooms costing US$6 for a double and camping at US$2. Another place that's been popular with travellers for some years is **St Peter's Guesthouse**, which is situated practically opposite the golf club in the grounds of the eponymous church. It has two double rooms, one triple, and three four-bed dorms, all with nets and at a cost of US$5 per person. The problem with both of these places is that bed space is limited, so you may well do the long walk from the bus station only to be turned away.

Two rather more expensive places are situated in the backroads behind St Peter's. The **Golden Peacock Hotel** (tel: 01 742638) has been around for years, sharing a property with the Korea Garden Restaurant, and it remains very popular with travellers. All rooms are doubles with nets and fans: rooms using communal showers cost US$9 and self-contained rooms with hot showers US$13.

If you are really desperate, there are numerous cheap lodgings along the backroads around the bus station and market. The **Council Resthouse** was a popular standby with travellers in the days before the backpacker hostels reached Lilongwe, and it remains about the best of the bunch. Rooms in the new wing cost from US$6 for an ordinary double to US$11 for a large, self-contained double. Of the 15-odd other hotels in this part of town, the **Crystal Lodge** next to the Council Resthouse looks acceptable, with rooms for US$5/7 single/double or US$10 self-contained double, as does the **Ambassador Resthouse**, with self-contained rooms in the US$8–10 bracket.

The campsite at the **Lilongwe Golf Club** is popular with travellers at US$5 per person – and this does include use of the club's facilities.

WHERE TO EAT

Not many travellers get to eat in the Capital City, as there are few reasonable restaurants to choose from. The long-standing **Golden Dragon Restaurant** near the British Council retains a good reputation. The restaurant in the **Capital Hotel** has meals in the US$10–12 range, and the meals at the snack bar near the hotel's pool are very good value – mostly around US$5.

There is greater choice in the old town. **Don Brioni's Bistro** near the post office has a varied international menu with an emphasis on Italian dishes. Pizzas are something of a speciality, and they cost around US$5–6, where most meat and fish dishes cost around US$8.

One of our favourite places to eat is **Modi's Restaurant** in the old town. This has an eclectic menu with items ranging from steaks to grilled fish and prawns, though the emphasis is on Indian dishes. Main courses are in the US$5–7 range, and the portions are large. The only other Indian restaurant in Lilongwe, **Hut's**, is close to Modi's, physically, in standard, and in price.

The **Korean Gardens Restaurant**, in the same building as the Golden Peacock Hotel, is highly rated for Korean food, with prices comparable to Modi's. A cheaper option is the **Ali Baba Take-Away**, which serves a variety of Lebanese dishes (hummus, kebabs, schwarmas) as well as burgers, steaks and the like. Portions are generous and very reasonably priced.

Annie's Coffee Pot serves hamburgers, piri-piri chicken, fried *chambo*, vegetable curry, etc for around US$2–3 per main course. The food is good and very reasonably priced, though the portions aren't particularly generous. There's definitely no reason to get excited about the coffee. If that's what you're after, head to the **Bohemian Café**; it's also a good place for breakfasts and lunches – cappuccino, fresh fruit juice, chocolate cake, pastries, pies and toasted sandwiches. It closes in the evenings and on Sundays. The coffee and cakes at **Lilongwe Hotel** are also pretty good.

Arguably the best restaurant in Lilongwe is **Mama Mia's**, an upmarket Italian trattoria in the new Old Town Mall off Chilambula Road. From gleaming stainless steel kitchen, to cosy corners and shaded patio, the place exudes class and is value for money too, serving pizzas at US$3.50 to US$5.50 and pastas at around US$6. **Harry's Bar** in the atmospheric old Imperial Hotel is a great place for a drink and pepper steak at only US$4.

Another good place for a drink, off Chilambula Road, is **Goodfella's**, a sportsbar with satellite television, a good selection of drinks, pool tables and pub meals – oxtail and chips at US$3.50 when I was there.

The **Shack**, next door to Lingadzi Inn in Chilambula Road, is a great pub- cum-social club started by the Round Table and supported by most of Lilongwe's expats. With volleyball outside on Wednesday evenings and Happy Hour on Fridays, it's a good place to make sporting and social contacts. **Legends** was the night club of choice in 2002, although it's difficult to find down the side streets off Chilambula Road, near to the Tambala Food Factory.

The cheapest places to eat out are the local restaurants around the market and bus station, where you can get a standard chicken and *nsima* or rice for less than US$1. The food at the **Council Resthouse** is of a slightly higher standard and still very cheap.

If you want to put together your own food, there's a good range of fruit and vegetables on sale at the market. For fresh bread and pastries, try the **Capital Bakery**, in the Asian town. Most supermarkets sell a limited range of foodstuffs – the best being the **PTC Hyperstore** in the Nico Centre. Across the road, in a shop-until-you-drop class of its own, is **Shoprite Supermarket**, where you can get anything. Both the PTC and Shoprite have adjoining fast-food outlets for good cheap chicken-and-chip-type meals.

TOURIST INFORMATION

The tourist office used to be conveniently situated in the old town, but has now moved to a semi-industrial area, where it shares offices with the National Parks Department opposite the Immigration office between Chilambula and Murray roads.

Airlines
Air Malawi NBS Building, Manadala Rd; tel: 01 753181; fax: 01 701008
Air Zimbabwe Mitco House; tel: 01 783804; fax: 01 783780
British Airways ADL House, Capital City; 01 771747; fax: 01 772747
Ethiopian Airlines Mitco House, Capital City; tel: 01 772001
KLM Capital Hotel; tel: 01 781413; fax: 01 784293
Kenya Airways Capital Hotel; tel: 01 774227
South African Airways see *Blantyre*

Books and newspapers

The main branch of the Times Bookshop is in the old town on Kamuzu Procession. There are also branches in the PTC supermarket in Capital City and in the foyers of the Lilongwe and Capital hotels. The branches in the hotels are open seven days a week. The Bookworm in Old Town Mall has a fabulous selection of books, including some very valuable Africana.

Car hire

Avis is the only international car-hire firm operating out of Lilongwe. The main office lies off Chilambula Road (tel: 01 756105) about 1km from the old town centre, so on foot it's more convenient to contact the branch offices in either the Lilongwe Hotel or the Capital Hotel.

Several local car-hire companies operate out of Lilongwe, including Ceciliana Car Hire (tel: 01 756055; fax: 01 756052) and SS Rent-a-car (tel: 01 751478; fax: 01 751529).

Email

There are email and fax facilities at the business centre in the foyer of the Capital Hotel, as well as at the ADL Building in the Capital City. The Capital Internet Café next door to Goodfella's charges US$0.16 per minute, while Licom in Mandala Road is US$0.20 per minute. They also do copies and faxes. The best internet connection in the most pleasant surroundings, though, is in the library at the British Council in Capital City ($1.35 per 15 minutes).

Embassies

China PO Box 30221; tel: 01 774181
Germany PO Box 30046; tel: 01 782555; fax: 01 780250
India PO Box 30348; tel: 01 780766; fax: 01 781332
Israel PO Box 30319; tel: 01 782933
Mozambique PO Box 30579; tel: 01 784100
South Africa PO Box 30043; tel: 01 783722
UK PO Box 30042; tel: 01 782400; fax: 01 782657
United States PO Box 30016; tel: 01 783166; fax: 01 780471
Zambia PO Box 30138; tel: 01 782100
Zimbabwe PO Box 30187; tel: 01 784988

Note that the German Embassy also handles visas for France, Belgium, Netherlands, Luxembourg, Spain, Portugal and Austria.

Foreign exchange

Foreign currency can be changed into kwacha at any of the main banks or at one of the private forex bureaux that dot the city centre. I found the best was Lee's in the Nico Centre. Outside normal banking hours, there is a 24-hour foreign exchange service at Lilongwe International Airport, though it's probably easier to change money at one of the tourist-class hotels or on the street. Individuals offering kwacha for dollars or rands cash can be found hanging around the post office in the old town or at the entrance to the golf club or the Council Resthouse; it's probably not advisable to change any more than you absolutely have to.

Immigration

The immigration office is a short way off Chilambula Road – the route is signposted from the Lilongwe Hotel. Visa and visitors' pass renewals are processed here in a matter of minutes.

Maps

The Department of Surveys' Map Sales Office sells a good range of 1:50,000 and 1:250,000 maps, covering most of Malawi. The office is in the old town near the golf club on a side road that radiates from the roundabout where Glyn Jones Road meets Kamuzu Procession. Maps cost between US$7 and US$12.

Medical

A laboratory called Medicore in the NBS Building in the old town opposite the Bohemian Café is the best place to go for tests of any sort. A malaria test, for instance, takes ten minutes to produce and costs US$5. Likuni Hospital, a few kilometres out of town on the Likuni road, is regarded as the best in the Lilongwe area, though Lilongwe Hospital on Nationalist Road is more central for simple routine checks. Dr Martin Huber has a surgery near the Likuni roundabout where his wife assists him, doing tests. There are also three pharmacies in the Nico Centre.

Post

The main post office is in the old town on Kamuzu Procession. This is where any post restante mail addressed to Lilongwe will be kept. If you want to collect your mail at the post office in Capital City, then have it addressed to Lilongwe Capital City. The post restante system in Lilongwe is reasonably efficient as these things go. Proof of identity is required to collect mail, and US$0.50 is charged for duration of stay.

Note that Lilongwe PO box numbers of four numerals or less are in the old town post office, while five numeral PO boxes are in Capital City post office.

Shopping

There are three new shopping complexes in Lilongwe, all with security guards for shoppers and their vehicles. The Shoprite Centre on the corner of Kamuzu Procession and Kenyatta has a supermarket, where virtually anything is available, as well as some small specialist shops. Across the road is the Nico Centre, with its PTC Hyperstore as well as three pharmacies and two forex bureaux. The most upmarket complex is the Old Town Mall, off Chilambula Road. Not only does it house the best restaurant in Lilongwe, Mama Mia's, but there are also the offices of Ulendo Safaris, an art gallery, a fascinating bookstore for new and antiquarian books, an exclusive wine and food emporium, video hire, a beautiful craft and curio gallery and trendy clothing stores. A treat to visit when you've had your fill of markets and poorly stocked superettes.

There are other smaller supermarkets and bakeries dotted around Lilongwe and there were no shortages when I was there in mid-2002. For a selection of camping gear and Camping Gaz, head for Land and Lake Safaris in the Bohemian Café on Mandala Road.

For motor spares and repairs, go to the industrial area bordered by Kamuzu, Kenyatta and Chilambula Roads. Look out for Halls (tel: 01 740677) for Landrover and Toyota Malawi (tel: 01 721566). Also try the Asian part of town.

The central market, next to the bus station, is the best place to buy fresh fruit and vegetables. It is also a good place to buy cheap clothes, cassettes of Malawian and Zairian music, and practically anything else you can think of.

The main cluster of curio sellers is outside the post office in the old town. There are also quite a few curios on sale in the main car park on Independence Drive in Capital City.

Tour operators

Several reliable tour operators have offices in Lilongwe. **Central African Wilderness Safaris**, one of the country's best and most reputable operators, is an affiliate of the Wilderness Safaris group that operates throughout much of southern Africa. They are also the concessionaires for Mvuu Camp in Liwonde National Park and the Chintheche Inn on the northern lakeshore, as well as having opened a new resthouse in Lilongwe itself. The office is in Bisnowaty Building, Kenyatta Road, Capital City (next door to a large new BP garage), PO Box 489, Lilongwe; tel: 01 771153; fax: 01 771397; email: info@wilderness-safaris.malawi.net; web: www.wilderness-safaris.com. South Africans can contact the Johannesburg office of Wilderness Safaris (tel: +2711 884 1458/9; fax: +2711 883 6255).

Another very reputable company is **Land & Lake Safaris** (PO Box 2140, Lilongwe; tel: 01 757120; fax: 01 754560; email: landlake@malawi.net; web: www.landlakemalawi.com), with an office in the old town behind the Bohemian Café. In addition to organising a wide variety of safaris, including to Zambia's South Luangwa National Park, they operate the forest lodges in Zomba and Dzalanyama and hire and sell camping equipment.

Ulendo Safaris (PO Box 30728, Lilongwe; tel: 01 754950; fax: 01 756321; email: info@ulendo.malawi.net) have offices in the Old Town Mall and offer a comprehensive travel service in Malawi as well as South Luangwa in Zambia.

Kiboko Safaris (Private Bag 295, Lilongwe; tel: 01 751226; fax: 01 754978; email: kiboko@malawi.net; web: www.kiboko-safaris.com) run the very popular Kiboko Backpackers Camp in Lilongwe and also organise budget tours around Malawi and into South Luangwa.

The **Nyika Safari Company**, the sole concessionaire for accommodation in Nyika National Park and Vwaza Marsh Wildlife Reserve, is the best place to arrange hiking and horseback trips in the Nyika and to get current information about these reserves. Contact them in advance at PO Box 2338; tel: 01 740579; tel/fax: 01 740848; email: nyika-safaris@malawi.net.

Other established tour operators include Soche Tours and Travel (PO Box 30406, Capital City; tel: 01 782377; fax: 01 781409), Makomo Safaris (tel/fax:

01 721536 or 01 723547; email: makomo@eo.wn.apc.org) and AMI Travel (PO Box 30074, Capital City; tel: 01 783220).

Wildlife and National Parks Office

The Wildlife Headquarters is in the old town next to the immigration office. All non-private accommodation in national parks and wildlife reserves can be booked there. The address is PO Box 30131, Capital City; tel: 01 753232; fax: 01 754427.

THINGS TO DO

Lilongwe is not the most inspiring of cities. For short stay visitors to Malawi, it's tempting to suggest you avoid Lilongwe altogether or, if you're forced to pass through, to hop off the bus and get straight on to one heading to your next destination.

If you find yourself with a spare day in Lilongwe, the place to head for is the excellent Lilongwe Nature Sanctuary, which lies between the new and old towns. Any minibus heading along this route can drop you near the entrance gate, where US$0.40 is charged for entrance and a small map and booklet is sold. You probably won't want to linger too long around the small zoo near the entrance (a few monkeys, hyenas and pythons); instead, devote a couple of hours to exploring the small network of trails that run through the reserve. These pass through pristine *brachystegia* woodland before descending to the riparian forest along the banks of the Lingadzi River.

A fair number of large mammals occur naturally in the reserve, including spotted hyena, otter, porcupine, bushpig, grey duiker and bushbuck. Of these, you'll be lucky to see more than the rump of a fleeing bushbuck. You can be more confident of seeing a few crocodiles next to the river, and the odd troop of vervet monkeys along the footpaths. But the main point of interest is birds: over 150 species have been recorded in the reserve, and the paths along the river in particular can offer quite excellent birding, especially at dusk (my list included three types of kingfisher, Hueglin's robin, brown snake eagle, a variety of weavers and finches, and the dazzlingly colourful Schalow's turaco).

When you've finished exploring the reserve, you might want to stop for a meal or drink at the restaurant outside the gate.

SHORT TRIPS FROM LILONGWE

Several short trips are possible from Lilongwe, though most are of more interest to residents looking for a weekend break than to tourists. Useful details of places of interest around Lilongwe (including areas like Dedza, Salima and Ntchisi which are covered elsewhere in this guide) are contained in the 60-page booklet *Day Outings from Lilongwe* (Judy Carter, Wildlife Society of Malawi, 1991). This costs around US$1 and can be bought at any Times Bookshop.

Tuma Forest Reserve

This 164km² forest reserve lies to the east of Lilongwe about 25km off the Salima road, and it is part of a much larger complex of protected areas which

SOUTH LUANGWA NATIONAL PARK, ZAMBIA

This low-lying park, which covers an area of 9,050km² in Zambia's Luangwa River valley, is widely regarded as one of the finest wildlife reserves anywhere in Africa. The reserve harbours innumerable elephant, buffalo and hippo, as well as a wide variety of antelope and other ungulates, substantial numbers of lion, leopard and spotted hyena, and smaller numbers of cheetah and wild dog. The entrance to South Luangwa and its main cluster of lodges lies little more than 100km from Mchinji on the Malawi–Zambia border west of Lilongwe, and since Malawi itself lacks any reserve comparable in size or in game viewing, South Luangwa is visited from Malawi with increasing frequency.

Any Lilongwe-based tour operator can organise an excursion to South Luangwa, either as part of a longer tour of Malawi or else as a self-contained trip out of Lilongwe. The cost of such an excursion will depend greatly on whether you camp at one of the cheaper sites or stay at an upmarket lodge. For a budget trip, try Land and Lake Safaris or Kiboko Safaris, while for lodge-based trips, you're best off using Central African Wilderness Safaris or Ulendo Safaris (all details under Lilongwe's tour operators). For visitors needing a Malawian visa, remember to get a double-entry one, so as to be able to return after your side trip to South Luangwa. Zambia also requires a yellow-fever certificate. The best months to visit are June, July and August.

For adventurous and patient backpackers, hitching to South Luangwa is a real possibility. The springboard for a hitching trip to South Luangwa is Chipata, a small town situated roughly 30km from the Mchinji border (see *Getting to Malawi from South Africa*, page 41). The best place to stick out your thumb is outside the Chipata Motel, and you are advised against accepting any lift that doesn't go all the way to Flatdogs, Croc Valley, Marula Lodge or Wildlife Camp, the only four places in the park that cater for budget travellers. All of these places have accommodation for around US$20 per person and allow camping for around US$5 per person, in addition to which the daily park entrance fee of US$15 must be paid, and they can organise game drives for visitors without transport. I would strongly advise you make advance contact before heading out this way: Flatdogs (tel: 062 45074), Wildlife Camp (tel: 062 21606) and Marula Lodge (tel: 062 45073).

More extensive details of South Luangwa and travel elsewhere in Zambia are to be found in *Zambia: The Bradt Travel Guide*, written by Chris McIntyre, who also supplied the information here.

until recently has seen little scientific exploration and even less tourist development. Tuma spans the Rift Valley Escarpment from an altitude of 575m to 1,550m, and it protects a corresponding variety of habitats, including *brachystegia* woodland, bamboo forest and evergreen forest.

Above Nkhotakota harbour
Left Mother and child on shore of Lake Malawi
Below Fishing dhow, off Likoma Island

Right Mulanje tea plantations, with Mulanje Mountain in the background

Below Mulanje boma, or administrative centre

The reserve is bounded by the Lilongwe River to the north and the Linthipe River to the south. Management of the reserve has been taken over by the Wildlife Action Group, who have managed to control poaching with the co-operation of local villagers, and hope to make Tuma something of a flagship reserve for their linked goals of protecting some of Malawi's lesser-known wilderness areas and opening them up to revenue-generating tourism.

In addition to having an untrammelled wilderness atmosphere, Tuma offers the opportunity to track a wide variety of large mammals on foot. Some 40-odd large mammal species have been recorded, including elephant, buffalo, leopard, baboon, vervet monkey, several antelope species (the magnificant greater kudu is particularly common) and a variety of small predators. A bird list is still in the process of being compiled, but the combination of habitats ensures that many notable birds are present, and the reserve has already thrown up one new record for Malawi in the form of the Natal francolin.

The person to contact for information on Tuma is Georg of Safari Beach Lodge, who is one of the trustees of the Wildlife Action Group (tel: 01 263142; fax: 01 263002; email: safwag@africa-online.net; web: www.wag-malawi.org).

Dzalanyama Forest Reserve

This forest reserve lies on the Mozambican border, 58km southwest of Lilongwe past Kamuzu Dam. Dzalanyama means 'place of animals'. The forest is rated to have the greatest diversity of *brachystegia* birds in Malawi, and also protects typical forest mammals including samango monkeys and leopards. The Dzalanyama Forest Lodge is privately operated by Land and Lake Safaris (see page 178 for contact details) and offers accommodation, with bedding, for eight people in four rooms. This self-catering lodge is staffed and contains all necessary equipment, including refrigerator and cooking facilities. You need your own transport to reach the lodge, and should be aware that the access road sometimes becomes impassable after rain.

Bunda Mountain and Dam

With your own vehicle, this would be a rewarding day trip from Lilongwe, though it's not really practical on public transport. Bunda Mountain is a large granite dome rising to 1,410m to the west of the M1. In addition to being the site of an important Chewa rain shrine (traditional rain ceremonies are still performed here twice annually), the mountain offers good views and the opportunity to see rock-nesting raptors such as the black eagle. Bunda Dam, which lies within the grounds of the Bunda College of Agriculture, is popular with birdwatchers, and the adjacent marshes can be a good place to see crowned crane, pelicans, and a variety of waterfowl, herons and waders.

To get to Bunda, follow the M1 south of Lilongwe for 10km, then turn right towards the Bunda College of Agriculture, the entrance gate of which lies about 20km from the M1. The dam lies 5km from the entrance gate; turn into the gate and ask directions from there. To get to the base of the mountain, continue past the gate for 500m, then turn left on to a track which follows the edge of a plantation forest, and then, when you reach a T-junction, turn right.

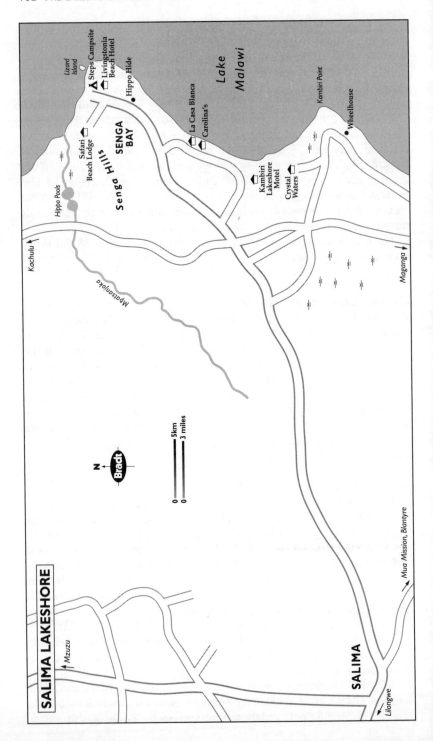

The Lakeshore around Salima

The Lake Malawi shore around Salima has become a popular weekend getaway for Lilongwe residents. As a result, the 5km stretch of beach between Senga Bay and Kambiri Point is as well developed for tourism as any part of the lake. The Salima area, it must be said, has neither the natural beauty of Nkhata Bay or Cape Maclear, nor the sense of isolation of some of the resorts on the northern lakeshore. It is popular simply because it is closer to Lilongwe than any other part of the lake. Nevertheless, it is an attractive enough spot, relatively rich in birds and mammals, and a very comfortable place to settle into for a few days.

Salima itself lies 15km from the lake; it is a thoroughly dull small town, and purely of interest as a route focus and as the gateway to Senga Bay on Lake Malawi. The only motivations for exploring Salima beyond its bus station are practical: it has a bank, a post office, a bustling market, and a couple of well-stocked supermarkets. Most visitors simply head straight on to Senga Bay.

Main points of interest around Senga Bay are the Mpatsanjoka River (excellent birding and resident hippos), Lizard Island, and the tropical fish farm near Kambiri Point.

CLIMATE

Salima has the hot, sweaty climate typical of the Lake Malawi shore.

GETTING AROUND

Salima is a major route focus, connected to Lilongwe by the recently tarred M14. The M14 intersects with the southern lakeshore road (to Cape Maclear, Mangochi, Zomba and Blantyre) about 2km west of Salima, and with the northern lakeshore road (to Nkhotakota, Nkhata Bay and Mzuzu) about 4km west of Salima.

Minibuses travel regularly between Salima and Lilongwe. All buses which follow the lakeshore road between points north and south of Salima stop there to pick up passengers. A steady stream of *matola* pick-up trucks runs between Salima's bus station and the market in Senga Bay. From the market, it's about 500m through the village to Hippo Hide, and about 2km along the tar road to the Livingstonia Beach Hotel and Steps Campsite.

The best way to reach any of the resorts towards Kambiri Point is to take transport towards Senga Bay, ask to be dropped at the appropriate turn-off (the resorts are all signposted from the Salima–Senga Bay road), and then walk or hitch to the lakeshore (between 30 minutes and an hour on foot, depending on the resort). The alternative is go right through to Senga Bay, continue along the tar road to the Livingstonia Beach Hotel, and then turn left on to the beach and follow it southwards. In terms of distance, there's not much in it, but walking along the beach will be more tiring and slower, especially if you have a heavy pack.

WHERE TO STAY
Salima
With Senga Bay only 15km away, it's difficult to think of a convincing reason why any traveller would actually choose to stay in Salima. On the other hand, its strategic position does mean that you might just end up there for a night at some point. Accommodation in town is limited to a few very ordinary resthouses dotted around the bus station.

Senga Bay
Livingstonia Beach Hotel (PO Box 11, Salima; tel: 01 263222; fax: 01 263452; email: livingstonia@lemeridienmalawi.co.mw) is the oldest hotel on Lake Malawi, built in the 1930s, when it was known as the Grand Beach Hotel, and with an overall shape and design instantly recognisable from the many old photos that line the walls of the public areas. The compact flower-filled grounds, beautiful private beach, comfortable rooms, and whitewash and creosote exterior vaguely reminiscent of the Cape Dutch style combine to make the Livingstonia arguably the finest hotel in Malawi. The atmosphere is certainly more sedate and exclusive than that of other major hotels on the lake. Facilities include watersport and snorkelling equipment hire, a swimming pool and tennis court, an atmospheric residents' lounge, a library, and an excellent first-floor restaurant. The management can arrange walking trips to the nearby hippo pool and view points, as well as boat trips to several islands and car trips to Mua Mission, the Stuart Grant Fish Farm and other local points of interest. The checklist of birds recorded in the grounds, available from reception, includes several interesting species. Rooms cost US$150/210 single/double, while chalets cost US$190/225 and suites US$205/245. Rates are inclusive of breakfast and all taxes. There is a discount of roughly 40% for residents of Malawi.

Next to the Livingstonia Beach Hotel and under the same management, the spacious **Steps Campsite** is widely reckoned to be one of the best campsites in Malawi, with a great position and good facilities, including a bar, laundry facilities, hot showers and credit card and money exchange facilities. Camping costs US$4 per person, and electricity is available for a small extra fee. Campers *are* welcome to eat at the neighbouring hotel, but they should be prepared to abide by the relatively formal dress code (no shorts or flip-flops).

In Senga Bay village, close to where the *matola* vehicles stop, **Hippo Hide Resthouse** offers basic but adequate rooms for US$2 per person, and you can pitch a tent in the compound for slightly less. Facilities include a communal shower and toilet, a fridge with cold beers and sodas, and meals can be ordered a few hours in advance. The two drawbacks are that you're some way from the beach, and we've heard several reports of people staying here being persistently hassled by the touts who hang out around the village. There are also a few rooms at similar prices at the **Top Hill Restaurant**, about 500m from the entrance to the Livingstonia Beach Hotel, and at the nearby **God is Guide Resthouse** – both of these places are similar in quality to Hippo Hide, but they're likely to be more peaceful because of the absence of touts.

To reach the upmarket **Safari Beach Lodge** (PO Box 312, Salima; tel: 01 263143; email: safwag@malawi.net), turn left just before the gates of the Livingstonia Beach Hotel and travel about 1km up the hill. Situated in a forestry reserve, this recently renovated lodge has two double en-suite rooms and five luxury tents with decks overlooking the lake. There is also a private beach, 10ha of forest to ramble through and the owners can organise safaris into the Tuma Forest Reserve. Rates are US$35/55 single/double including breakfast.

Towards Kambiri Point

South of the Livingstonia Beach Hotel, several resorts, hotels and campsites stretch along the beach towards Kambiri Point. These resorts can be accessed from the tarred Salima–Senga Bay road by a series of signposted side roads. On foot, they can also be reached along the beach, though – if you have a pack – this is probably a tougher walk than along the roads.

The southernmost cluster of accommodation lies about 5km from the Livingstonia Beach Hotel as the crow flies. By road, the turn-off to these places is about 8km towards Salima, and clearly signposted. From the turn-off, it's a further 4–5km, depending on where you're heading, and there is no public transport.

The **Red Zebra Fish Farm** offers comfortable, self-contained accommodation at US$15/20 single/double, as well as offering sundowner cruises (US$15) and guided tours of the tropical fish farm (US$0.50).

For campers, the best place to head for here is the **Wheelhouse** (tel: 01 261485), best known for its raised wooden bar overlooking a reed-lined (ie: high risk of bilharzia) beach. Good rooms and meals are available at **La Casa Blanca**, which lies next to the tropical fish farm and charges US$15/25 single/double. For cheaper accommodation, **Crystal Waters** (tel: 01 263169) has self-contained double rooms with hot water for US$16. The smartest place in this area is the **Kambiri Lakeshore Motel** (tel: 01 263052), which, despite being set further back from the beach than its name suggests, offers immaculate self-contained rooms at US$35/45 single/double as well as good meals.

A separate cluster of chalet-type accommodation lies about 20 minutes' walk north along the beach from the Kambiri Motel and perhaps 40 minutes' walk south of the Livingstonia Beach Hotel. This cluster can also be reached from the main Salima–Senga Bay road via a 3km-long turn-off signposted 'Carolina's'. The most appealing of the options here *is* **Carolina's** (tel/fax: 01 263220), which offers comfortable self-contained triple chalets with nets and hot water for US$38–50, as well as inexpensive camping and excellent meals. Next door, **Chimpango Chalets** and **Baobab Chalets** have more basic chalets for around US$12 per unit.

WHERE TO EAT

The restaurant at the **Livingstonia Beach Hotel** is the most upmarket in the area. Meals cost US$20 and are available to non-residents of the hotel provided that they dress reasonably smartly.

On the main tar road about 500m from the Livingstonia Beach Hotel, the **Top Hill Restaurant** is an idiosyncratic little place with walls plastered with raves from passing travellers. The banana pancakes here have acquired something close to legendary status. Main meals such as fish or chicken with mashed potatoes, chips or rice must be ordered in advance, at US$2.50 per plate.

The **Red Zebra Café** next door to Top Hill was much more pleasant, with a garden and good food, and excellently served. Most meals cost about US$3.50.

In Senga Bay village, 100m from the market, the restaurant next to the Third World Bar serves local food for around US$1.

Further afield, **Carolina's** and to a lesser extent **Crystal Waters** have varied menus with most dishes in the US$3–4 range – tempting lunchtime goals if you're looking for an incentive to stroll down the beach.

If you're cooking for yourself, the market in Senga Bay is pretty basic. It would be better to stock up in Salima, where there are PTC and Kandodo supermarkets. The market has a fair range of vegetables, fruit and fresh meat, and you can get fresh bread at the Tiara Bakery.

THINGS TO DO

Lazing around on the beach, or perhaps hiring some watersport equipment at the Livingstonia Beach Hotel, will be enough to occupy many people's time at Salima. There are, however, a couple of options for those who want to explore.

Lizard Island

This small rocky island, which lies just off the beach in front of the Livingstonia Beach Hotel, is known for its dense population of monitor lizards, and also as the breeding ground for large numbers of white-breasted cormorants. It's easy enough to organise a day trip to the island (inclusive of a fish barbecue) with children in Senga Bay village – expect to pay around US$10 per person, depending on group size and to a lesser extent your negotiating skills.

Mpatsanjoka Dambo

The lush and seasonally marshy Mpatsanjoka River runs in an arc north of Senga Hill, before emptying into Lake Malawi about 2km north of Senga

Bay. The river is home to a small resident population of hippos, crocodiles and water monitors, and is also noted for its prolific birdlife. The simplest way to reach the hippo pools is to adopt a local child as your guide (ask around in the village), though if you're stubborn about such things (or prefer birding without having to explain your curious behaviour to children) it's not too difficult to find your own way there. Take the path crossing the hill from the road to Safari Beach Lodge, then descend to the beach and follow it northwards for about 20 minutes to the river mouth. From here, it's about 3km upriver to the area where you're most likely to see hippos (you know you have gone far enough when you connect with a dirt road that bridges the river).

Seeing the hippos requires a little luck: we could hear them and approached them within metres, but they remained submerged beneath thick overhanging vegetation. Especially in the morning, it would be wise to be very cautious (at least two people have been killed by hippos in this area in the last ten years). If you don't see the hippos, you can be certain of seeing plenty of birds – they are everywhere, even when the water is low. I saw a good variety of hornbills, kingfishers, weavers and finches, and it's a good pace to see the localised and very colourful Boehm's bee-eater, as well as the secretive rufous-bellied heron.

In the wet season, you could cross the bridge and continue north along the road for about 2km to an area of rice cultivation, where several unusual birds (including crowned crane and common pratincole) are regular.

Enthusiastic birders may want to explore the several other seasonal marshes in the Senga area; good directions and a map are included in the booklet *Day Outings from Lilongwe*.

Tropical fish farm

This farm near Kambiri Point was established by Stuart Grant to breed various cichlid species for the European tropical fish market. A huge variety of cichlids can be seen in the tanks, many of them rare species, and visitors are welcome – cost US$0.50. Tel: 01 263165; fax: 01 263407; email: redzebra@lakemalawi.com.

Mua Mission

This Catholic Mission is one of the oldest in Malawi, established at the base of the Rift Valley Escarpment by the so-called 'White Fathers' in 1902. Over the last few years, Mua has set itself up as something of a tourist attraction. The main point of interest here is undoubtedly the ethnographic museum, reputedly the best in Malawi. A two- to three-hour tour of the museum costs US$5 per person. The historical murals on its outside walls are worth a look, and the mission also boasts a highly regarded craft centre, a dismal zoo, an impressive church dating to the first decade of the 20th century, and a showroom and shop selling woodcarvings.

The museum, which is closed on Saturday afternoons and Sundays, offers courses, seminars and retreats for interested individuals or groups wishing to explore more detailed aspects of the local culture and its interaction with

Christianity. Bookings should be made in advance. Casual accommodation is available at US$4 for dorm beds, US$12 for double rooms and US$15 for en-suite double rooms, inclusive of breakfast. Meals are also available at the Father's house for US$4.

Mua lies about 45km south of Salima along the main tar road to Balaka. The roughly 1km-long dirt turn-off to the mission is clearly signposted 'Mua Parish'. Note that Mua lies at the base of the scenic road through the Mua-Livulezi Forest Reserve, making it the terminal of a route that already has much to offer keen hikers and cyclists.

If you get stuck and need accommodation between Salima and Mua, then the little lakeside town of Chipoka is your best bet. The lake ferry also sometimes stops here. Situated right on the beach, the smart **Chipoka Lake View Lodge**'s rooms range from US$3.50 for a basic single to US$13 for a luxury double. Meals cost US$2.

Ntchisi and Surrounds

14

The dirt road connecting Lilongwe to Nkhotakota via Dowa and Ntchisi is one of the most obscure routes in Malawi, but it is also one of the most rewarding, giving access to the excellent Ntchisi Forest Reserve as well as passing through the heart of the scenic Nkhotakota Wildlife Reserve for around 30km. Most visitors to Malawi prefer to travel between Lilongwe and Nkhotakota on the zippy surfaced route through Salima, and this is certainly the better route if speed or comfort are your prime considerations. If, on the other hand, you're aching for some off-the-beaten-track hitching, and even more so if you have your own vehicle, you might think seriously about trying the slower and dustier route covered in this chapter.

CLIMATE
This is yet another part of Malawi with dramatic climatic variations. Ntchisi and the forest reserve have cool pleasant climates, while the Nkhotakota Wildlife Reserve, riddled with tsetse flies, can be extremely hot.

GETTING AROUND
With your own vehicle, you want first to head north of Lilongwe along the M1 past the airport towards Kasungu. After about 20km, in the middle of a small village, a left turn signposted for Dowa takes you on to the M7. From this turn-off all the way to Nkhotakota you'll be following rough dirt roads (perfectly navigable in a saloon car if taken slowly); you will pass through only one town of note, Ntchisi (Dowa lies some kilometres off the M7). The turn-off to Ntchisi Forest Reserve lies about 12km south of Ntchisi town, while Nkhotakota Wildlife Reserve lies between Ntchisi and Nkhotakota.

Using public transport, there is at least one bus daily in each direction between Lilongwe and Ntchisi. There are reputedly buses between Ntchisi and Nkhotakota town during the dry season, and you'll definitely find a few *matola* vehicles cover this route daily. In 2002 the road was being rebuilt all the way between Kasungu and Nkhotakota through the Nkhotakota Wildlife Reserve, and when it is finished, will be a good route for own-vehicle travellers and public-transporters alike. It will also make a good loop from Lilongwe, through the Kasungu National Park, the Nkhotakota Wildlife

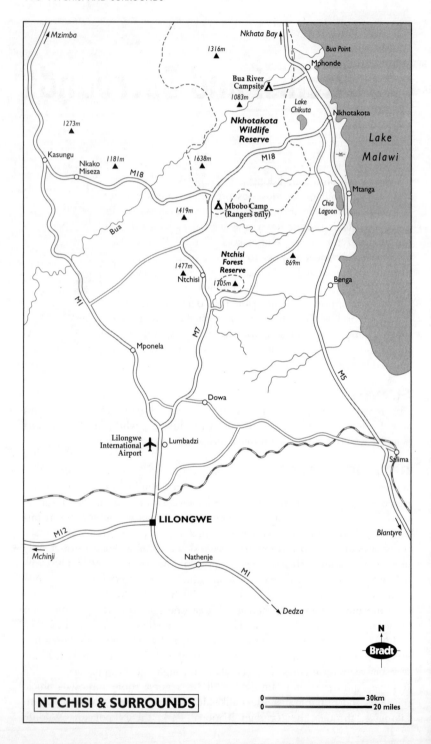

NTCHISI & SURROUNDS

Reserve, down to the lake at Nkhotakota and back along the lake via Salima. Note that transport to Ntchisi and Nkhotakota leaves Kasungu not from the main bus station but from the junction of the M1 and the Nkhotakota road. By the same token, all transport leaving Nkhotakota town for Ntchisi or Kasungu waits for passengers in front of the PTC supermarket. On the way between Kasungu and the junction with the Ntchisi–Nkhotakota road, you may want to stop at Kamuzu College. Founded by Banda as the self-styled 'Eton of Africa', the students (all Malawian, mostly scholarship students from remote villages) once wore a bizarre colonial uniform of shorts and a boater, and learnt Latin and Greek, at Banda's specific insistence.

NTCHISI FOREST RESERVE
Ntchisi Forest Reserve protects one of the most extensive patches of montane forest remaining in Malawi. There is an excellent resthouse at the reserve entrance, which means it is easy to explore the forest and its surrounds over a day or two. The main stand of evergreen forest covers the upper slopes of the 1,655m high Ntchisi Mountain. It is home to a variety of large mammals including samango and vervet monkey, red and blue duiker, bushpig, porcupine and leopard. I gather that the occasional elephant has been known to stray into the forest from the neighbouring Nkhotakota Wildlife Reserve. The forest also protects a wide variety of forest birds and butterflies, while the densely wooded lower slopes around the resthouse protect characteristic *brachystegia* birds.

Getting there and away
Coming from Lilongwe, the turn-off to Ntchisi Forestry Resthouse is signposted about 40km along the M7, and about 12km before Ntchisi Town. The signpost isn't particularly obvious if you're coming from Lilongwe as it's posted on a tree and faces in the direction of Ntchisi Town. There is a small village at the turn-off, and a tall radio mast on a hilltop about 1km closer to town, so if you pass the radio mast you know you've gone too far.

The resthouse is at the entrance to the forest reserve, about 16km from the turn-off along a poor dirt road. There are signposts at all intersections along this road so you can't get lost. You should get through in a saloon car in the dry season, but a 4WD is necessary after rain.

If you are using public transport, buses between Lilongwe and Ntchisi will drop you at the turn-off to the resthouse. The bus stage you need is called Chindembwe, which is the name of the small village about 5km along the road to the resthouse. It shouldn't be difficult to find a *matola* ride from the turn-off to Chindembwe, but you'll probably have to walk the final 11km to the resthouse.

Where to stay
The newly privatised **Ntchisi Forestry Resthouse** lies just within the forest reserve entrance. It was built as a holiday residence by a colonial district commissioner. There are five self-contained rooms in the resthouse (a total of

14 beds), all with wood-heated hot showers, at a cost of US$5 per person. There is also a communal lounge, a dining room and an equipped kitchen with a resident cook. The lovely veranda overlooks a well-tended garden and offers great views across to Lake Malawi. There is no electricity in the lodge, but hurricane lamps are provided at night, and there is even a paraffin fridge. You should bring all the food you need with you.

You can camp in the resthouse grounds for US$7 per person.

Walks

The walking possibilities from the resthouse are practically unlimited, and not just restricted to the forest reserve – the surrounding countryside is also very beautiful, with good views over the lake. If you're spending a while in the area, it would be well worth buying a 1:50,000 map.

The obvious route if your time is limited is to follow the road past the resthouse uphill towards the edge of the evergreen forest. This road passes through moss-covered *brachystegia* trees, then through alternating patches of plantation forest, boulder-strewn grassland and isolated stands of indigenous forest. From the road head, which is about 3km from the resthouse, a clear path leads into the forest, past tortuously-shaped strangler figs, lush fern-bordered watercourses and mossy rocks. The variety of habitats along this walk makes for excellent birdwatching (my list included red-throated twinspot, East African swee, starred robin, and a variety of bulbuls, canaries and sunbirds). I also saw baboons and red squirrels.

NTCHISI

One Malawian described Ntchisi to me as the most remote town in the country. The town is really too nondescript to live up to this sort of mystique, but it is certainly very isolated – the kilometre-long stretch of tar road along which it sprawls seems absurdly misplaced. Nevertheless, Ntchisi is the sole piece of urban punctuation along the M7, and travellers using public transport may well end up staying there for a night. There are a few resthouses, and even a rather well-stocked PTC supermarket, and ... well, that's Ntchisi.

NKHOTAKOTA WILDLIFE RESERVE

The oldest wildlife reserve in Malawi protects the scenic, well-watered Rift Valley hills west of Nkhotakota Town. The *brachystegia* woodland of Nkhotakota Wildlife Reserve supports a rich diversity of mammals including elephant, buffalo, sable antelope, warthog, lion and leopard, but the undulating terrain and thick vegetation make animal spotting difficult. Nkhotakota Wildlife Reserve is poorly developed for tourism, the only road through the reserve being the main road between Ntchisi and Nkhotakota towns.

Getting there and away

Since Chipata Camp, in the southwest of the reserve, burnt down and is no longer open to the public, and nearby Mbobo Camp is for game rangers only, access from the Kasungu/Ntchisi side is limited to driving through the park on the M18 down to Nkhotakota. This rough and lonely road is being rebuilt – watch out for the memorial marking the spot where an unfortunate woman, walking through the reserve, was caught and eaten by a lion one night early in 2002.

Access from the lakeside M5 road is via a turnoff 12km north of Nkhotakota at a village called Mphonde. A rough 4WD track then leads to the Bua River Camp. A good way to see the best of the reserve is to contact John Grosart of Njobvu Safari Lodge, 13km south of Nkhotkota (see page 205). Very knowledgeable and involved in the conservation and promotion of the area, he runs safaris into the reserve at US$50 per person, per day.

Where to stay
Bua River Camp is an attractive site on the river bank, but is for camping only and one must be completely self-sufficient. A 4WD track, which is only passable in the dry season, leads to the even more basic **Tongoli Camp**. Fortunately, the unique bush experience fully makes up for the difficulty in getting there.

Walks
The best way to explore the reserve is on foot, but you must walk with an armed guide; this can easily be arranged for around US$2 per walk.

The evergreen forest protects a variety of unusual birds, notably moustached green tinkerbird, starred robin, yellow-streaked bulbul and grey-olive bulbul. Forest mammals include blue and vervet monkeys, and such secretive nocturnal creatures as leopard and bushpig. The mammals most frequently seen in the *brachystegia* woodland are warthog, bushbuck and baboon. The latest game census counted about 2,000 elephants and 45 lions, and recent additions to the reserve have been a salt lick and tree hide. Nkhotakota Wildlife Reserve is a gem just waiting to be discovered.

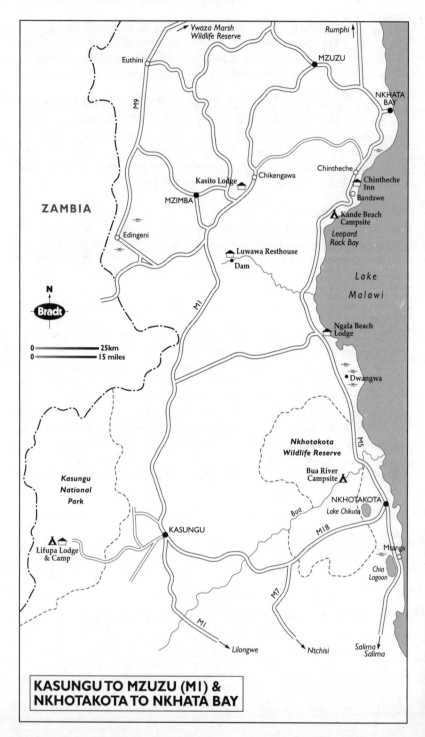

**KASUNGU TO MZUZU (M1) &
NKHOTAKOTA TO NKHATA BAY**

The MI between
Lilongwe and Mzuzu

This is the fastest and most direct route between Lilongwe and Mzuzu, though it is less popular with tourists than the lakeshore road as it offers relatively little in the way of tourist attractions. The major towns along this route are Kasungu and Mzimba; the former is the gateway to Kasungu National Park and the latter is close to two excellent and reasonably accessible forestry resthouses in the Viphya Hills.

CLIMATE
Kasungu and surrounding areas lie at a medium altitude and have a similar climate to the capital city. Mzimba and the Viphya Plateau are high and cool.

GETTING AROUND
In a private vehicle, the 367km stretch of the M1 between Lilongwe and Mzuzu is a straightforward four- or five-hour drive along a generally well-maintained tar road. Shire express buses also do the run in around six hours, stopping at Kasungu, Mzimba, Chikengawa and a handful of other large settlements, while country buses take around eight hours, as they stop at local bus stages every few kilometres. Hitching is certainly possible, though slower than you might expect: private vehicles are less numerous than they are on other major routes. Both times I tried to hitch I waited a couple of hours without success and eventually boarded a bus.

KASUNGU
Basically, Kasungu is a typically bland and unmemorable small Malawian town, and of no interest whatsoever to tourists. That said, if you arrived in Lilongwe late in the day and intended heading north the next morning, you might think of hopping on a bus as far as Kasungu for the night.

Getting there and away
All buses between Lilongwe and Mzuzu stop at Kasungu. The ride takes around two to three hours, depending on whether you take an express or country bus. A few *matola* vehicles connect Kasungu to Nkhotakota daily.

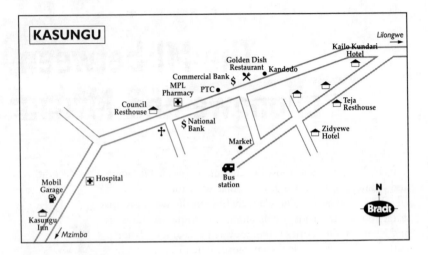

Where to stay

Kasungu Inn (tel: 01 253306), a short walk out of town along the Mzimba road, has large, self-contained twin rooms with mosquito nets and hot showers costing US$30/40 single/double occupancy.

The **Council Resthouse**, on the main road next to the MPL pharmacy, is the best value in the budget range, with twin rooms for less than US$2. The resthouse has clean communal showers and toilets. Several private resthouses are clustered about 200m from the bus station. The **Teja Resthouse** is the most savoury of the bunch, with ordinary doubles for US$4 and self-contained doubles for US$5.

Where to eat

Most of the resthouses around the bus station do the standard stews with chips, rice or *nsima* for around US$1. More interesting and not a great deal more expensive (most items on the menu cost less than US$2) are the meals at the Kasungu Inn: steak, roast chicken and the like.

You can buy fresh bread and a reasonable range of tinned and dry foodstuffs at the PTC supermarket.

KASUNGU NATIONAL PARK

This 3,727km² national park is the second largest in Malawi, protecting an area of *brachystegia* woodland along the Zambian border west of Kasungu town. Several rivers run through the park, the most significant of which are the Dwangwa and Lingadzi. Kasungu probably supports a greater number of large mammal species than any other reserve in Malawi, but populations have been heavily thinned out by poaching, which along with the dense nature of the vegetation means that general game viewing is rather poor by comparison with Liwonde, Lengwe or Nyika national parks, though recent clampdowns on poaching give some cause for future optimism. The elephant population, for instance, rose from a late 1980s low of about 300 to 450 in the census of

1995, and one of the rangers we spoke to felt the figure in 2002 was probably well in excess of 700. Large predators are represented by lion, leopard, cheetah and a small, presumably resident population of African wild dog, though none of these is likely to be seen on a casual visit. Kasungu was once regarded as the best place in Malawi to see black rhinoceros, but these are now locally extinct. Common ungulates include Burchell's zebra, warthog, buffalo, puku, sable antelope, roan antelope, kudu, reedbuck and the very localised Lichtenstein's hartebeest. In addition to the wildlife, Kasungu boasts several prehistoric sites, including an iron-smelting kiln, rock paintings, and the remains of fortified villages.

Based on our visit in June 2002, and the excellent facilities offered at Lifupa Lodge notwithstanding, it is difficult to recommend Kasungu National Park as an upmarket safari destination with total conviction. That said, game viewing *is* reputedly very seasonal and things might be different towards the end of the dry season (August to November), which is when the vegetation thins out and animals tend to concentrate near Lifupa Dam. And the park does boast an untrammelled wilderness feel, since visitors are relatively few.

Kasungu will be very attractive to budget travellers with a broad interest in natural history and some time on their hands. Access is relatively straightforward, entrance and camping fees are inexpensive in comparison with most other African countries (the combined cost of camping and entrance and a taxi in either direction for two people spending three days in the park would work out at less than US$50 a head), and the self-catering facilities mean you needn't spend a fortune on meals. Best bet of all, the campsite on Lifupa Dam is an excellent place to chill out for a few days, waiting for the game to come to you – in addition to the certainty of sighting hippo, puku and several varieties of bird, large herds of elephant tend to visit the dam daily in the dry season.

The best source of current information about accommodation, access and game viewing in Kasungu is the Lifupa Lodge office in the foyer of the Capital Hotel in Lilongwe. The people who work here are used to the idea of travellers on a budget making their own way to the camp, and their advice is refreshingly down-to-earth and useful.

Getting there and away

The national park entrance gate lies roughly 38km from Kasungu Town along the dirt D187, and from the entrance gate it's another 22km to Lifupa Lodge. The turn-off from the M1 is clearly signposted opposite an Oilcom filling station as you enter Kasungu Town. Until recently, the D187 was very rough, but it was rebuilt in 1998 and at the time of writing is navigable in any vehicle – in fact, the main danger along this road is not getting stuck so much as skidding off it, so do drive carefully. There's no telling how the road will look after a couple of rainy seasons have passed.

Without private transport, trying to hitch into the park would be somewhat optimistic but by no means impossible. More reliable, however, to charter a private taxi from Kasungu Town, which is not prohibitively expensive though you will need to bargain over prices (we were initially asked US$60 but settled at US$25 with a minimum of fuss). When you're ready to leave, the lodge vehicle will give you a lift to Kasungu Town, assuming it's already heading that way. If not, then you can ring through to Kasungu to arrange for a taxi to collect you – assuming that you got a good price on the way there, you'll be glad to have jotted down a phone number for the same driver.

Where to stay

Recently privatised and renovated, **Lifupa Lodge** consists of several semi-detached bungalows with a private balcony overlooking Kasuni Dam, which supports a number of hippos and several types of large bird (including fish eagle) as well as attracting animals coming to drink. The most attractive feature of the lodge is the communal bar and dining area, with its dramatic thatched upper deck, and the food is as good as any we tasted in Malawi. The lodge runs morning game drives and night drives, the latter – seriously chilly in winter – offering the opportunity to see a variety of nocturnal predators. Full-board accommodation inclusive of game drives costs US$120 per person.

Under the same management, and only 200m away, **Lifupa Camp** consists of several basic but comfortable reed chalets at US$15 per person, or you can pitch your own tent for US$5 per person. The camp grounds are well wooded, teeming with birds, and face the dam. Facilities include a well-stocked bar, hot showers and a cooking area with cook on request (bring your own food). Camp residents can organise game drives through the lodge at US$18 per person, guided walks at US$10 per person, and meals from between US$11 and US$14.

Reservations for Lifupa Lodge and Camp can be made through any recognised tour operator in Malawi, or by phoning the lodge's office in the Capital Hotel in Lilongwe on tel: 01 773388.

Do note that in addition to camping or lodge fees, a park entrance fee must be paid by all visitors to Kasungu. This fee is US$5 per person per day and US$2 per car. The fees are not prohibitively expensive if you've just arrived from East Africa, where most parks ask US$25 per person per day!

MZIMBA

From Kasungu, the M1 runs north through the koppie-strewn central plateau before ascending gently through dense *brachystegia* woodland into the Viphya Hills and the leafy, breezy town of Mzimba. Lying some 15km west of the main highway to Mzuzu, Mzimba feels slightly isolated, but it's a well-equipped and pleasant little place, and very friendly. The town itself lacks any obvious points of interest, but it's the best base from which to visit the excellent forestry resthouses at nearby Luwawa Dam and Kasito, and could also be a possible stopover before catching an early morning bus to Vwaza Marsh Wildlife Reserve (see pages 234–6).

Getting there and away

Some buses between Lilongwe and Mzuzu divert to Mzimba. A bus leaves Mzimba for Rumphi every morning at 07.00, stopping at Kazuni Tented Camp in Vwaza Marsh Wildlife Reserve.

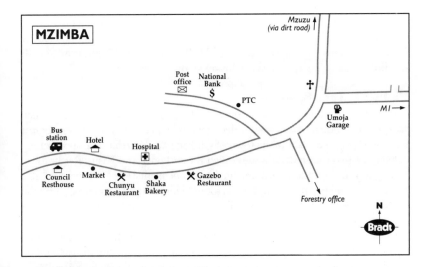

Where to stay

The **Council Resthouse** was closed for renovations in mid-2002. The nearby **Kanjoji Resthouse** has brighter rooms at a similar price, but there are bucket showers only. If these resthouses are full, there are a couple less conveniently situated resthouses out towards the forestry office.

Where to eat

There are plenty of restaurants scattered around town; I had a good beef stew for less than US$1 at the **Chunyu Restaurant**. If you're stocking up for a visit to one of the forestry resthouses or to Vwaza Marsh, there's a fair selection of goods at the PTC supermarket, and fresh bread every morning at the Shaka Bakery.

FORESTRY RESTHOUSES AROUND MZIMBA

The Forestry Department runs two excellent and inexpensive resthouses in the Mzimba area on the Viphya Plateau near Chikengawa. These resthouses see few tourists, but they are highly accessible to travellers using public transport. For motorised visitors travelling between Lilongwe and Nyika, the forestry resthouses are a good place to break the trip over two days. Enquiries about the resthouses may be made at the Forestry Office in Mzimba.

Luwawa Dam

This artificial lake lies east of the M1 and south of Mzimba, and its main attraction is the Luwawa Forest Lodge. This is the privatised and upgraded forestry resthouse and is situated overlooking the Luwawa Dam, only three hours from Lilongwe. The best access road is off the M1, 128km from Kasungu and signposted to Luwawa D73. Promoted as an environment-friendly outdoor adventure centre, activities such as hiking, abseiling, mountain biking, sailing, canoeing and orienteering are offered with suitable equipment for hire. The forest walks and birding are very rewarding and accommodation costs US$80 for a self-contained chalet sleeping four. Camping is US$3 per person and dorms US$7.50. Booking is through Central African Wilderness Safaris (tel: 01 771153; fax: 01 771397) or email: wardlow@malawi.net; web: www.luwawalodgemalawi.com).

Viphya Forest Reserve

North of Mzimba, as the M1 continues climbing on to the Viphya Plateau, thick *brachystegia* woodland gives way to the exotic pine plantations of Viphya Forest Reserve. About 4km before the town of Chikengawa, at an altitude approaching 2,000m, lie two forestry resthouses called Kasito Lodge and Kasito Resthouse.

The area around Kasito is dominated by exotic plantations, but there are also some significant patches of indigenous forest. This is lovely walking country: the scenery is beautiful and there is still some game around. Duiker and vervet monkeys are likely to be seen by visitors, but bushpigs and even a few leopards are also resident. The area offers excellent birdwatching, with several species that are otherwise restricted to the less accessible Nyika Plateau. With the right frame of mind, keen walkers and birders could easily settle into Kasito for several days.

Getting there and away

Any country bus running along the M1 between Mzimba and Mzuzu will drop you at the Kasito Lodge bus stage, which lies about 20km north of Mzimba and 4km south of Chikengawa. Kasito Resthouse is directly opposite the bus stage, while Kasito Lodge is about 500m further down the road towards Mzuzu.

When you're ready to leave, you may find buses are reluctant to pick up passengers at the Kasito bus stage. It's better to walk about 1km up the M1 towards Mzimba and wait at Macdonald's bus stage (named after a Scottish forestry officer who camped on the site for several years in the colonial era). To pick up an express bus, it's best to walk the 4km to Chikengawa.

Where to stay

Kasito Lodge is little short of perfect, a one-time colonial residence overlooking a lovely pine-covered valley. It has attractive grounds where you should look out for the African citril, a type of canary. The rooms in the lodge are comfortable and well maintained, and facilities include a fridge, electric lighting, a large communal lounge with a log fireplace, communal hot baths, and a fully equipped kitchen with the free services of a cook. The lodge sleeps up to 20, but as often as not it's completely empty. Rooms cost US$6.50 per person, and you can camp in the grounds for US$3 per person.

Kasito Resthouse is more rustic in character, and a bit run down, but it has similar facilities to the Lodge. Rooms cost US$5.50 per person. You should bring all the food you will need from Mzimba or Mzuzu. A very limited range of goods (sodas, vegetables and rice) can be bought at the market in Chikengawa.

An attractive overnight stop is the lodge at the giant **Raiply Sawmill**, 21km past the Mzimba turn-off. From the gate they will direct you to the neat Holiday-Inn-styled rooms with private bathrooms costing US$15/25, single/double. Camping is US$6 per person. The attached restaurant serves a selection of dishes at around US$3.50.

What to do

There is plenty of good walking around Kasito. From the garden of the lodge, you can follow a clear path to the base of the valley and over a small stream, where, after about 200m, it connects with a disused road. Turn left into this road, and after perhaps 2km, passing through plantation forest and dense undergrowth, rich in butterflies and notable for several immense communal webs built by a type of spider with a bright purple body the size of a thumb, you should come to a five-point junction.

Running clockwise from this junction, the fork to your immediate left curves downhill into a thick patch of indigenous forest which can be extremely good for birds: among the more interesting species I saw here were olive-bellied mountain bulbul, Fulleborne's black boubou and golden weaver. The next fork – basically straight ahead – peters out after about 500m without doing anything very interesting.

The next fork, the one to your right at roughly 90°, meanders without any great complications to Kasito Dam, an attractive spot set in a pine plantation, and reasonably rewarding for birds. It takes about 15 minutes to walk from the junction to the dam, and once there you can follow a motorable track past the dam for another ten minutes or so to reach the M1, where a left turn will take you back to the lodge, passing the resthouse en route.

We didn't try the last fork from the junction, which runs at about 45° to your right, but I'm told that after about 1–2km it leads to the top of Wozi Hill, where there is a lookout tower offering great views over the surrounding hills. The caretaker at the lodge or resthouse can give you full directions.

If you don't fancy bashing through these often rather overgrown paths, a more straightforward short walk involves following the M1 from the lodge towards Mzimba for about 1km, then turning right into the side road for Kasito Dam (this is no longer signposted, but as the first motorable road leading to your right it is difficult to miss).

Also worth a look is the riverine forest which runs along a stream about 100m west of the M1 towards Chikengawa. There are several side roads off the M1 in this area which you could explore.

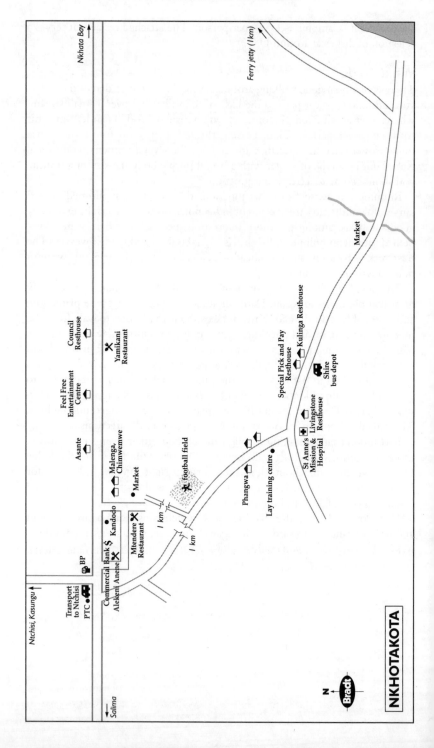

NKHOTAKOTA

The Lakeshore from Nkhotakota to Nkhata Bay

This chapter follows the Lake Malawi shore, starting in the south at the old slaving centre of Nkhotakota, then passing a string of isolated lakeshore resorts to the very popular resort town of Nkhata Bay in the north.

CLIMATE
Hot and sticky.

GETTING AROUND
The lakeshore road between Salima and Mzuzu is now surfaced in its entirety and it is generally in excellent condition. If you have a private vehicle, getting around is straightforward, though some of the side roads between the main road and the various lakeshore resorts should be taken with care, particularly if you don't have a 4WD. Unfortunately, the bridge over the Dwambazi River between Ngala Beach Lodge and Kande Beach was washed away in 2001, which temporarily broke this route into two sections. A Bailey bridge was being constructed in 2002 as well as a big new bridge at a site further inland – so I am assuming that the route is now open.

There is plenty of public transport: express buses and minibuses run between Lilongwe and Salima, and at Salima you can pick up the express buses which travel between Blantyre and Mzuzu via Nkhotakota and Nkhata Bay. These stop at all large towns but not at more obscure bus stages, so you'll be dependent on slower country buses if you plan on stopping at some of the more isolated resorts along the lake. Hitching along this route is erratic, but it's generally easier than along the M1 between Lilongwe and Mzuzu.

The lake steamer MV *Ilala* provides a popular way of travelling along this stretch of the lake, connecting Monkey Bay in the south to Nkhotakota, Nkhata Bay and Likoma Island, among other places. For full details, see *The Lake Ferry and the Islands*, page 213.

NKHOTAKOTA
Nkhotakota is a town of considerable historical note. For much of the 19th century, it was the largest slave market on Lake Malawi: the terminus from which as many as 20,000 slaves were shipped every year across the lake to Kilwa Kivinje on the Tanzanian coast. The slave trade at Nkhotakota was

founded in the early 19th century by an Arab half-caste called Jumbe. The Jumbe dynasty ruled Nkhotakota for several generations, and a descendent of Jumbe was still the local chief at the end of World War II.

When, in late 1861, Livingstone led the first European expedition on Lake Malawi, he described the area around Nkhotakota as an 'abode of lawlessness and bloodshed ... literally strewed with human bones and putrid bodies'. On September 10 1863, Livingstone returned to Nkhotakota in a futile attempt to convince the incumbent Jumbe ruler to abandon the trade in slavery. The 'magnificent fig tree' under which Jumbe and Livingstone met is still standing in the mission compound. The slave trade out of Nkhotakota was only stopped in the 1890s, when Commissioner Harry Johnston persuaded the ageing Jumbe to sign a treaty in exchange for British protection.

Historical claims aside, it is only the attractive stone mission (the church here, built in 1894, is the burial place of the first bishop of Likoma, Chauncey Maples) and a strong Muslim influence that distinguish Nkhotakota from any other similarly sized Malawian town. Several writers have noted the brooding sense of evil that still pervades the town, a century after the last slaves were shipped out of its port, and certainly it is difficult not to see Nkhotakota's present in the light of its cruel history. More obtusely, Nkhotakota is often referred to as the largest traditional market village in East and Central Africa, a label which is thoroughly meaningless as the modern market is, thankfully, quite unexceptional.

Like many Malawian towns, Nkhotakota is divided into two sections. The modern town, with a PTC supermarket, bank, post office and the charmingly named Feel Free Entertainment Centre, sprawls along the main lakeshore road, about 1km inland of the lake. A shady avenue, planted in the slaving era, connects the lakeshore road to the older part of town, where you'll find the ferry jetty, the mission, the bus station and a cluster of cheap resthouses.

Getting there and away

All buses between Nkhata Bay and Salima stop at Nkhotakota. The town can also be approached via Ntchisi (see also page 189). Nkhotakota is the last port of call for northbound lake steamers before they cross to Likoma Island. In 2002, the MV *Ilala* stopped at Nkhotakota in the early hours of Saturday on its northbound leg.

Where to stay

My first choice of accommodation in Nkhotakota is the **Livingstone Resthouse**, which lies in the 'old' part of town, in the grounds of St Anne's Mission, opposite the historical church and in the shadow of the 'Livingstone Tree'. Clean and quiet, the resthouse has three single rooms with net and fan for US$1.50, including use of the communal showers. There is also one self-contained double room costing US$2. The **Lay Training Centre** opposite St Anne's has rooms for US$2 per person, and might be worth a try.

About 100m from these places, directly opposite the Shire bus station, the **Special Pick and Pay Resthouse** has been popular with travellers for years. Recently repainted, it is certainly one of the better options in town, though none of the rooms appears to have nets or fans. Prices range from US$2 for a small single to US$4 for a self-contained double, and camping is permitted for the usual pittance. The **Kulinga Resthouse** next door is similar in standard and price.

Most of the accommodation along the main road through the 'new' town consists of grotty resthouses, but the **Council Resthouse** stands out as something of an exception, and it's very good value at US$1.50 for an ordinary double and US$3 for a large self-contained double with net and fan.

Ten kilometres south of Nkhotakota town and about another five down to the lake is the **Sani Beach Resort** with self-contained chalets for US$13/25 single/double, and camping for US$1.50.

A more interesting and upmarket option is **Njobvu Safari Camp** (PO Box 388, Nkhotakota; tel: 01 292506; fax: 01 292418; email: njobvusafaris@ eomw.net; web: www.njobvusafarismalawi.com). Lying 1km south of Sani Beach, it offers attractively furnished self-contained chalets at US$25 per person and camping for US$2.50. The camp offers guided tours into the nearby Nkhotakota Wildlife Reserve as well as birdwatching boat trips to the Chia Lagoon and Lake Chilingale. A new development is catch-and-release-fishing for sea trout with barbless fly or spinner.

At 15km south of Nkhotakota and 90km north of Salima is a well sign-posted turn-off to **Nkhotakota Potteries**. Another 4km takes you down to this lakeside branch of **Dedza Potteries** (tel: 01 292444 or contact Dedza Potteries, PO Box 54, Dedza; tel: 01 223069; fax: 01 223131) which offers some very attractive options. You can use the pottery workshop, which is fully equipped with electric and foot-driven potter's wheels and offers raku and electric-kiln firing, for an hourly fee of US$2. If you're looking for accommodation, stay in their very comfortable en-suite chalets for US$10 per person and eat at the spotless little coffee shop. Better still, if you're keen on learning more about pottery, sign up for an all inclusive weekend. You'll get two nights' accommodation, tuition and use of the workshop as well as a session with local village potters making traditional pots – all for US$60.

Halfway between Dwangwa and Dwambazi river mouth (where the bridge was washed away) lies the attractively renovated **Ngala Beach Lodge**. The beautiful beach, bar and restaurant, and individually decorated en-suite chalets and bungalows are very popular – especially with honeymooners. Rates are US$35 per person, including breakfast (presumably late, if you're on honeymoon) and they can be contacted on email: ngala@malawi.net; web: www.ngalabeachlodge.co.za. If you are using public transport (definitely not on honeymoon), ask for Ngala bus stage.

Travelling north up the coast, a couple of smaller lodges have recently closed down, which means that the next establishment you reach is the well-known **Kande Beach Campsite**.

Where to eat

There is not much variety of food available in Nkhotakota, but plenty of choice of where to eat it. On our most recent visit, several people pointed us towards the **Alekeni Anene Restaurant** in the 'new' town, and we were quite happy with this recommendation – the whole fried *chambo* and chips is good value at US$3 per plate.

Of the rest, the restaurant at the **Special Pick and Pay Resthouse** picks up quite a bit of *mazungu* custom, largely because so many travellers stay there, but the food is pretty ordinary. In the 'new' town, the **Yamikani Restaurant** looked worth a try, while the **Mtendere Restaurant**, despite its flashy new sign, is a bit of a dump and served nothing but fish and *nsima* when we looked in.

THE LAKESHORE BETWEEN NKHOTAKOTA AND CHINTHECHE

The 150km-odd stretch of lakeshore north of Nkhotakota has seen a good deal of tourist development since 1993. The majority of places in this area used to be in the budget category, with camping and/or cheap rooms designed to cater to the steady flow of backpackers making their way between East and southern Africa, but many of them have been smartly upgraded.

Starting in the south, the first place of interest along this stretch of the lake is **Dwangwa**, a fair-sized town sprawling around the large Kasasa Sugar Estate. Dwangwa is an odd little place, notable as much as anything for the odour of molasses that clings to the air, and it is rather short on aesthetic appeal. It would take a perverse nature to actually want to spend a night in one of the identikit resthouses clustered along Dwangwa's main road. Rather more inviting is the one relatively upmarket option in the area, the Kasasa Club, a sports club with a golf course, swimming pool, and attractive clubhouse with television, bar and restaurant. Although the club is aimed primarily at estate workers, visitors are welcome to stay in one of the pleasant self-contained chalets in the grounds at a charge of US$20 for a double. In theory, accommodation here should be booked in advance (PO Box 46, Dwangwa; tel: 01 295266), but the chalets are rarely full and when we popped in to take a look the receptionist seemed quite put out that we didn't want to stay. To get to the club, take the left turn next to the filling station about 1km south of the town centre, and follow it for 3km.

Traditionally the favoured backpackers' haunt along this stretch of lake, **Kande Beach Campsite** (PO Box 22, Kande; tel: 01 347765) lies about 20km south of Chintheche. Positioned on a beautiful stretch of beach, and run with the permission and co-operation of the local chief, Kande has the sort of atmosphere which tempts travellers into staying on for weeks (in many respects, it is reminiscent of the legendary Twiga Lodge near Mombasa in Kenya): busy and sociable when a few overland trucks pull in, peaceful and intimate when the trucks are absent. There is a large open bar and a kiosk, while the new restaurant is up and running. The highly regarded PADI diving school attached to the site offers five-day courses for US$180 per person, day dives for ticketed divers at US$25 per person, and day 'resort courses' for unticketed divers at US$35. Also available for hire are catamarans, canoes, pedal-boats, windsurfers and snorkelling equipment. A games room has table tennis, a pool table and dart board. Camping costs US$2 per person, with an additional US$2 per night if you want to hire a two-man tent. Dorm beds cost US$4 and the twin-bedded beach-front chalets, US$11. Horse-riding can also be arranged with nearby stables where they have 12 horses, suitable for novices or experts. Two-hour rides through the bush and villages, ending up with horse and rider swimming in the surf, cost US$30.

Kande Beach lies 3km from the main road; the turn-off is signposted from Kande village (the bus stage here is used by both express buses and country buses).

CHINTHECHE

This small trading centre lies just west of the main lakeshore road about 40km south of Nkhata Bay. The town (if you can call it that) was fairly important in the colonial era, and several old buildings from this time remain, notably the post office. But today Chintheche isn't anything to shout about, especially as it lies a kilometre or so inland of the lake. The surrounding beaches, on the other hand, are paradise: perfect white sand rescued from picture postcard anonymity by jagged rocky outcrops, patches of *brachystegia* woodland, and even some remnant forest. Chintheche lies on the widest part of the lake, with the Mozambican shore an indistinct blur on the horizon; here more than anywhere on Lake Malawi it is easy to be lulled into the feeling you are at the ocean.

In 1880, Dr Robert Laws moved the Livingstonia Mission from its temporary site at Cape Maclear to Bandawe, on the lakeshore about 10km south of Chintheche. At this time the Tonga people of the lakeshore lived in terror of the murderous annual raids of the Mombero's Ngoni clan, which generally resulted in village after village being razed to the ground and hundreds of Tonga people being killed. Dr Laws at first had an uneasy relationship with Mombero, but when one of the missionaries was asked to pray for rain during a severe drought and a thunder storm ensued, Mombero became more friendly and allowed Laws to persuade him to cease harassing the Tonga. The other major achievement made by Laws at Bandawe was in the field of education; one of the most influential products of the mission school was Edward Kamwama, who in 1908 founded the Ethiopianist Watch Tower Church in Bandawe.

In the end, the mission site at Bandawe proved to be as unhealthy as the one at Cape Maclear, despite Laws' practice of facing all buildings inland (he believed that malaria was caused by 'miasma' rising from the lake). In 1894, Bandawe was abandoned for Khondowe on the Rift Valley Escarpment, where the Livingstonia Mission still operates today. The Bandawe Mission can be reached via a 2.5km sand road, clearly signposted from the main lakeshore road about 2km south of the Chintheche Inn. The original church, a somewhat warehouse-like brick construction built between 1886 and 1900, is still standing, and the priest welcomes visitors – he has in fact compiled a short history of the mission, illustrated with period photographs. There is no entrance fee but a small donation will be appreciated. Roughly 500m from the main mission building lies a small cemetery, a literal 'White Man's Graveyard', where several of the early

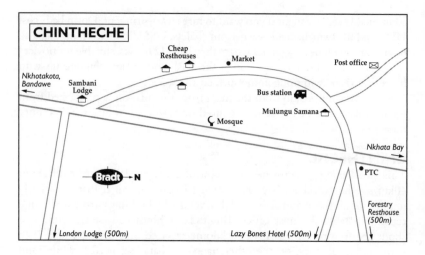

Scottish missionaries are buried, most of them victims of malaria, many of them in their early twenties. A more recent grave is that of 'Mama' Jane Jackson, the owner of a nearby lodge who died tragically in a paragliding accident in Zimbabwe in 1997. Close by is the grave of an unidentified *mazungu* who drowned on the nearby lakeshore in 1986.

Getting there and away

All express and country buses between Nkhotakota and Nkhata Bay stop at Chintheche, from where it's a short walk to Lazy Bones Hotel and the Chintheche Forestry Resthouse.

The turn-offs to other resorts mentioned under *Where to stay* are between 2km and 10km south of Chintheche, so it might be better to board a country bus and ask to be dropped at the bus stage nearest to the resort you want.

Where to stay

There are a few basic resthouses in Chintheche Town, though it's rather difficult to think of a convincing reason why any traveller would want to stay at one of them. A better option for those on a budget is **London Lodge**, which lies on the beach about 500m from town, and has self-contained rooms with net for US$5/7 single/double as well as flat camping sites for US$2.50 per tent. Meals are available.

The **Chintheche Forestry Resthouse** (tel: 01 357210) is situated in a patch of thick woodland only ten minutes' walk from town and costs US$7 per person, inclusive of use of a communal lounge and equipped kitchen.

The **Lazy Bones Hotel**, which lies on the lakeshore about 200m from the Forestry Resthouse, was being renovated in 2002.

There are several other resorts a bit further out of town. The closest is **Flame Tree Lodge** (PO Box 150, Chintheche; tel: 01 357276), an attractive, easy-going place set on a shady wooded peninsula. The lodge has self-contained rooms for around US$12/18 single/double, and camping costs

US$2.50 per person. The restaurant is very good, reasonably priced, and boasts a remarkably varied menu. To reach Flame Tree Lodge, you can either walk for 15 minutes south along the beach from London Lodge, or else follow the main lakeshore road south of Chintheche for about 2km, then take a signposted 3km turn-off to the lodge.

About 5km south of Chintheche is the signposted 2km turn-off to **Sambani Lodge** (PO Box 89, Chintheche; tel: 01 357290), which lies on a pretty beach surrounded by thick forest teeming with birds and monkeys. Sambani Lodge is similar in standard to Flame Tree Lodge, but the rooms, which cost US$13/20 single/double, are larger. Camping costs US$2 per person.

The only truly tourist-class hotel in this part of Malawi is the **Chintheche Inn** (PO Box 9, Chintheche; tel: 01 357211), a former government property which has been thoroughly renovated and redecorated since it was taken over by Central African Wilderness Safaris in 1997. Rooms cost US$55/80 self-contained single/double with nets and fans, inclusive of a hearty breakfast. Facilities include snorkel hire for US$6 per day (there is good snorkelling in the nearby rocks) as well as boat hire, a book exchange service, and a good range of literature about Malawi. Organised excursions include a trip to the Bandawe Mission (US$10 per person), bird walks (US$5 per person) and a trip to a fishing village (US$5 per person). The restaurant serves substantial à la carte meals in the US$2–5 range as well as a three-course set dinner for US$12. The campsite and ablutions are the nicest I saw in Malawi – with grass, trees and a separate beach bar – and costs only US$5 per person. With a swimming pool, tennis court and warm welcome for kids, it's the ideal family resort. Bookings and enquiries can be addressed to Central African Wilderness Safaris (PO Box 489, Lilongwe; tel: 01 771153; fax: 01 771397; email: info@wilderness.malawi.net; web: www.wilderness-safaris.com).

There are two lovely lodges just south of Chintheche, both run by hospitable husband and wife teams – always the best formula for a good place to stay. The turn-off to the first, **Nkhwazi Lodge** (PO Box 120, Chintheche; satellite tel: 871 76 265 8745), is 10km south of the village and then another 2km down to the shady, grassed site above two little coves. A ski-boat is available for diving, fishing and snorkelling, and there's a small reef just offshore. The attractively decorated split-level bungalows are brick-built and can sleep four people at US$27 per chalet. The campsite is very neat and comfortable with clean ablutions and is great value at US$2.50 per person

The next little piece of paradise is **Makuzi Beach** (Private Bag 12, Chintheche; tel/fax: 01 357296; email: makuzibeach@sdnp.org.mw), which is about 2km past Nkhwazi. The rondavels and campsite overlook a private bay and the service is friendly and attentive. The owners are involved in the upliftment of the local community and have established a trust fund which has already built a new school at the old Bandawe Mission Station, next door. En-suite chalets are US$42/68 and rooms with shared facilities US$18/28 single/double, all inclusive of breakfast. Camping is US$3.50 per person and email and internet access is available for guests.

NKHATA BAY

Nkhata Bay's attractions are manifold. The lakeshore is gloriously lush and scenic: a twin pair of bays spilling into the wooded mainland and separated by a long, narrow peninsula. Just as alluring to many is the strong sense of traveller community that has developed in the village. The place is addictively laid back, to the extent that it seems to paralyse the will of many travellers, but Nkhata Bay's fortunes have fluctuated. From being one of the best-kept secrets on Malawi's backpackers' trail, this small port overtook Cape Maclear as the most popular travellers' congregation point on the lakeshore, if not anywhere between Zanzibar and Victoria Falls. Lately however, visitor numbers have dwindled and the old vibe has gone. Of course, the World Trade Centre attack, Zimbabwe's land issues and local food shortages were affecting tourism in the entire region in mid-2002, so one can only hope that the slump is temporary. The security problems of the mid to late '90s have improved and lodge owners are now working together with a better motivated police force to contain crime against tourists. It is advisable, however, to avoid dark areas on your own at night (the better lodges will organise guards to escort you) and go easy on the marijuana-based 'space cake' – people have been hospitalised, people have died.

A final and altogether more mundane point is that many travellers are caught out by the absence of foreign exchange facilities in Nkhata Bay, and are consequently forced to make a day trip to Mzuzu to change money.

Getting there and away

Regular buses connect Nkhata Bay to Nkhotakota and points south. There are also plenty of buses between Nkhata Bay and Mzuzu: a spectacular 50km stretch of road, which sees you whizzing down or puffing up the Rift Valley Escarpment past expansive grassland and *brachystegia* woodland, with the lake glittering in the sun hundreds of metres below.

Where to stay

There is no shortage of affordable accommodation in Nkhata Bay, with something to suit most tastes, though nothing that genuinely attempts to cater to upmarket tourists.

A very popular place close to town is **Big Blue**, beautifully situated on a rocky beach about 500m from the market (you'll see it signposted from the main road as you come into town). Accommodation here consists of bamboo huts costing US$4 per person, you can pitch a tent for US$1.50 per person, or dorms cost US$3 per person. Recently, Big Blue was fully renovated and new huts extend on stilts over the water. Good food is available for about US$3 a dish in the comfortable bar/restaurant, which also boasts a pool table. Email and internet access are available to guests. Contact friendly Bryn Evans on tel: 01 353370; email: bigblue@sdnp.org.mw. As with all the better lodges in and around Nkhata Bay, watchmen patrol the premises day and night.

On the opposite side of the road to Big Blue, **Backpackers Connection** has rooms for US$3.40/5 single/double and dormitory accommodation for US$2. Facilities include a pool table and hot showers. Close by, **Kupenja**

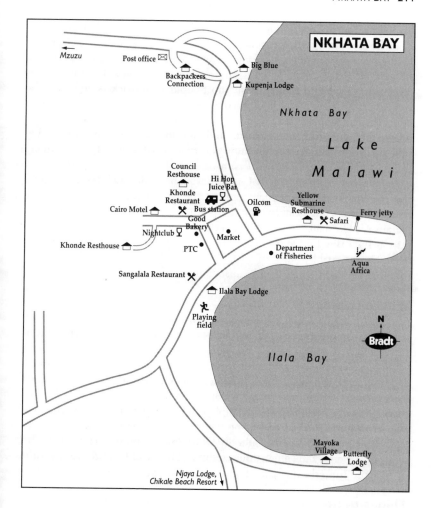

Lodge is a relatively new place offering unremarkable rooms at US$3.50/4 single/double with nets.

Near Nkhata Bay is **Njaya Lodge** (tel: 01 352342; fax: 01 335025; email: easymail@sdnp.org.mw), which lies 20–30 minutes' walk from the town centre at Chikale Beach. Good food is available in the buzzing bar/restaurant area, which also commands an excellent view, and has a pool table and great music. Huts costs around US$4.50 per person, and camping space is also available. Credit cards are accepted.

Sharing a beach with Njaya, the **Chikale Beach Resort** (PO Box 199, Nkhata Bay; tel: 01 352338) offers a number of comfortable chalets ranging in price from US$15 to US$25. The shady campsite costs US$2 per person.

Actually in the town centre, the German-owned **Yellow Submarine Resthouse** has clean rooms for US$2.20/3.20 single/double. The **Cairo Motel**, also very centrally located, is a somewhat dingy and atmospherically challenged triple-storey monolith offering acceptable rooms at US$1.60/2.40 single/double.

Three new lodges have opened recently, all around Ilala Bay. **Mayoka Village** (email: caredotcom@sdnp.org.mw for attention Majoka Village) is situated on a steep slope down to the water's edge at Mayoka Point, and is deservedly proving to be one of the most popular backpackers' lodges in the area. Snorkelling and the use of dugouts are free and camping excursions are often arranged up the coast in a motor boat. The menu in the bar/restaurant is imaginative with steak, fish, baguette, and even authentic hummus and freshly squeezed fruit juice. Accommodation is very reasonably priced with camping at US$1 and huts US$2.50 per person.

Another new place, **Butterfly Lodge**, next door to Mayoka Village, was under construction in 2002. Although some of the chalets seemed to be strangely designed around huge sunken baths, the position is beautiful. Accommodation in A-frames is US$4.50, dorms US$2 and camping US$1. Quite an upmarket new place is **Ilala Bay Lodge** (tel: 01 352362), next to the Department of Fisheries. A large, comfortable, but somewhat soulless establishment, it offers en-suite rooms at US$14/20 single/double, including breakfast.

Where to eat

Aside from the backpacker lodges and resthouses, most of which serve food, there are a few decent restaurants in Nkhata Bay. The longest running of these, which recently changed its name to **Sangalala Restaurant**, serves a variety of Western-style dishes for around US$2.50, as well as fresh fruit juice and excellent chocolate cake. Another long-serving place is the **Safari Restaurant**, where you can get anything from steak and chips to pizza or pasta, all at around US$3 for an ample plateful. A new restaurant called the **Hip Hop Juice Bar** has opened on the corner next to the market and serves fresh fruit juices (US$0.75), muesli (US$1.25) and burgers (US$2). It also sells beads, books and some ethnic clothing. The small **Khonde Restaurant** up the road from the bus station serves local dishes at under US$1.

Things to do

For most travellers, activity in Nkhata Bay comprises mainly eating, drinking, sitting on the beach, recovering from hangovers, and generally just hanging out. For the more active, Aqua Africa's highly regarded week-long diving courses are US$150 all inclusive. I heard only praise from several people who'd done the course. If a week's diving isn't enough, a high proportion of people sign on for a second week's advanced course.

Operating from the boat shed on Chikale Beach, Monkey Business offers kayak trips at US$30 per person per day, deepwater fishing (including all equipment and breakfast) at US$10, or a full day of activities around Nkhata Bay – bushwalk, kayak ride and diving – for US$35.

The nightclubs that were in favour in mid-2002 were Sankhani and Mbakajiso, both near to the PTC superette. The curio sellers are hard to avoid and all have their stalls on the Ilala Bay side of town, while a great selection of printed Malawian cloths is available in the market at about US$1.50 per piece.

Above Horseback safari,
Nyika Plateau

Below Likhabula waterfall,
Mulanje Mountain

Top Old mission church, Blantyre

Right Old cathedral, Likoma Island

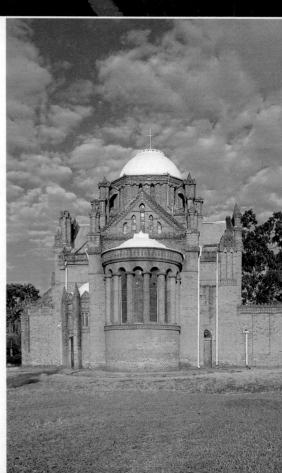

The Lake Ferry and the Islands

17

This chapter covers ferry transport on Lake Malawi, as well as Likoma and Chizumulu islands, both of which lie within Mozambican waters on the eastern side of the lake. They are destinations that have long held something of a special fascination for travellers, largely because they can only realistically be reached by using the ferry. For local people, the ferry forms the only connection between the mainland and the islands, and the crowded lower deck is testament to its importance to the islanders. For travellers, who mostly can afford to use the spacious first-class deck, the attraction of the ferry is primarily aesthetic. This is one of Africa's great public transport rides, a leisurely cruise on one of the continent's largest and most scenic lakes, offering fantastic sunsets and night skies, as well as a welcome break from the grind of bus travel. Although many travellers do use the ferry as a means of visiting one of the islands, a far greater number travel on it for its own sake, as an alternative means of transport between the popular lake resorts of Cape Maclear (near the southern ferry terminus at Monkey Bay) and Nkhata Bay further north. A few intrepid travellers even cross into Mozambique.

Due to the unusual nature of the subject matter covered in this chapter, the format deviates somewhat from that used elsewhere in the guide.

THE LAKE FERRY

The Malawi Lake Services has recently been privatised and will hopefully now be more reliable. They use the MV *Ilala* for their weekly service, which runs from a Friday through to the next Wednesday. Mbamba Bay in Tanzania has been dropped as a port of call and the ferry now calls at Cobue and Metangula on the Mozambique side of the lake, making it possible for travellers to enter that country via this new and adventurous route.

Since 1957, the MV *Ilala* has run up and down the lake once a week. Its present route is as follows: Starting at Monkey Bay in the south, it runs up the lake's western shore to Nkhotakota, across to the Mozambique ports of Metangula and Cobue, then to the Malawian islands of Likoma and Chizumulu, back across to Nkhata Bay, right up the west coast to Chilumba, returning to Monkey Bay using the same route in reverse. Sometimes stops are also made at the smaller ports of Makanjila and Chipoka in the south and

213

Mangwina, Usisya, Ruarwe, Tcharo and Mlowe in the north.

Four types of ticket are available for the *Ilala*. By far the cheapest is deck class, with ticket prices comparable to bus transport (around US$6 from Monkey Bay to Nkhata Bay), but the lower deck is very crowded and sweaty, and there's a real risk of theft. Many travellers do use deck class, but, to quote one reader: 'vomiting children, chickens on your lap, cockroaches on your backpack and spiders on your legs without any space to move for 15 hours might sound very romantic, but it can cause frustration in the long run.' For many travellers, the compromise between cost and comfort is a first-class ticket which works out at around US$30 from Monkey Bay to Nkhata Bay, or US$7.50 to travel directly between Likoma or Chizumulu and either Nkhata Bay or Nkhotakota. First-class passengers sleep on the breezy, uncrowded upper deck, where there is a shaded bar, as well as a restaurant below. There is no need to book tickets for deck or first class, and if you embark anywhere but Monkey Bay or Nkhata Bay, tickets can only be bought once you are on the boat.

If you can afford it, the most comfortable way to travel on the *Ilala* is cabin class, which works out around 20% more than first class (unless you take the solitary owner's cabin, which is self-contained and costs about double the first-class price). Cabin space *is* limited, so it's advisable to book in advance. You're unlikely to get a cabin berth without a booking, unless you embark at Monkey Bay or Nkhata Bay, where a lot of travellers will disembark. Cabin bookings can be made at the Malawi Lake Services office in Monkey Bay (tel: 01 587311) or through a tour operator such as Soche Tours in the Mount Soche Hotel in Blantyre or Central African Wilderness Safaris in Lilongwe. The latter company tells me that they are increasingly reluctant to make ferry bookings, because many customers have blamed them for delays which are totally out of their control. Perhaps it's worth pointing out the obvious, which is that booking through the most reliable tour operator won't affect the ferry's punctuality (or lack thereof), and you probably shouldn't be using the ferry if you aren't prepared for the delays which are almost inevitable. Vehicles can be taken on the ferry at surprisingly reasonable prices (around US$30 from Monkey Bay to Nkhata Bay, less for shorter journeys).

So far as facilities go, there is a well-stocked bar on the upper deck, normally selling biscuits and other packaged snacks. The restaurant serves good three-course meals for around US$4, and it is advisable to reserve lunch and dinner a few hours in advance. The first-class toilets are clean, and the communal showers have hot water. At ports other than Monkey Bay and Nkhata Bay, there is no jetty, and the Bay is too shallow for the ferry to come in close, so passengers and goods are transported to and from the ferry on a smaller boat. If you are embarking at a port where the ferry docks at some distance from the town (for instance Nkhotakota) you might well want to bring along something to nibble and drink while you wait.

Aside from the *Ilala*, the only reasonably reliable ferry on the lake at the time of writing was the Tanzanian MV *Songea*. It connects two ports in Tanzania, Mbamba Bay (on the eastern shore) and Itungi Port (near Kyela on the lake's northwestern tip). The ferry leaves Itungi at 07.00 on Mondays and Thursdays

THE MV ILALA TIMETABLE (2002)

	day	arrives	departs
Monkey Bay	Friday		10.00
Chilinda	Friday	12.10	13.40
Nkhotakota	Saturday	05.30	07.00
Metangula (Mozambique)	Saturday	10.30	12.00
Cobue (Mozambique)	Saturday	15.45	17.00
Likoma Island	Saturday	17.25	19.30
Chizumulu Island	Saturday	20.45	22.45
Nkhata Bay	Sunday	05.00	07.00
Chilumba	Sunday	18.30	02.00 (Monday)
Nkhata Bay	Monday	14.45	20.00
Chizumulu Island	Monday	23.30	02.00 (Tuesday)
Likoma Island	Tuesday	03.15	06.15
Cobue (Mozambique)	Tuesday	06.40	08.30
Metangula (Mozambique)	Tuesday	12.15	14.15
Nkhotakota	Tuesday	17.25	19.20
Chilinda	Wednesday	10.15	12.00
Monkey Bay	Wednesday	14.00	

This timetable has not changed significantly for several years, except for the dropping of Tanzanian ports in favour of Mozambican ones, but is flexible and subject to delays. For simplicity's sake, it includes only the larger ports. For details of minor ports visited (these include Makanjila and Chipoka in the south and Mangwina, Usisya, Ruarwe, Tcharo and Mlowe in the north), or to confirm that the times given here still hold good, you are advised to contact the Malawi Lake Services' office in Monkey Bay (PO Box 15, Monkey Bay; tel: 01 587311; fax: 01 587203; email: ilala@malawi.net).

and arrives at Mbamba Bay at around midnight the same day, after stopping at Lupinga, Manda, Lundu and Liuli. After arriving at Mbamba Bay, the ferry turns around almost immediately, to arrive back at Itungi at 17.00 the next day. Please note that this ferry no longer crosses to Nkhata Bay nor connects with any other Malawian port.

LIKOMA ISLAND

The island of Likoma, 8km long and 3km wide, lies within Mozambican waters but is territorially part of Malawi, mainly as a result of its long association with Scottish missionaries. In 1886, Likoma became the site of an Anglican mission, established by Bishop Chauncey Maples with the help of his close friend and fellow Oxford graduate, the Rev William Johnson. Maples was consecrated as the first bishop of Likoma in London in 1895, but he never actively assumed this post as he drowned in a boating accident near Salima,

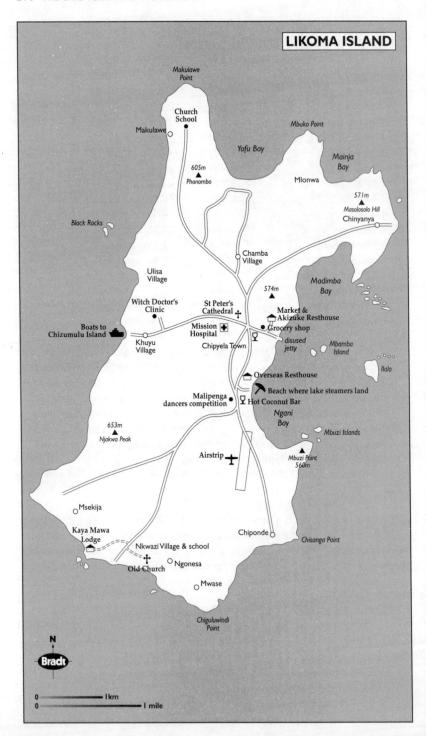

LIKOMA ISLAND

Makulawe
Point

Church
School

Makulawe

Mbuko Point

Yofu Bay

Mainja
Bay

605m
Phonombo

Mlonwa

571m
Masolosolo Hill
Chinyanya

Black Rocks

Chamba
Village

Ulisa
Village

574m

Madimba
Bay

Witch Doctor's
Clinic

St Peter's
Cathedral

Market &
Akizuke Resthouse
Grocery shop

Boats to
Chizumulu Island

Mission
Hospital

disused
jetty

Mbamba
Island

Khuyu
Village

Chipyela Town

Ilala

Overseas Resthouse

Beach where lake steamers land

Malipenga
dancers competition

Hot Coconut Bar

Ngani
Bay

653m
Njakwa Peak

Mbuzi Islands

Airstrip

Mbuzi Point
560m

Msekija

Kaya Mawa
Lodge

Chiponde

Chisanga Point

Nkwazi Village & school

Old Church

Ngonesa

Mwase

Chiguluwindi
Point

N

Bradt

0 — — — 1km
0 — — — 1 mile

caused by his enthusiasm to return to Likoma despite stormy weather. Maples was buried in the church at Nkhotakota. Johnson went on to become one of the most fondly remembered of all the missionaries who worked in Malawi. He arrived at the lake in 1882 and for 46 years he preached from a boat all around the lakeshore, despite being practically blind and well into his 70s when he died in 1928. Johnson's grave at Liuli (on the Tanzanian part of the lakeshore) remained for several decades a popular site of pilgrimage for Malawian Christians.

The Likoma Mission founded by Maples and Johnson remained the headquarters of the Anglican Church in Malawi until after World War II. During this period, the educational zeal of the missionaries ensured that Likoma was probably the only settlement in Africa with a 100% literacy rate. The most obvious physical legacy of the missionaries work is the large and very beautiful St Peter's Cathedral (similar in size to Westminster Cathedral) designed by Frank George and built between 1903 and 1905 in a cruciform shape using local granite. The site of the church, chosen by Maples before his death, is where in 1889 he witnessed and was unable to prevent three witches being burnt to death. Notable features of the church include carved soapstone choir stalls, some fine stained-glass windows, and a crucifix carved from a tree which grew near Chitambo (the village in Zambia where David Livingstone died in 1873).

Historical interest aside, Likoma's main attraction for travellers is its isolation and mellow atmosphere. This is no conventional tropical island paradise, though the beaches really are splendid with the mountainous Mozambican shore rising above them, while the interior has a certain austere charm, particularly the southern plains which are covered in massive baobabs and shady mango trees and studded with impressive granite outcrops. Likoma has always generated a great deal of interest among travellers, but it remains surprisingly little visited. Above all, perhaps, Likoma has an overwhelmingly friendly mood, making it a good place to get to know ordinary Malawians.

Most visitors to the island are content to while away their time on the beaches or exploring Chipyela, the island's largest town. Chipyela lies between the cathedral and the jetty, and is named after the spot where witches used to be burnt (Chipyela translates as *the place of burning*). It is an unusual town: the neat, cobbled roads and stone houses have, according to one resident, led to it being nicknamed 'Half London', a strange epithet for a metropolis that not only lacks an underground but boasts a grand total of one car, the ambulance belonging to the mission hospital. The central market is dominated by a massive strangler fig with a hollow base large enough to stand in. Worth asking about are the regular *malipenga* dancing competitions held on most weekends about 500m out of town opposite the Hot Coconut Bar – these are generally held in the afternoon, and are rather boozy affairs, notable both for the interesting traditional instruments that are used and for the bizarre colonially-influenced costumes the men wear.

Further afield, a half-hour walk eastwards from Chipyela takes you to the village of Khuyu, where visitors are normally welcome at the witch doctor's clinic. Reputedly one of the most important 'witch doctors' in Malawi, he is regularly visited by people from as far away as Tanzania and South Africa, and his influence over the islanders is immense, despite the superficial trappings of Christianity associated with Likoma. Another good excursion is a boat trip to Cobue on the Mozambican shore of the lake, where there is a large ruined church – this is best organised through the management of Kaya Mawa, and visas aren't a problem for day trips.

Getting there and away

Unless you can afford to charter a plane or boat or Air Malawi suddenly makes good a long-standing threat to introduce scheduled flights to Likoma, there is only one way of reaching the island from the Malawian mainland. This is with the MV *Ilala*, which is scheduled to stop at Likoma on Saturday evening on its northbound trip and on Tuesday morning on the southbound trip. Allowing for delays, this means that you need to allocate at least five days to the round trip, spending three or four nights on the island. The *Ilala* docks a few hundred metres offshore at a beach about five minutes' walk from Chipyela. It is usually docked here for about two hours, which means, in theory, that ferry passengers who are travelling on could still hop off the boat and take a quick look around the cathedral. In practice, however, the complexities of transporting passengers between the *Ilala* and the beach make this inadvisable, unless you're prepared to risk the boat sailing away without you.

Other than the MV *Ilala*, it is possible to travel between Likoma and Chizumulu islands and Cobue on the Mozambican mainland using a local fishing boat. Boats to Cobue are probably best organised through the staff of Kaya Mawa (see below), who can also advise you on the current situation with Mozambican visas. Should you be crossing into Mozambique rather than just paying a day visit, you might also want to ask them about the current transport situation on the road connecting Cobue to Lichinga – for more details of this little-used crossing between Malawi and Mozambique, see page 45.

Where to stay and eat

The **Akizuke Resthouse** is in Chipyela, facing the central market, about five to ten minutes' walk from the beach where the ferry docks. Basic but clean rooms with mosquito nets cost US$3/5 single/double, and facilities include a flush toilet, running showers and a spasmodically functional generator. The bar attached to the resthouse serves cold beers and sodas when the generator is running, and the restaurant prepares basic meals by advance order, generally fish, beans and rice, though you can also ask them to buy you a chicken.

So far as we could establish, the only other accommodation close to Chipyela is the run-down **Overseas Resthouse** next to the beach where the ferry lands. There is nowhere else to eat in town, but a couple of stores on the road between the mission and the Akizuke Resthouse sell tinned provisions and cold sodas and mineral water. Opposite the entrance to the Likoma Mission (next to a volleyball court) is a building housing a bar with a fridge, but nowhere to sit. The closest thing to a nightspot in this neck of the woods is the **Hot Coconut**

Bar, an open-air bar with a fridge and shaded tables, about ten minutes' walk from town, not far from the beach where the ferry lands.

Kaya Mawa, a wonderfully laid-back spot, the name of which translates somewhat appropriately as *maybe tomorrow*, is set on an idyllic beach, book-ended by large rocky outcrops and stands of baobab, near Nkwazi village on the southwestern end of the island facing the Mozambican shore. This popular old backpackers' place has been completely changed and rebuilt as the spectacular and exclusive Kaya Mawa Lodge, and offers luxury accommodation, including a tiny honeymoon island just offshore, accessible only by boat. Rates are US$208/320 single/double, full board and include government taxes and all non-motorised watersports (kayaking, sailing and snorkelling). They also generously offer residents of any African country rates at approximately half the above. Boat transfers to and from the island can also be arranged at US$200 per person, one way. Contact details are: PO Box 79, Likoma Island; satellite tel: +87 176 168 4670; email: kaya01@bushmail.net.

Backpackers are well catered for at the new **Mango Drift**. Run by Kaya Mawa, and about 1km north of them, this idyllic spot with a bar under a mango tree and grass huts on the beach offers camping at US$2, dorms at US$3 and accommodation in the huts at US$4, all per person. Dinner is about US$3. They also run a PADI dive school which offers the four-day Open Water course for only US$150, including free camping. Contact details are the same as for Kaya Mawa.

CHIZUMULU ISLAND

Smaller than Likoma, and even more remote, the island of Chizumulu is noted for excellent diving and snorkelling in the surrounding waters, and for attractive beaches lined by large, ancient baobabs. Like Likoma, this is essentially a place to chill out, free of roads, cars, electricity and hassle, and widely regarded to offer the most beautiful sunsets in Malawi. Few travellers make it to Chizumulu, but those who do invariably regard it as a highlight of their time in Malawi.

Getting there and away

Most people travel to Chizumulu on the MV *Ilala*, which stops there between Likoma and Nkhata Bay on both the northbound and southbound parts of its weekly circuit. If the timing works, travellers who want to visit both islands can use the *Ilala* to get between them. Alternatively, a fishing boat ferries passengers between Likoma and Chizumulu daily for around US$12 per person. This boat leaves Khuyu Beach on Likoma in the early morning (generally at around 05.00) and it arrives at Same Beach on Chizumulu roughly two hours later. It generally starts the return trip some time between 10.00 and 12.00, though timings are pretty vague and it doesn't run at all in rough weather.

Where to stay

The only place to stay on the island is the excellent **Wakwenda Retreat** (PO Box 23, Chizumulu Island; tel: 01 357286), a backpacker-friendly lodge set on the beach a few hundred metres from where the *Ilala* stops and about 1km from Same Beach, where fishing boats from Likoma set anchor. Wakwenda offers simple but comfortable accommodation and camping, as well as drinks and meals. Scuba diving can be arranged (for experienced divers only), and snorkelling equipment is available for hire at reasonable rates. Camping US$1.20; dorms US$2.40; grass huts US$3; and rooms US$3.50, all per person per day.

18

Mzuzu, Nyika and Vwaza Marsh Wildlife Reserve

Mzuzu is the largest town in northern Malawi and the region's major route focus, lying on the junction of the M1 between Lilongwe and the Tanzanian border and the lakeshore road from Nkhata Bay. Mzuzu and the nearby town of Rumphi hold little of interest to tourists, but they are springboards for visits to two of Malawi's finest conservation areas: Nyika National Park and Vwaza Marsh Wildlife Reserve. Nyika is the better known of these reserves, a beautiful, rolling highland plateau where visitors can walk freely amongst a variety of big game species. Vwaza Marsh is less publicised than Nyika, and sees very few tourists, although it is readily accessible both to motorised travellers and to backpackers, and it offers exceptional game viewing, elephants being particularly numerous.

CLIMATE

Mzuzu has an attractive moderate climate, and it's one of the few towns in Malawi where rain can fall at almost any time of the year. The Nyika Plateau lies at an altitude of over 2,000m and is thus one of the coldest parts of Malawi. Vwaza Marsh, on the other hand, is low-lying, hot and humid, and mosquitoes and tsetse flies are abundant.

GETTING AROUND

Mzuzu is a major public transport hub. There are regular buses between Mzuzu and Lilongwe, Karonga and Nkhata Bay. Between Mzuzu and Rumphi (the gateway town to Nyika and Vwaza Marsh) buses are supplemented by a steady stream of minibuses.

There is not much public transport west of Rumphi. One bus runs daily in each direction between Rumphi and Mzimba (on the Viphya Plateau), passing within 1km of Kazuni Tented Camp at Vwaza Marsh, and there is also a reasonable amount of *matola* traffic between Rumphi and Kazuni. Nyika is more difficult to reach without private transport, and you have to hitch or walk the last 16km to Chelinda Camp.

If you have private transport, it's advisable to check the current condition of the roads to Vwaza and Nyika at the Wildlife Office in Mzuzu or Rumphi, especially if your vehicle is not a 4WD and you are travelling during the wet

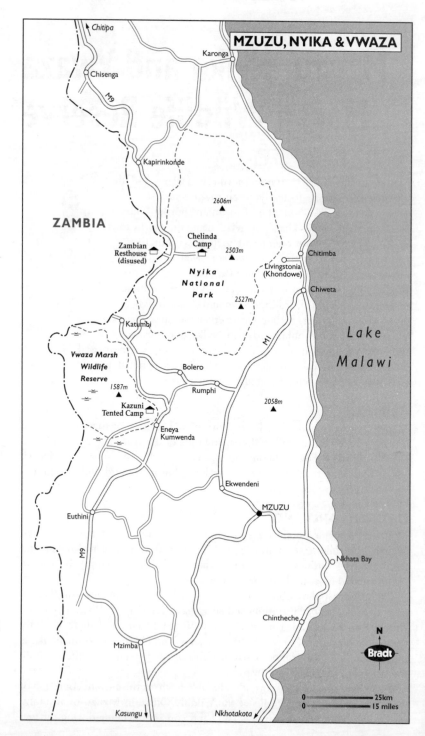

MZUZU, NYIKA & VWAZA

season. Assuming the roads are passable, it will take less than an hour to reach Vwaza from Rumphi, and perhaps four hours to reach Chelinda Camp in Nyika.

Air Malawi now flies between Lilongwe, Mzuzu and Karonga two or three times a week.

MZUZU

Mzuzu, the official capital of Malawi's Northern Province, has a sleepy provincial atmosphere, compared with which even Lilongwe and Blantyre seem positively cosmopolitan. This is not surprising when you discover that less than 50 years ago Mzuzu was merely the name of a stream running through rural hillside. Even until the time of Malawi's independence, Mzuzu was practically inaccessible during the rainy season; the highlight of the expatriate social calendar was the arrival every Friday of a Beaver plane from Lilongwe.

Despite this, or perhaps because of it, I thought Mzuzu was the most likeable of Malawi's three regional capitals. In size and atmosphere, it fits somewhere between small town and city (it only officially received city status in 1991); climatically it occupies a mid-altitude (1,200m) niche between the lakeshore humidity of nearby Nkhata Bay and the breezy highland chill of the Viphya Hills, while an average annual rainfall of around 1,750mm ensures the town and the surrounding hills are green and fertile all year through.

As for tourist-related facilities, Mzuzu has a good tourist-class hotel, several small resthouses, a few decent restaurants, four PTC and Kandodo supermarkets, a Times Bookshop, a couple of internet offices and several banks. For all that, few travellers do more than pass through Mzuzu, and, pleasant as the town may be, it's difficult to think of any compelling reason to do otherwise.

Getting there and away

Reasonable surfaced roads connect Mzuzu to Lilongwe in the south, Karonga in the north, and Nkhata Bay on the lakeshore. There are regular buses along all these routes. A Shire bus connects Lilongwe and Mzuzu, leaving from the Capital Hotel in Lilongwe and the Mzuzu Hotel in Mzuzu at 07.00 daily in both directions.

Where to stay

Set in attractive grounds on the outskirts of town, the **Mzuzu Hotel** offers the only tourist-class accommodation in Mzuzu. The self-contained rooms are large and clean, with satellite television and 24-hour room service, and they cost US$111/145 single/double. Suites are available at US$131/186 single/double. Facilities include a good restaurant and bar with pool table, airport transfers, car hire, photocopy, fax and secretarial services, and foreign exchange at a good rate for hotel residents only. Rooms can be booked through the Le Meridien Head Office in the Mount Soche Hotel (see *Blantyre*, page 103), or directly at PO Box 231, Mzuzu; tel: 01 332622. Air Malawi and DHL offices are here.

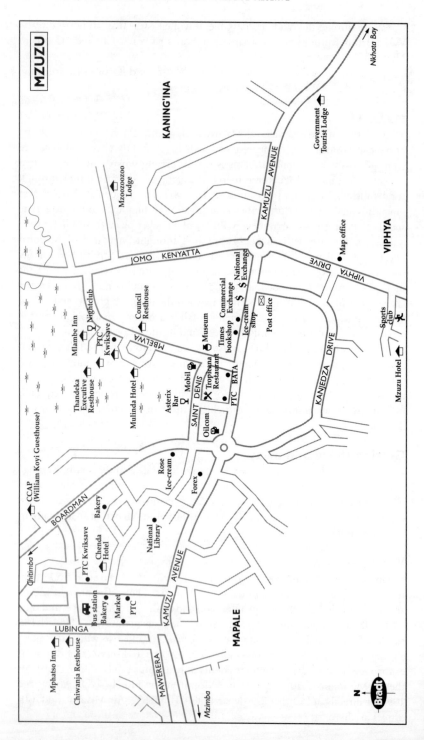

Recommended in the mid-range, the pleasantly rustic **Government Tourist Lodge** (PO Box 485, Mzuzu; tel: 01 332097) lies about 1km out of town on the Nkhata Bay road. The large, comfortable rooms with fans are good value at US$25/40 single/double. Similar in standard, though very different in style and more central, the **Chenda Hotel** (PO Box 314, Mzuzu; tel: 01 335255) has acceptable self-contained rooms with hot showers for US$14/16/19 single/double/twin.

Probably the best option in the budget range is the **William Koyi Guesthouse** in the CCAP compound, which offers dormitory accommodation at US$2.50 per person and has two self-contained doubles costing US$5 each. Unfortunately, it is often full, though it's still worth checking out as it's not too far from the bus station. Camping costs US$1.

The main cluster of budget accommodation lies in the backstreets behind the banks and supermarkets. Here, the **Council Resthouse** is the obvious stand out, with scruffy rooms in the old wing for around US$1/2 single/double and much better doubles in the new wing for US$3. Otherwise, there are close on ten resthouses in this area, most of which charge around US$2/4 single/double. The **Mlambe Inn** looks to be one of the better options, and it has hot showers, but its position – sandwiched between two nightclubs – doesn't bode well for a peaceful night. The pick of the bunch is the **Thandeka Executive Resthouse**, which seems clean and secure, and is sufficiently distant from the noisier hangouts that you've a chance of sleeping.

Better than these are two adjacent resthouses on the Karonga road, only five minutes' walk from the bus station. The cheaper of these is the **Chiwanja Resthouse**, which offers a variety of basic but clean rooms at around US$3–5 in price. The smarter **Mphatso Inn** has ordinary rooms for US$7/10 single/double and excellent self-contained doubles with hot water at US$12. The restaurant at the Mphatso Inn serves a good selection of meals in the US$2–4 range.

An interesting development in 2002 was the **Mzoozoozoo Backpackers Lodge and Campsite** (tel: 01 864493). Still being sorted out, it was to offer camping at US$1, dorms at US$1.50 and an en-suite double room for US$5.50. There was a legal battle going on over the use of the Tropicana Restaurant name, but food and drinks were already on offer. I struggled to find the place down past the churches from the Nkhata Bay roundabout, but hopefully signs have now been erected.

Where to eat

The **Tropicana Restaurant** used to be really good value, serving decent steaks, piri-piri chicken and fried *chambo* for less than US$2 per main course. It's still very cheap, and well worth a try, but on the basis of our last meal there appears to have been a decline in standards of late. We didn't try the new **Sombrero Restaurant** around the corner, but are told that it serves similar dishes at similar prices, and is much better. The restaurant at the **Chenda Motel** might also be worth a try, though it looks rather uninspiring.

The restaurant at the **Mzuzu Hotel** serves decent meals in the US$5–6 range, but your best bet for a good wholesome cheap meal has got to be the **William Koyi Guesthouse** at US$1.50.

RUMPHI

This small town, attractively ringed by hills, is of little intrinsic interest to travellers, and – lying as it does quite a long way off the main Mzuzu–Karonga road – it could be bypassed altogether were it not the springboard for visits to Nyika National Park and Vwaza Marsh Wildlife Reserve, the two prime game-viewing areas in northern Malawi.

As far as travel practicalities go, most of the essentials are to be found in Rumphi. In addition to a few resthouses and restaurants, Rumphi boasts Kandodo and PTC supermarkets (though not nearly as well stocked as those in Mzuzu), a bank, and a decent market. There is also a Wildlife depot a short distance out of town, back towards the main Mzuzu–Karonga Road.

Getting there and away

Minibuses between Mzuzu and Rumphi leave regularly in either direction on a fill-up-and-go basis. Buses between Mzuzu and Karonga generally divert to Rumphi.

Where to stay and eat

The closest thing to upmarket accommodation in Rumphi is the **Luninya Motel**, which has ordinary rooms with three-quarter beds and mosquito nets for around US$2 and very pleasant self-contained doubles (hot showers, fans) for US$4. Of the more local resthouses in Rumphi, the **Yangotha Hide-away Resthouse** is certainly the best, with clean rooms for US$1/2 single/double, and communal baths. Cheaper still are the basic **Fumbauzi Resthouse** and **Thuluwa Resthouse**, with rooms for around US$1.

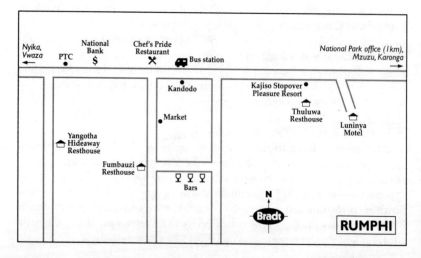

The best place to eat is the new **Mbakajiso Restaurant** (part of the Kajiso Stopover Pleasure Resort), though you could also try one of the several local eateries around the bus station, of which the **Chef's Pride Restaurant** is recommended. And *don't* miss out on a cold beer at the **Kajiso Stopover Pleasure Resort**, a riotous pick-up joint which, with its blaring sound system, flashing lights and myriad bar girls, wouldn't look out of place in downtown Nairobi, particularly during the tobacco season when local farmers roll into Rumphi to drink away their profits.

NYIKA NATIONAL PARK

Malawi's largest national park, Nyika was gazetted in 1965 and extended to its modern size of 3,134km² in 1978, though parts of what are now the national park have been under government protection since the 1940s. At the heart of the park, averaging over 2,000m in altitude, lies the gently undulating Nyika Plateau, where montane grassland and fern heather communities, notable for their prolific wild flowers during the rainy season, are interspersed with isolated stands of indigenous forest and exotic pine and eucalyptus plantations. Although the Nyika Plateau is very much the centrepiece of the park, and the only part of it which is readily accessible to tourists, the *brachystegia*-covered lower slopes of the Nyika range also lie within its boundaries.

Nyika's main attraction is the wonderful montane scenery, a landscape unlike any other in Malawi, and one which reminds many visitors of Europe (an impression reinforced by the extensive pine plantations in the Chelinda area and the chilly winter nights characteristic of the plateau). The park is also notable for being one of the few African national parks with horse-riding facilities, and for allowing visitors the freedom to walk as they please along a vast network of dirt roads and footpaths. Of particular interest to botanists are the roughly 200 orchid species which generally flower in January and February; of these, 11 species are endemic to Nyika and a further 27 are found nowhere else in Malawi.

Nyika also protects a rich diversity of mammals: almost 100 species have been recorded, including an endemic race of Burchell's zebra (*Equus burchelli crawshayi*) and what is widely regarded to be the densest leopard population in Central Africa. Game viewing is good all year round, and the open nature of the plateau ensures excellent visibility. Due to extensive poaching in more remote areas, animal populations are concentrated around Chelinda (sometimes spelt Chilinda) Camp, where visitors are practically guaranteed to see roan antelope, scrub hare, Burchell's zebra, reedbuck, bushbuck and eland, and stand a good chance of encountering one of the leopards that haunt Chelinda Forest. The *brachystegia* woodland of the lower slopes supports significant populations of buffalo and elephant, though – perhaps fortunately for walkers – these animals only rarely move up to the grassy plateau. Lion and cheetah are listed as infrequent visitors to the plateau, and although they haven't been seen in years, visitors do stand a good chance of encountering hyenas and smaller nocturnal predators on night drives out of Chelinda Camp.

With well over 400 species recorded, Nyika supports the greatest diversity of birds found anywhere in Malawi, though this figure is rather deceptive as many

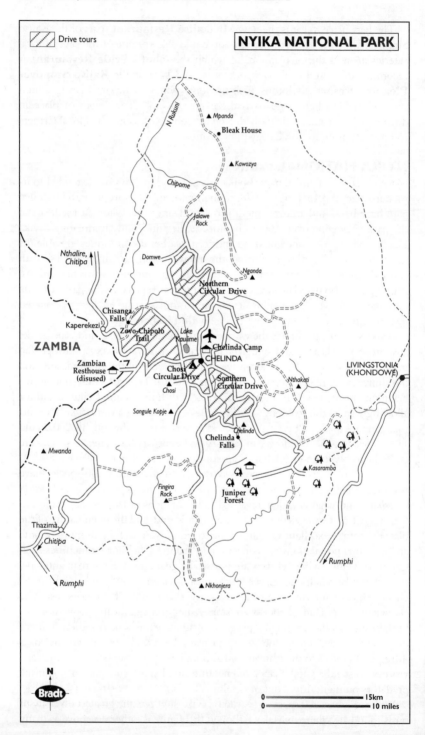

NYIKA NATIONAL PARK

of the species included on the checklist occur only in the inaccessible *brachystegia* woodland of the lower slopes and are thus unlikely to be seen by visitors who stick to the plateau. Nevertheless, the grassland around Chelinda Camp is inhabited by several tantalising birds. Foremost among these is the wattled crane, a large, striking bird which is internationally endangered; nowhere in its wide range is this very localised species as likely to be seen as it is in the marshes around Chelinda. The dam in front of Chelinda is a good place to pick up the yellow and black mountain marsh widow, a species restricted to a handful of montane areas in Central Africa. Other grassland birds of note include the localised Denham's bustard and the exquisite scarlet-tufted malachite sunbird. More rewarding than the grassland for general birding are the forests, particularly the large Chowo forest near the Zambian Resthouse, where localised species such as Sharpe's akalat, bar-tailed trogon, olive-flanked robin, white-breasted alethe and a variety of other robins and bulbuls may be seen. Four birds found at Nyika have been recorded nowhere else in Malawi (yellow mountain warbler, churring cisticola, crackling cloud cisticola and mountain marsh widow), while the Nyika races of red-winged francolin, rufous-naped lark, greater double-collared sunbird and Baglafecht weaver are endemic to the plateau. There are also three butterfly species endemic to the plateau, and one species each of chameleon, frog and toad which are found nowhere else.

From a practical point of view, 1997 was a time of great change at Nyika. Chelinda Camp was leased by the government to the private Nyika Safari Company, which also has the sole concession for organising activities such as night drives, horse-riding, overnight wilderness trails and the granting of fishing permits. Access to the reserve has also improved, with the road from Rumphi being graded for the first time in five years in 1998. In addition, the German KFW bank has provided funding of US$8 million towards the improvement of tourist facilities and an anti-poaching service, in the hope that Nyika might yet generate enough profit through tourism and timber production to satisfy the requirements of the government, the private sector and local communities.

An entrance fee of US$5 per person per 24 hours is charged for visiting Nyika, and there is also a small daily fee for private vehicles (US$2).

Further information

A highly recommended purchase is Sigrid Anna Johnson's 150-page *A Visitor's Guide to Nyika National Park, Malawi* (Mbabazi Book Trust, Blantyre), which is available at most good bookshops in Blantyre and Lilongwe as well as at Chelinda Camp for around US$4. This book provides a detailed historical and ecological background to Nyika, 20 pages of special-interest sites and recommended walks and hikes, as well as complete checklists of all mammals, birds, butterflies and orchids which are known to occur in the park. A range of other books, pamphlets and maps relating to Nyika is sold at the shop in Chelinda Camp.

The best source of current practical information is the Nyika Safari Company (PO Box 2338, Lilongwe; tel/fax: 01 740848 or 01 740579, email: nyika-safaries@malawi.net). The address of their new website, covering both Nyika and Vwaza Marsh, is www.nyika.com.

Getting there and away

By road, Chelinda Camp lies roughly 100km from Rumphi, and is reached along recently regraded dirt roads which shouldn't present any problem in the dry season but which may require a 4WD vehicle after heavy rain. The route is clearly signposted: from Rumphi you need to follow the S85 westwards for around 50km, then turn right into the S10 to Chitipa. Thazima Entrance Gate is 8km along the S10. About 30km past the entrance gate, a signposted turn-off to the right leads to Chelinda, a further 16km away. If you are driving yourself, take note that the last place where you can buy fuel before reaching Chelinda is at Rumphi. The drive between Lilongwe and Nyika cannot be done in a day during the rains, and it's a long slog even in the dry season. Many tour companies break the trip with a night at the Kasito Lodge or Resthouse on the Viphya Plateau (see page 200), an option which is recommended to independent travellers with private transport.

Without private transport, getting to Chelinda cheaply by road can be problematic (the Nyika Safari Company does offer road transfers from Mzuzu, but at US$100 per person this isn't an option for budget travellers). There is no public transport all the way through. In the dry season, a twice-weekly bus between Rumphi and Chitipa can drop you at the last turn-off, from where you'll either have to walk the last 30km to Chelinda (it's reasonably flat!) or else hope to hitch a lift. In the rainy season, there is no bus but you can easily get a *matola* lift from Rumphi along the S85 (ask for a vehicle heading to Katumbi), and then walk the 8km from where you will be dropped at the entrance gate. Provided you have a tent, it is permitted to camp at the entrance gate, though facilities are basic. Frankly, if you want to hitch, you'd be wiser trying to do so directly from Rumphi, so that you can be sure of not getting stuck along the way. The best days to hitch are Fridays and Saturdays, which is when Malawian residents tend to head to the park.

One of the options for backpackers leaving the park is to hike to Livingstonia over two or three days (see *Things to do* below).

If you're privileged enough to have your own plane, there is an airstrip at Chelinda. In 2002 there were no scheduled flights into the Park, but the Nyika Safari Company was planning on setting up charter flights.

Where to stay and eat

A brand new upmarket stone lodge was opened in Chelinda at the end of 1999, where eight luxurious en-suite log cabins command stunning views across the high plains. Rates are US$200 per person inclusive of all meals and game drives. Other accommodation is available lower down overlooking an attractive small dam and – like many resthouses built in the colonial era – encircled by an extensive plantation of exotic pines rather than indigenous vegetation. The camp consists of six comfortable self-contained double rooms, each of which costs US$80 per person full-board. In addition to the rooms, there are four private self-catering chalets costing US$120 per unit. Each chalet has two double bedrooms, a large lounge, an en-suite shower and toilet, and a fully equipped kitchen. About 2km from the main camp there is a campsite with a large ablution block, where you can pitch your own tent for US$5 per person.

Visitors who stay in the rooms are normally accommodated on a full-board basis. People staying in the chalets or campsite have the option of preparing their own food, but they are strongly urged to bring all they need with them as the only shop at Chelinda cannot be relied upon to have any provisions whatsoever. Should you want to eat in the lodge's dining room, it is best to give them some notice – breakfast and lunch cost US$10 per person and dinner costs US$15.

It should be stressed that Chelinda does not cater to budget travellers unless they have their own tent: the standing tents mentioned in some guidebooks have been taken down, and the nearby youth hostel is no longer open to tourists. Likewise, the private 'Zambian Resthouse' near the turn-off 16km before Chelinda shut down a couple of years ago, though the ranger station nearby may let you pitch a tent. The rustic cabin near the Juniper Forest 40km from Chelinda is effectively inoperative at the time of writing, and even if it is renovated will only be a feasible target for those with private transport.

Any bookings and enquiries can be addressed to the Nyika Safari Company (see page 229).

Things to do

Nyika National Park is rich in scenic spots, archaeological sites, mammals and birds, and the extensive network of roads and trails within the park gives visitors a practically unlimited number of hiking and driving options. The following synopsis of major attractions serves as a taster only; visitors to Nyika are strongly urged to supplement it with the more detailed information included in the book *A Visitor's Guide to Nyika National Park*.

Note that while visitors are free to walk where they please by day (and to explore the park by road if they have private transport), all guided activities and night drives *must* be organised through the management of Chelinda Camp.

Unguided walks around Chelinda

Plenty of roads radiate from Chelinda Camp, and it would be quite possible to spend four or five days in the area without repeating a walk. The marshy area immediately downstream of Chelinda Dam (which lies right in front of the camp) is a good place to see bushbuck and a variety of birds, and the dam itself attracts nocturnal predators such as hyena and leopard. A good short walk for visitors with limited time is to the two dams near Chelinda. The road here follows a dambo and the area offers good game viewing, as well as frequent sightings of wattled crane. The round trip covers 8km and takes two hours.

Another good short walk (about an hour) is from behind Chalet Four to the Kasaramba turn-off and then left along Forest Drive through the pine plantation back to Chalet Four. At dusk, there is a fair chance of seeing leopards along this walk.

A longer walk takes you to Lake Kaulime, which lies 8km west of Chelinda. This is the only natural lake on the plateau and is traditionally said to be the home of a serpent which acts as the guardian to Nyika's animals. More certain attractions than legendary serpents are migratory waterfowl (in summer) and large mammals, particularly roan antelope and zebra, coming to drink. It is also a very attractive spot, circled by indigenous trees.

Horse safaris
A stable of around 20 horses is kept at Chelinda, with animals suitable both for novices and experienced riders. Visitors can do anything from a short morning ride to a ten-night luxury riding trail. Shorter rides can be arranged at a moment's notice, and are an excellent way of getting around, as well as getting close to game – eland in particular allow horses to approach them far more closely than they would a vehicle or pedestrian. Horse rides cost US$15 per hour or US$60 for a full day.

Longer riding safaris should be booked well in advance, and cost around US$200 per person per day inclusive of everything but park fees and drinks. Contact the Nyika Safari Company for details, page 229.

Night drives
Spotlit night drives out of Chelinda cost US$15 per person, and are highly recommended as they offer the best opportunity to see nocturnal predators. Leopard and serval are often seen on the fringes of Chelinda Forest, while spotted hyena and side-striped jackal are common in grassy areas. When we last visited, we were lucky enough to see a pair of honey badgers crossing the road – a first for both of us. Especially in winter, the plateau gets really cold at night, and you should take all your warm clothing with you in the vehicle.

Angling
The rivers and dams on the Nyika Plateau are stocked with rainbow trout, and are thus popular with anglers. The dams are closed to anglers from April through to September, but the rivers are open throughout the year. Fishing permits must be arranged through the Nyika Safari Company at Chelinda. Licences cost US$4 per day and rods can be hired for US$10.

Places of interest further afield
Many of the more interesting points in Nyika are too far from Chelinda to be reached on a day walk, though they are accessible to visitors with vehicles.

Perhaps the most memorable viewpoint anywhere in Malawi, Jalawe Rock lies about 1km (to be done on foot) from a car park 34km north of Chelinda. The views here are spectacular, stretching over a close range of mountains to Lake Malawi's mountainous Tanzanian shore. With binoculars, it is often possible to see buffaloes and elephants in the brachystegia woodland of the Mpanda Ridge below. A variety of raptors, as well as klipspringer, are frequently seen around the rock, and the surrounding vegetation includes many proteas and aloes.

At 2,606m Nganda Peak is the highest point in northern Malawi. It lies about 30km northeast of Chelinda, and can be reached by following the Jalawe

Rock road for about 25km, then turning left on to a 4km-long motorable track. It's a steep 1.5km walk from the end of the track to the peak.

Kasaramba Viewpoint lies 43km southeast of Chelinda. You can motor to within 1.5km of the viewpoint and then walk the final stretch. When it isn't covered in mist, the views to the lake are excellent, and you can also see remnants of the terraced slopes built by the early Livingstonia missionaries. The most extensive rainforest in Nyika lies on the slopes below Kasaramba, and visitors frequently see the localised crowned eagle and mountain buzzard in flight. From Kasaramba, a 3km road leads to the top of the pretty, 30m-high Nchenachena Falls.

Further along the road to Kasaramba, also 43km from Chelinda, is a large juniper forest, the most southerly stand of *Juniperus procera* in Africa, and the first part of the Nyika Plateau to be afforded official protection back in the 1940s. There is a rustic cabin on the edge of the forest, but it is currently in a state of disrepair. A short trail through the junipers offers the opportunity of sighting forest animals such as leopard, elephant shrew, red duiker, bushpig and a variety of forest birds. The forest can also be explored from the firebreaks which surround it.

The Zovo Chipola Forest lies on the Chitipa Road near to where the Zambian Resthouse used to be. It is of special interest to birdwatchers, and harbours several mammal species, the most commonly seen of which are bushbuck, blue monkey and elephant shrew. An unmarked trail runs through the forest, which is best visited with a local guide, at least if you hope to pick up the calls of such elusive forest birds as the bar-tailed trogon. The larger Chowo Forest, which lies in the Zambian part of the park, used to be popular with people staying at the Zambian Resthouse, but it is now somewhat off the beaten track.

Fingira Rock is a large, granite dome lying 22km south of Chelinda. On the eastern side of the rock, an 11m-deep and 18m-long cave was used as a shelter by humans around 3,000 years ago – excavations in 1965 unearthed a complete human skeleton and a large number of stone tools. Several schematic rock paintings can be seen on the walls of the cave. A motorable track runs to the base of the rock, 500m from the cave.

The *brachystegia* woodland around Thazima Entrance Gate is the most accessible in the park. The area is rich in birds, and noted for harbouring unusual species. Walking here, you are also likely to see mammal species which are rare at higher altitudes.

Guided wilderness trails

Six wilderness trails have been designated within Nyika National Park, ranging from one to five nights in duration. Visitors wishing to use these trails must supply their own camping equipment and food, and are required make an advance booking through the Nyika Safari Company, page 229.

The most popular of Nyika's wilderness trails is the Livingstonia Trail, which leads from Chelinda all the way to Livingstonia on the Rift Valley Escarpment east of the national park. This three-day, two-night guided hike is recommended only in the dry season, and it costs US$80 for one or two people and another US$10 for every additional person. It is not permitted to hike this route in reverse, as a guide and park fees cannot be organised at Livingstonia, though the Nyika Safari Company hopes to find a way around this at some point.

Of particular interest for wildlife viewing is the four-night Jalawe and Chipome River Trail, passing through the *brachystegia* woodland in the northern part of the park and offering the opportunity to see elephant, buffalo, greater kudu and a variety of other mammals which are generally absent from the plateau. This and all other trails cost US$30 per person for the first night for the first two people, and an additional US$20 per night thereafter for the first two people. Additional people are charged at a rate of US$5 per person per night. In other words, one person would pay US$50 for a two-night trail, two people would each pay US$70 for a three-night trail, and four people would each pay US$55 for a four-night trail.

Porters are available for all trails at a small extra charge.

VWAZA MARSH WILDLIFE RESERVE

This underrated and little-visited reserve covers an area of 1,000km² along the Zambian border west of Rumphi and south of Nyika National Park. It is, without doubt, Malawi's best-kept game viewing secret, a highly attractive and surprisingly accessible and affordable target to anybody with an interest in natural history. Rich in wetland habitats, Vwaza may be named after a rather inaccessible marsh in the northeastern corner of the reserve, but the main focus for tourism is Lake Kazuni in the southeast, which lies on a public transport route and offers inexpensive hutted accommodation and camping.

Aside from the wetlands, Vwaza Marsh primarily consists of flat terrain supporting mixed *brachystegia* and mopane woodland. The large mammal populations have suffered badly at the hands of poachers in the past, and they are to some extent seasonal, but the reserve remains reasonably well stocked because animals can move freely between it and the neighbouring Luangwa ecosystem in Zambia. Some 2,000 buffalo and 300 elephant are thought to be resident in Vwaza Marsh, and a variety of antelope are present, including roan, greater kudu, Liechtenstein's hartebeest, eland, puku and impala. Lion and leopard are around, but they are not often seen by tourists, while a few recent sightings of African wild dog suggest this endangered creature may be in the process of re-colonising the reserve from Zambia.

Because the camp looks over Lake Kazuni, you can see plenty of game just by sitting on the veranda of your hut. It is, in any case, an atmospheric and sumptuously African setting: an expanse of flat water surrounded by low hills and *brachystegia* woodland, with hippos splashing, crocodiles basking and a steady stream of mammals coming down to the shore to drink. It is emphatically worth paying the small charge to take a guided game walk out on to the floodplain, where it's reasonably easy to approach animals on foot. The 1998 animal census estimated there to be 545 hippo living in the lake in 17 pods, and they are generally very approachable on foot (provided that they are already in the water). A couple of substantial elephant herds visit the lake on most days. Other large mammals that currently visit the lake include baboon, impala, puku and greater kudu, while three herds of buffalo are resident in the area. It should be stressed that walking out towards the lake without an armed ranger is forbidden, not to say foolhardy, as there is a real risk of being charged by buffalo or hippo.

The Kazuni area also offers some good birdwatching. The lake itself supports a great many waterfowl, waders and storks, and I've seen osprey, fish eagle and palmnut vulture there on different occasions. The thick woodland around the camp is rattling with birds, especially in the morning – we noted around 50 species in a few hours on our most recent visit, including trumpeter hornbill, Carp's black tit, Hueglin's robin and a number of attractive small warblers. According to *Newman's Birds of Malawi*, this should be a good place to see the extremely localised babbler-like, white-winged babbling starling, though nobody locally seems to know much about it. If you feel like taking an unguided stroll, you stand a good chance of seeing some animals by walking along the 1km stretch of public road between Kazuni gate and the village (there's an electric fence, so it's safe to walk here unescorted). Even if you don't see much, it's quite interesting to look at the mudfish traps along the South Rukuru River as it flows out of the park near the gate.

Visitors with private vehicles can explore the network of internal roads within the reserve, though they are advised to check conditions with the warden at Kazuni before doing so.

Getting there and away

Kazuni Camp at the reserve's entrance gate lies approximately 25km from Rumphi along the 'old' dirt road that connects Rumphi to Mzimba. To get there, follow the S85 out of Rumphi towards Nyika for about 10km, then turn left on to the S49, which is signposted for the reserve. You can normally reach the gate in a saloon car, though a 4WD may be necessary after rain. Internal roads are generally closed during the rainy season.

Access to Vwaza Marsh on public transport is surprisingly easy. In the dry season, there is at least one bus daily between Mzimba and Rumphi, leaving Mzimba at 07.00 and arriving in Rumphi at roughly 11.00, shortly after which it starts the return trip to Mzimba. This bus doesn't stop right at the gate, but at Kazuni village, which is about 1km from the gate in the direction of Mzimba. A better option coming from Rumphi is to look for a *matola* lift to Kazuni. There seems to be a steady stream of pick-up trucks travelling between Rumphi and the tobacco farms in the Kazuni area, and you shouldn't have to wait longer than an hour for a lift. Private vehicles will generally drop you right at the gate, from where it is a five-minute walk to the camp. The best place to wait for a lift out of Rumphi is under the trees directly opposite the PTC supermarket.

Where to stay

Kazuni Safari Camp lies 500m inside the entrance gate, where it sprawls attractively in a grove of evergreen woodland overlooking Lake Kazuni. Recently leased by the Nyika Safari Company, and given a thorough overhaul, the camp now accommodates eight guests in four luxury en-suite reed huts at US$80 per person, on a full board basis. Near by are five smaller self-catering huts, each of which lies on a raised concrete block with a thatched roof, and has two beds with mosquito netting, two chairs, a table, and a small veranda. The huts cost US$10 per person, which is excellent value. Alternatively, you can pitch your own tent for US$5 per person. An additional park entrance fee of US$5 per person per 24 hours is levied. Facilities at the camp include clean long-drop toilets, showers, and a fireplace with grid, firewood and cooking utensils provided. You must bring your own food; the nearest place to stock up is at the supermarket in Rumphi, though there is a better selection of goods on sale in Mzuzu. The staff will cook for you on request. Beer and sodas are normally available at a kiosk just outside the reserve entrance, while a limited range of goods can be bought at Kazuni village 1km back towards Mzimba. The night-time atmosphere at Kazuni is utterly compelling: just you, the trumpeting of elephants if you're lucky, snorting hippos, fluttering fruit bats and swooping owls. And, it must be said, rather a lot of mosquitoes – so cover up!

Camping is permitted at three other sites in the game reserve: **Zaro Pool** in the southwestern corner of the reserve, **Turner Camp** on Vwaza Marsh, and **Khaya Camp** on the Luwewe River. None of these sites has any facilities worth speaking of, and they are only accessible in a private vehicle.

As with Nyika National Park, the best source of reliable up-to-the-minute information about all practicalities surrounding a visit to Vwaza Marsh is the Nyika Safari Company office in Lilongwe (see page 229).

Livingstonia and the Northern Lakeshore

This chapter covers the far north of Malawi. The main town in this region, Karonga, is the gateway to and from northern Zambia and southern Tanzania, and as such it is many backpackers' introduction to Malawi. The established tourist attraction in this part of Malawi is the turn-of-the-century Scottish mission of Livingstonia, perched on top of the western Rift Valley Escarpment overlooking the lake, but Karonga, with its recent hominid and dinosaur finds and its interesting World War I history, is just waiting to be discovered. The Lake Malawi shore north of Livingstonia is arguably the most dramatic stretch of the lake, with immense mountains rising to either side, and although it has not in the past seen tourist development to match that on the southern lakeshore, a burgeoning number of low-key resorts have recently been built around the beautiful Chombe Bay.

CLIMATE

The Karonga area has a typical lakeshore climate – hot, sunny and humid. Of the other places mentioned in this chapter, only Livingstonia and Chitipa have moderate climates, as they are both at higher altitudes.

GETTING AROUND

Most places mentioned in this chapter lie along the surfaced M1 which connects the regional capital of Mzuzu to Songwe on the Tanzanian border. There are plenty of buses along this road as far north as Karonga, and several minibuses and *matola* pick-up trucks daily between Karonga and Songwe. Livingstonia lies 16km west of the M1 by road: many travellers walk there, but you can generally get a *matola* ride if you prefer.

BETWEEN RUMPHI AND CHITIMBA

There are a couple of attractions along the road between Rumphi and Chitimba, of particular interest to those travelling in their own vehicle.

The first, a double-storey building constructed using a variety of improbable scraps, and easily visible from the west side of the main road about 20km north of the Rumphi turn-off, is the home of Mr Ngoma. An idiosyncratic and somewhat morbid soul, Mr Ngoma is fixated on his death to

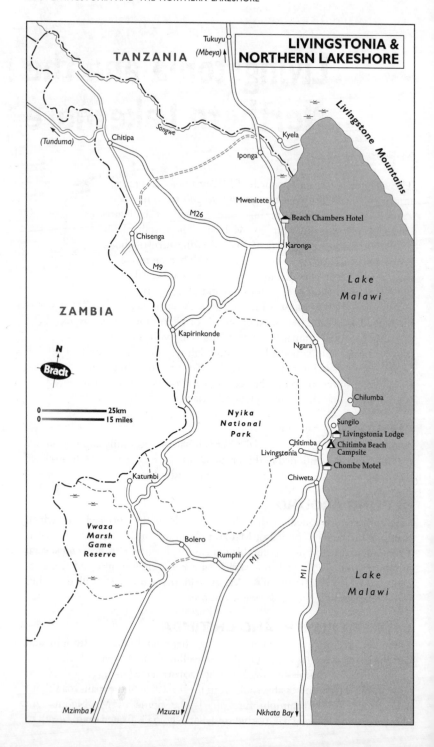

the extent that several years ago he prepared his own grave, coffin and tombstone. The house itself is also rather unusual: in addition to the conventional bed and living rooms, it boasts what he refers to as a mortuary, a hospital and a chapel, not to mention a telephone with a direct line to the Lord and the recently departed. Visitors are welcome provided that they leave a small donation – which might lead a sceptic to question just how much Mr Ngoma's eccentric behaviour has been cultivated as a preferable source of income to selling groceries (the house used to be a shop). Charlatan or eccentric, either way Mr Ngoma is amiable company, and well worth visiting.

Also on the west side of the road, another 10km or so further towards Chitimba, the Zuwurufu Hanging Bridge was initially constructed in 1904 to connect the village to a school on the opposite side of the Rukuru River. Made with bamboo, and regularly repaired, the bridge is still used by villagers today, and visitors are welcome to wobble across it. The bridge lies no more than 100m from the main road, but it is not visible from the road, so you'll need to ask directions (I've been told it lies precisely 32km north of the Rumphi turn-off, and while I'm not able to verify this, it might be worth setting your kilometre reading to zero at this turn-off).

There is enough traffic along this road that backpackers could ask to be dropped at either of these places and then catch the next vehicle when they've finished looking around.

THE LAKESHORE AROUND CHITIMBA

North of Rumphi, the M1 follows the course of the North Rukuru River in a breathtaking descent of the Rift Valley Escarpment which brings you out at Chiweta on the northern shore of Lake Malawi. There is a drama to the northern lakeshore that is lacking further south, with both the Malawian and Tanzanian shores flanked by the precipitous and thickly wooded mountains of the Rift Valley Escarpment. Until recently, this area was largely undeveloped for tourism, but the last couple of years have seen a rapid development of low-key campsites and more commodious chalets and motels along Chombe Bay, which lies between the villages of Chiweta and Sungilo.

The most serious boating accident ever recorded on Lake Malawi occurred in Chombe Bay in 1946, when a passenger ship, the *Vipya*, sank in storm-related circumstances which have never been satisfactorily explained. The tragedy resulted in the death of all but 49 of the 200 or more passengers and crew. The hulk of the *Vipya* reputedly still lies submerged in the bay.

The largest settlement along Chombe Bay is Chitimba, which consists of little more than a few resthouses and homesteads concentrated between the beach and the M1 (where it forms a T-junction with the road to Livingstonia). Chitimba is often and inaccurately marked on maps as Khondowe. Khondowe is actually the traditional and official name for the village which is more often referred to as Livingstonia (after the Livingstonia Mission that lies within it).

Getting there and away

All express and country buses between Mzuzu and Karonga stop at Chiweta and Chitimba. If you want to be dropped elsewhere along Chombe Bay, you need to use a country bus. The road between Mzuzu and Karonga is reasonably hitchable, though most lifts will be *matola*.

Where to stay

Chombe Bay is a beautiful place to spend a few days, with a marvellous beach and fabulous scenery. In general, accommodation is less crowded than it is further south along the lake and, after looking at empty resort after empty resort, I couldn't help but wonder if the rapid mushrooming of accommodation along the bay isn't a result of wild optimism on the part of developers. In 2002 the road through these parts was being rebuilt, which meant the disruption and even closure of some resorts; others were occupied by road construction crews. When the new road is complete, business should revert to normal, but names and details could change.

The first place you'll pass, perhaps 15km past Chiweta, is **Nyathumbata Travellers Lodge**. Situated on a great stretch of beach, the double rooms here are good value at US$6, and you can also camp for US$2 per person. There are communal showers, and basic meals can be prepared by the staff.

Right next door, the **Chombe Motel** has comfortable, nicely furnished rooms which are reasonably priced at US$12 double. Unfortunately, the motel's setting, well back from the beach, makes few concessions to aesthetics, and the staff seem to be rather disorganised.

About 3km further towards Chitimba, **Namiashi Holiday Resort** (PO Box 28, Chitimba) and **M'Buta Tourist Lodge** (PO Box 106, Chitimba) are altogether more attractive. Namiashi in particular has a wonderful setting, and large, comfortable double rooms (using communal showers) with mosquito nets for US$8/14 single/double, and camping for US$2 per person. M'Buta had been taken over by the road construction company, and has self-contained doubles with hot water for a similar price, and slightly cheaper camping. There is also a very comfortable double cottage with private hot showers, air conditioning, a cooker and fridge, and a lounge – great value for money at US$14. Both these places have a restaurant and bar.

Chitimba itself is rather dull, despite its proximity to the lake, and there's little reason to stay there unless you happen to be heading up to Livingstonia. If you need a room, there are several cheap resthouses, of which the **Brothers-in-Arms Resthouse**, a short way up the hill towards Livingstonia, is the only one that can be recommended. Right on the junction, the **Florence Resthouse** also has cheap rooms and it allows camping for well under US$1per tent, but I've heard several negative reports of late. It does, however, serve reasonable meals, and is one of the few places where I've been offered cassava chips.

A far more attractive option, clearly signposted only 1km from Chitimba, is the **Chitimba Beach Campsite** (formerly Des's Place), which has been taken over by a group of ex-overland truck drivers and has become the main backpacker focus on this part of the lakeshore. Set on the beach, this place currently offers inexpensive camping facilities for US$2, dorm beds at US$3, accommodation for two in reed huts for US$10, and self-contained double rooms at US$12. Meals and drinks are available at an attractive beach bar and trips can be arranged up to Livingstonia Mission.

LIVINGSTONIA (KHONDOWE)

The Livingstonia Mission was founded in 1875 at Cape Maclear by Dr Robert Laws. It was named in honour of Dr Livingstone, and its original purpose was to further the famous explorer's goal of using Christianity and commerce to end the slave trade which had caused so much suffering in the Lake Malawi region. In 1881, the mission moved to Bandawe. Finally, due to the high incidence of malaria around the lake, Laws decided to move the mission to a higher altitude. He settled on the small village of Khondowe, 900m above the lakeshore, for its healthy climate, fertile land and abundant supply of water. The modern mission was built in 1894, and many of its stone buildings are still in use today, one of which houses a very interesting museum.

The Scottish missionaries of Livingstonia have been highly influential on modern Malawi. In the early days, under Laws, they played an important role in stopping the slave trade and the Ngoni raids on neighbouring tribes. More recently, they provided education to many influential members of the African nationalist movement, so much so that Banda himself once referred to Livingstonia as the 'seed-bed' of the Malawi Congress Party.

Livingstonia, according to every publicity brochure and travel guide ever written about it, is the most scenic place in all of Malawi, if not in the whole of Africa. In fact, there are several no less attractive vistas in Malawi, but Livingstonia *is* without doubt a very beautiful spot, and the views from the edge of town, across the plummeting escarpment and lake to the Livingstone Mountains in Tanzania, are quite breathtaking, particularly at dusk.

Livingstonia Town is also less atmospheric than many descriptions might have you believe. The town is curiously unfocused: the resthouses, a school, a technical college and turn-of-the-20th-century hospital are dotted along the escarpment, and in the vicinity are a couple of poorly stocked grocery shops, a few scattered patches of plantation forest, and a rather bizarre stone circle and clocktower surrounded by blooming flower beds. The overall effect is as if somebody started transporting a Victorian English village on to the edge of the Rift Valley Escarpment, but got bored before they finished the job. Livingstonia's charm lies in its peculiarity rather than in any great antiquity.

If hyperbole should be attached to any single aspect of Livingstonia, it is the magnificent 300m-high Manchewe Waterfall which crashes down the Rift Valley Escarpment about 2km outside of town. Surrounded by lush rainforest, this waterfall is truly spectacular, and crawling to its edge is a vertigo-inducing experience. To get to the falls from Livingstonia Town, walk back towards Chitimba for about 2km until you see the Manchewe Falls Grocery. A short path directly opposite the grocery leads to the edge of the waterfall.

Getting there and away

The 16km road between Chitimba and Livingstonia is arguably as much of a tourist attraction as Livingstonia itself. Climbing over 700m in altitude along a series of precisely 20 switchback bends (the bends were numbered so you could count them as you ascended, but most of the numbers have now disappeared), the road passes through dense *brachystegia* woodland, with spectacular views back to the lake. It is without doubt one of the most exciting roads I've been on in Africa – no less so if you discover, as I did after I was offered a free lift halfway down to Chitimba, that you're cruising down the Rift Valley Escarpment in a vehicle that doesn't have any brakes!

There is no public transport between Chitimba and Livingstonia, but a few vehicles switchback up and down every day, and with an early start you can be reasonably confident of finding a *matola* lift. Alternatively, the people at Chitimba Beach Campsite offer regular Land-Rover trips to Livingstonia, and motorised excursions to the mission can be organised at Nkhata Bay. Do not attempt this road in your own vehicle, unless it is tough and has high ground clearance. Preferably it should be a 4WD, as the road is steep, rough and often wet or washed away.

The walk to Livingstonia used to be popular with fit travellers, but several travellers have been mugged along this road. Should you decide to risk the walk, you might feel more secure taking a local guide, though we have heard of travellers being mugged by their guide along the way! Whatever else you do, you'll enjoy the walk a lot more if you leave as much luggage as possible at the base (Chitimba Beach Campsite would be your safest bet). I would also resist the temptation to make use of the steep short cuts that plunge between the switchbacks, not so much because of the environmental degradation caused by using short cuts (over 99% of the pedestrian traffic on this route is local people, so a couple of tourists is neither here nor there), but because they are impossibly steep. And don't get overexcited when you pass bend 20 – you still have around five (admittedly relatively flat) kilometres to cover before you reach Livingstonia.

Where to stay

There are two resthouses in Livingstonia, both of them run by the CCAP church. The **Stone House**, the original house built by Robert Laws, is by far the most atmospheric, and not prohibitively expensive at US$2.50 per person. The other resthouse, which is known simply as the **Resthouse**, is also very pleasant, and a bit cheaper at US$1.50 per person. Both resthouses have verandas offering amazing views down to the lake, there are communal showers, and the kitchens can provide basic meals if you order before 15.00 or thereabouts (cost US$1.50).

An alternative to staying in Livingstonia itself is to pitch a tent at the new and highly regarded **Lukwe Permaculture Camp** (PO Box 20, Livingstonia; email: ecologique2000@hotmail.com), which lies 2km back towards Chitimba close to the Manchewe Falls. Three chalets with spectacular views are available at US$5 per person, camping is US$2 and meals are prepared, using their own organically grown ingredients. The best view of the

Manchewe Falls is from here too. Proceeds from the camp go towards the development of permaculture (sustainable agriculture) projects in the area.

CHILUMBA

This small harbour village is situated on a peninsula several kilometres from the M1 towards Karonga. Chilumba is not without natural charm, though, rather surprisingly, there is nothing in the way of tourist development. True, there's no obvious reason to stop over in Chilumba – but neither is there any obvious reason not to, especially as all buses between Mzuzu and Karonga divert to Chilumba, and it's also the northern terminus of the ferry service on Lake Malawi. There are several dollar-a-night resthouses to choose from.

KARONGA

Karonga is the largest town on the northern lakeshore and the springboard for overland crossings into northern Zambia and southern Tanzania. The fertile hills around Karonga are home to the Nkonde, an agricultural people who were considered by early visitors to be the most peaceful and hospitable in Central Africa. Consul Elton described Nkondeland as the 'finest tract of Africa [he] had yet seen', comparing its climate and fertility favourably to Natal in South Africa; while the explorer Joseph Thomson, who passed through the area in 1878, described it as 'an enchanted place' and 'a perfect Arcadia'.

The favourable impression made by the Nkonde is perhaps because this was one of the few parts of Central Africa not to have been devastated by the slave traders or the Ngoni. All this was to change, however, when a Swahili trader called Mlozi arrived in the area from the Luangwa Valley in Zambia. In 1886, Mlozi set up base about 10km from Karonga and proceeded to raid Nkondeland for human booty. Monteith Fotheringham, the manager of the African Lakes Company (ALC) store at Karonga, attempted to negotiate with Mlozi in order to stop the slave raids, but to no avail. From 1887 onwards, the

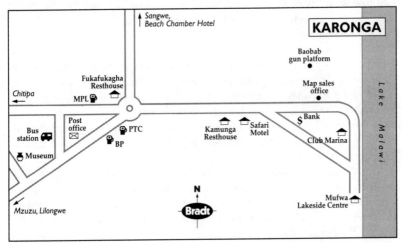

Karonga area became the setting of a largely forgotten war between Fotheringham and Mlozi.

This war was initiated in October 1987, when Mlozi ordered the massacre of hundreds of defenceless Nkonde who had been lured by his spies to congregate at the marshy mouth of the Rukuru River (a few kilometres north of Karonga). A distraught Fotheringham watched the massacre helplessly, and he was further enraged when, a month later, Mlozi declared himself the Sultan of Nkondeland and then tried to capture the ALC fort in Karonga. In June 1888, a British raid on Mlozi's stockade was repulsed and almost resulted in the death of its leader, Captain Lugard (who 30 months later was to be instrumental in Britain's capture of Kampala in Uganda, for which effort he was made Lord Lugard). In 1889, Harry Johnston restored temporary peace to the region by signing a treaty with Mlozi. But, over the next six years, even as Johnston managed to conquer or negotiate with every other slave trader in the land, Nkondeland remained in the terrible grip of its self-styled sultan, who became more prosperous and powerful than ever in the first half of the 1890s.

In 1895, Johnston returned to Karonga, and on December 3 he led a successful attack on Mlozi's fort. When Johnston's troops entered the fort, they found it littered with Nkonde bodies, victims of Mlozi's most recent raid. Over 500 people were found alive but imprisoned in the slave stockade, awaiting shipment towards the coast. The next day, Mlozi was tried by a group of Nkonde elders, and Johnston had him hanged from a tree in Karonga. With the capture of Mlozi, Johnston effected the last blow to organised slavery in Malawi.

During World War I, Karonga was the focus of hostilities between the adjoining German East African Colony (later Tanganyika) and British Nyasaland. War in the region commenced with a 'naval victory' that was almost certainly the first of the war, and without doubt the most comic. When the British Commissioner in Zomba received news of declaration of war, he decided the first priority must be to sink the *Hermann Von Wessman*, Germany's only ship on Lake Malawi. HMS *Gwendolyn* was dispatched into German waters under Captain Rhoades, its only gun manned by a Scotsman who hadn't seen battle in over a decade. Rhoades found the *Wessman* docked in Liuli harbour and, when finally the rusty aim of the Scottish gunner and a live shell coincided, the German boat was sunk. Rhoades was then startled to see his enraged German counterpart and old drinking partner, Captain Berndt, leap into a dinghy and climb aboard the *Gwendolyn* screaming curses and questioning Rhoades' sanity. It transpired that news of the war had not reached Liuli. Rhoades sat Berndt down with a whisky, explained the situation, then led away his angry prisoner of war – who was by now loudly berating the German officials at Songea for not having informed him of developments in Europe.

The Germans at Songea did indeed know of the war. Immediately after securing his naval victory, Rhoades was dispatched to Karonga to repulse the German troops gathered at Nieu Langenberg (now Tukuyu). The Battle of Karonga of September 8–9 1914 proved to be almost as farcical as the naval battle – the opposing troops marched straight past each other on the Nkonde

Plateau and when they finally met the next day they were facing each other in the wrong direction. However, the skirmish resulted in tragic loss of life, mostly on the German side, with 19 out of 22 German officers being killed in the most bloody battle, and even heavier losses among the African conscripts. That Britain won was more a matter of luck than judgement (it so happened that the British troops accidentally stumbled on the Germans from behind, forcing them to flee into an ambush which would otherwise have been ineffective) but win they did, and after the Battle of Karonga, Nyasaland was never again seriously threatened by the neighbouring German territory.

Few relics of Karonga's history remain. In the mission cemetery lies the grave of James Stewart, who was commissioned by the ALC to build the Stevenson road between lakes Malawi and Tanganyika (the road was abandoned after Stewart's death). The Armstrong gun in front of the District Commissioner's Office is the one used by Captain Lugard in his abortive raid on Mlozi's fort. British and German war graves from the Battle of Karonga lie in the small cemetery behind the District Council Office. Another World War I relic is a large baobab tree (outside the old post office) which was used as a gun platform and which now has a mango tree growing out of it.

To add to all this fascinating history is the recent local discovery of a virtually intact 12m skeleton of a *malawisaurus* dinosaur that roamed the area 100 million years ago. Under the enthusiastic leadership of Professor Friedemann Shrenk, a team of archaeologists has also unearthed a 2.5 million year old jawbone, one of the oldest remains found of genus *Homo*. A new museum is under construction in Karonga town to house these remains. Situated opposite the town assembly, it should be open in early 2003. Don't miss it. The museum will also be offering tours to all the other places of interest around the town. Contact the Cultural and Museum Centre, Private Bag 16, Karonga; tel/fax: 01 362579; email: uraha@malawi.net.

Beautiful clay pots are brought across the lake by dugout canoe from the renowned pottery community at Matema Beach in Tanzania and sold on the beach opposite Club Marina. They are not 'tourist junk', but well crafted and wonderfully decorated pots for cooking and carrying water and used by the local people in their everyday lives. They cost very little (US$1–2) and make a great gift or memento of Malawi.

Of more practical interest to travellers is the good PTC supermarket near the main roundabout. There is also a well-stocked map sales office on the road to the Club Marina, which you should definitely visit if you've just arrived in Malawi from Zambia or Tanzania.

Getting there and away

There are several express and country buses daily between Lilongwe and Karonga, passing through Mzuzu. There are also several buses daily between Mzuzu and Karonga.

Matola pick-up trucks and minibuses ply back and forth all day between Karonga and the Tanzanian border post at Songwe. After crossing into

Tanzania, it is easy to get a lift on a bicycle-taxi through to the main Mbeya–Kyela road, where you can pick up a bus in the direction of your choice.

If you're heading towards Zambia, you need first to get to the remote highland town of Chitipa. Although there are plans to upgrade this road, it is currently (2002) atrocious and one of the worst in Malawi. No buses run this route, only pick-ups and trucks, which cost US$4. The best accommodation is at the Chitipa Inn, which has rooms and camping, a bar and restaurant and safe parking.

Where to stay

Club Marina (PO Box 16, Karonga; tel: 01 362391) is a very reasonably priced mid-range hotel situated on the lakeshore about ten minutes' walk from the town centre. Self-contained rooms with fans, nets and hot water cost US$10/15 single/double. The restaurant serves reasonable meals, certainly the best in town (which isn't saying a great deal) and not at all expensive. Practically next door to this, the **Mufwa Lakeside Centre** doesn't quite achieve the Club Marina's standards, but it's reasonable value at US$3.50 for a basic single, US$7.50 for a self-contained double and US$3 per person camping.

In the town centre, the **Fukafukagha Resthouse** is an above-average budget hotel, with basic rooms at US$1/2 single/double. The **Kamunga Resthouse** is a little cheaper and a lot sleazier. The **Safari Motel** offers rooms at US6/8 single/double including breakfast, though the Club Marina is far better value in this range.

About 5km out of town, on the road to the Tanzanian border, the **Beach Chamber Hotel** (PO Box 293, Karonga; tel: 01 362534) is a pleasantly isolated place with self-contained rooms for US$6/8 single/double and slightly more expensive VIP suites with satellite television. Camping is permitted, though the site is nothing to write home about. The restaurant serves fair meals for around US$2. Any pick-up truck heading between Karonga and Songwe can drop you at the hotel, which lies right on the main road.

Appendix 1

LANGUAGE
Pronunciation
In Chichewa, as in most Bantu languages, almost all words and syllables end with a vowel. There are five vowel sounds, represented by A, E, I, O and U. These vowel sounds have no close equivalents in the English language; they are, however, practically identical to the vowel sounds of A, E, I, O and OU in French. Where two vowels follow each other, they are not compounded but instead each retains its pure sound.

Consonants generally have a similar sound to their English equivalent, though 'j' is always pronounced as 'dj'; 'ch' is far softer than the English 'ch'; 'ph' is pronounced as a breathy 'p' as opposed to an 'f', and 'r' is often interchangeable with 'l'. To give some examples, Rumphi is pronounced more like Rumpi than Rumfi, and Karonga may sometimes be pronounced in a way that sounds closer to Kalonga.

Grammar and tense
The grammar and use of tenses in Bantu languages is very different from that of English or any other European language. It is not something that tourists wanting to know a few basic words and phrases need concern themselves with. People who want to familiarise themselves with Chichewa grammar and tenses are advised to buy a copy of Rev Salaum's *Chichewa Intensive Course* (Likuni Press), which was first published in 1969 and went into a third edition in 1993. If you can't find it in a bookshop, then contact the publishers directly at PO Box 133, Lilongwe; tel: 01 721388; fax: 01 721141.

Greetings and phrases
Hello	*Moni*
How are you?	*Muli bwanji?*
Fine (and you?)	*Ndiri bwino (kaya inu?)*
Thank you	*Zikomo (or ziko)*
What's your name?	*Dzina lanu ndani?*
How much (price)?	*Ndalama zingati?*
I don't understand	*Sindikumva*
Where are you going?	*Mukupita kuti?*
I'm going to Lilongwe	*Ndikupita ku Lilongwe*
I want ...	*Ndikufuna ...*
I don't want ...	*Sindikufuna ...*
Goodbye	*Khalani Bwino*

Some useful words

animal	*nyama*	hyena	*fisi*
arrive	*fika*	journey	*ulendo*
baboon	*nyani*	large	*kula*
banana	*nthochi*	meat	*nyama*
buffalo	*njati*	milk	*mkaka*
cattle	*ngombe*	mosquito	*udzudzu*
chicken	*nkhuku*	mountain	*phiri*
egg	*dzira*	name	*dzina*
elephant	*njobvu*	near	*pafupi*
English (language)	*Chizungu*	no	*ai*
enough	*basi*	person	*munthu*
European	*Mazungu*	rain	*mvula*
far	*kutali*	salt	*mchere*
fish	*nsomba*	small	*ngono*
food	*kudya*	swamp	*dambo*
friend	*bwenzi*	tent	*hema*
goat	*mbuzi*	today	*lero*
god	*mulungu*	tomorrow	*m'mawa*
government	*boma*	water	*madzi*
hippo	*mvuu*	yes	*inde*
honey	*uchi*	yesterday	*dzulo*
house	*nyumba*		

Glossary of vernacular and scientific words

acacia A genus of thorny trees dominant in many parts of Africa, but not in Malawi where acacia woodland is largely replaced by *brachystegia*.

bakkie South African word for a pick-up truck.

banda In some African languages, this literally means home, but in hotel-speak it can refer to any detached accommodation unit.

boma In Malawi and other parts of Central Africa, the *boma* is the administrative part of town, often a discrete entity to the commercial centre of that town. Some game lodges use the word *boma* to refer to a stockaded outdoor dining area.

braai Afrikaans word meaning 'barbecue', used widely in southern Africa.

brachystegia The type of woodland that is dominant in Malawi, characterised by trees of the genus *brachystegia* and often referred to as '*miombo* woodland'.

buck Any antelope.

chamba Marijuana.

chambo The main eating fish caught in Lake Malawi.

chiperone Heavy mists that occur seasonally in highland areas such as Mount Mulanje.

chitenga Sarong-type cloth worn by most Malawian women.

dambo Seasonal or perennial marsh, normally fringing a river.

endemic In the context of this guide, a race or species found nowhere else but in the area or country to which it is allocated.

exotic	A term that may cause some confusion as it is often abused in travel literature. An exotic species is one that has been introduced to an area; in Malawi, the pine plantations on Nyika are exotic, the palms that line the Shire River are indigenous.
koppie	Small hill, an Afrikaans term widely used in this part of Africa.
matola	A light vehicle or truck that carries paying passengers, often informally.
mazungu	Term used throughout East Africa for a white person, plural *wazungu*.
mielie	Term used throughout southern Africa for maize (corn).
nsima	Maize porridge that is the staple diet of most Malawians.
nyama	Any meat, but especially beef.
rondawel	Used by hotels to refer to a *banda* built in the round shape of an African hut.
south	South Africa – a lot of Malawians will tell you they used to work 'south'.
trading centre	Any village large enough to have a market or small shop.

Appendix 2

FURTHER READING
Travel guides

The only quality coffee-table guide to Malawi is Frank Johnston and Vera Garland's *Malawi: Lake of Stars* (Central Africana Ltd, 1991), an attractively photographed and presented book, and available in most bookshops in Malawi.

David Stuart-Mogg's *Guide to Malawi* (Central Africana Ltd, Malawi) is perhaps more of a travel companion than a guidebook, but it's well organised and readable, easy to get hold of in Malawi, and very reasonably priced – a recommended buy.

Lonely Planet's *Malawi* (Lonely Planet, 2001) is sound and well written, worth carrying if you want a second source of practical travel information.

Travellers visiting Malawi as part of an extended African trip have a number of useful regional guides to choose from. Philip Briggs' *East and Southern Africa: The Backpackers' Manual* (Bradt Travel Guides Ltd, 2001) is the only guidebook dedicated purely to the popular backpacking circuit that runs between East and South Africa. Bradt also publishes one-country guides to most countries in this region.

Several guidebooks to specific regions or places of interest in Malawi are available in the country. Generally these books are inexpensive and easy to get hold of in Lilongwe and Blantyre. Absolutely essential if you are visiting the places they cover are Frank Eastwood's *Guide to the Mulanje Massif* (Lorton Communications, 1988), H & K Mundy's *Zomba Mountain: A Walkers' Guide* (Montfort Press) and Sigrid Anna Johnson's *Visitor's Guide to Nyika National Park, Malawi* (Mbabazi Book Trust).

The Wildlife Society of Malawi publishes a range of inexpensive booklets and bird checklists covering all the main national parks and game reserves. Also published by the Wildlife Society, and of particular interest to walkers, birdwatchers and Malawian residents, are Judy Carter's *Day Outings from Lilongwe* (1991) and Peter Barton's *Day Outings from Blantyre*, the latter updated in 1997.

Central Africana Limited are the publishers of regional guides to *Blantyre and the Southern Region of Malawi*, *Lilongwe and the Central Region of Malawi* and *Mzuzu and the Northern Region of Malawi*. These books include some good pictures, but the editorial tends towards tourist-brochure hyperbole. They're not really worth spending your money on.

History and background

One of the better general books written about Malawi is *Livingstone's Lake* by Oliver Ransford (John Murray, 1966). Ransford's accessible writing style and anecdotal approach to history make this book a pleasure to read, even if some of the views expressed by the author seem a little culture-bound 30 years after they were written. This book is out of print but is easily found in libraries in the UK and South Africa.

For a general overview of Central African history, try one of the following: *History of Central Africa* by P Tindall (Longman, 1985); *From Iron Age to Independence: A History of Central Africa* by Needham, Mashingaidze & Bhebe (Longman, 1974 & 1984); or *A History of South and Central Africa* by D Wilson (Cambridge University Press, 1975). All these books are slightly on the dry side; I found the most informative and readable to be the one by Needham, Mashingaidze & Bhebe. You can buy these books in most bookshops in Malawi.

Two biographies of Livingstone have been published in the last 30 years. The better is Tim Jeals' *Livingstone* (Heinemann, 1973), which was recently updated and reprinted in paperback. Oliver Ransford's *David Livingstone: The Dark Interior* (John Murray, 1978) is also a good read, but more difficult to get hold of.

For a general overview of the colonisation of Africa, you can't do better than Thomas Packenham's award-winning and wonderfully readable *The Scramble for Africa* (Weidenfeld & Nicholson, 1991).

The definitive biography of Dr Hastings Banda is Philip Short's *Banda* (Routledge & Kegan Paul, 1974), though this doesn't cover the later years of Banda's presidency. More current, though arguably a little one-sided in its approach, is *Kamuzu Banda of Malawi: A Study in Promise, Power and Paralysis* by John Lwanda (Dudu Nsomba Publications, 1993).

An interesting book if you want to know more about traditional Malawian beliefs is *Land of Fire: Oral Literature from Malawi* by Matthew Schoffeleers & Adrian Roscoe (Popular Publications, 1985).

Novels
Paul Theroux, *Jungle Lovers* (Ballantine Books, 1989)
Paul Theroux, *My Secret History* (Penguin, 1990)
Laurens van der Post, *Venture to the Interior* (Vintage, 2002)

Health
Dr Jane Wilson-Howarth, *Healthy Travel: bites, bugs and bowels* (Cadogan, 1999)
Dr Jane Wilson-Howarth and Dr Matthew Ellis, *Your Child's Health Abroad* (Bradt Travel Guides Ltd, 1998)

Field guides
A number of excellent field guides to African mammals have been published in the last few years. If weight is a consideration and you're content to stick with identifying large mammals, the one to go for is Chris & Tilde Stuart's *Southern, Central and East African Mammals: A Photographic Guide* (Struik, South Africa, 1992), which despite being very compact covers 150 large mammal species found in the region. *The Larger Mammals of Africa* (Struik, 1997) is a more comprehensive tome by the same authors, and a better buy for those who aren't carrying their luggage on their back. For those whose interest extends to small mammals, Jonathan Kingdon's *Field Guide to African Mammals* (Academic Press, 1997) is highly recommended. The publication of the above books has made Haltenorth & Diller's *Field Guide to the Mammals of Africa (including Madagascar)*

(Stephen Greene Pr, 1988) and Dorst & Dandelot's *Field Guide to the Larger Mammals of Africa* (Collins, 1986) look a bit dated.

Rather more bulky than any of the above guides, but highly recommended if weight isn't a consideration, is Richard Este's *The Safari Companion* (Russell Friedman Books, South Africa; Chelsea Green, USA; Green Books, UK, 1999), which is most aptly described as a field guide to the behaviour of African mammals.

No one volume provides comprehensive coverage of birds found in Malawi. The recommended combination is that of Kenneth Newman's *Birds of Malawi* (1999) and the same author's *Birds of Southern Africa* (Southern Book Publishers, South Africa, 2002). *Birds of Malawi* describes and illustrates only those species which have been recorded in Malawi but not in southern Africa (which is why you also need a southern African field guide) but it does include a full checklist of every bird that has been recorded in Malawi, complete with comprehensive details of distribution and status as well as giving the page number on which the bird is described in Newman's *Birds of Southern Africa*. There is no reason why you couldn't use another South African field guide instead of Newman's (several are available), but it helps that Newman's Malawi guide has been designed to be used in conjunction with his southern Africa guide. For serious birders, especially South Africans visiting Malawi in the hope of picking up a few lifers, the booklet *Bridging the Bird Gap* by Johnston-Stewart and Heigham details the species found in Malawi but not listed in the southern African guides. The line drawings are black-and-white only, but it has far greater detail on distribution of these species than Newman's *Birds of Malawi*.

There is no comprehensive field guide to the fishes of Lake Malawi, but Lewis, Reinthall & Trendall's *Guide to the Fishes of Lake Malawi National Park* (Worldwide Fund for Nature) is comprehensive within the confines of the national park, and pretty useful elsewhere in the lake. It can be bought in Malawi for about US$7.

Clare Shorter's *An Introduction to the Common Trees of Malawi* (Wildlife Society of Malawi) is widely available in Malawi, and excellent value at around US$4. For orchid enthusiasts, there is La Croix's *Malawi Orchids Volume 1: Epiphytic Orchids* (NFPS, 1983).

Except for the fish and tree guides, it is advisable to buy all field guides before you arrive in Malawi; they are not easy to get hold of once you are in the country.

Internet sites

www.malawi.net Lots of official information.

www.allafrica.com Fitting Malawi into context with the rest of Africa.

www.malawihere.com Good news site.

www.malawicichlidhomepage.com Great site to find out more about Lake Malawi's unique fish.

www.getawaytoafrica.com General travel information and recent magazine articles on countries in Africa.

MEASUREMENTS AND CONVERSIONS

To convert	Multiply by
Inches to centimetres	2.54
Centimetres to inches	0.3937
Feet to metres	0.3048
Metres to feet	3.281
Yards to metres	0.9144
Metres to yards	1.094
Miles to kilometres	1.609
Kilometres to miles	0.6214
Acres to hectares	0.4047
Hectares to acres	2.471
Imperial gallons to litres	4.546
Litres to imperial gallons	0.22
US gallons to litres	3.785
Litres to US gallons	0.264
Ounces to grams	28.35
Grams to ounces	0.03527
Pounds to grams	453.6
Grams to pounds	0.002205
Pounds to kilograms	0.4536
Kilograms to pounds	2.205
British tons to kilograms	1016.0
Kilograms to British tons	0.0009812
US tons to kilograms	907.0
Kilograms to US tons	0.000907

5 imperial gallons are equal to 6 US gallons
A British ton is 2,240 lbs. A US ton is 2,000 lbs.

Temperature conversion table
The bold figures in the central columns can be read as either centigrade or fahrenheit.

°C		°F	°C		°F
−18	0	32	10	50	122
−15	5	41	13	55	131
−12	10	50	16	60	140
−9	15	59	18	65	149
−7	20	68	21	70	158
−4	25	77	24	75	167
−1	30	86	27	80	176
2	35	95	32	90	194
4	40	104	38	100	212
7	45	113	40	104	219

NOTES

NOTES

Index

*Page references in **bold** indicate main entries; those in italics indicate maps.*

accommodation 66–7
AFORD 4, 22
airlines 106, 175
airport tax 38

Banda, Hastings Kamuzu 16–22
Bangula 116–17
Bantu 77, 247–9
baobab tree 24
bargaining 69–70
bilharzia 92–3
birds 34
black market 60
Blantyre **100–11**, *100, 104, 112*
  accommodation 103–5
  climate 102
  getting there 102–3
  information 106–8
  orientation 101–2
  restaurants 105–6
  things to do 109–11
Blantyre Mission 12
Bocarro, Gasper 8
books 107, 176
Booth, Rev Joseph 14
brachystegia woodland 24
bribery 73–4
Bua River Camp 193
budgeting 48–9
Bunda Mountain and Dam 181
bureaucracy 73–4
buses 63–5

camera equipment 54
camping 49, 53
Cape Maclear **154–9**, *148, 156*
  accommodation 156–7

Cape Maclear *continued*
  getting there 156
  restaurants 158
  things to do 158–9
capital 3
car hire 61, 107, 176
Chelinda Camp 230
Chembe Village *see* Cape Maclear
Chichewa 247
Chikwawa 114
Chilembwe, Rev John 15–16
Chilumba 243
Chinguni Hills Camp 146
Chintheche **207–9**, *208*
Chipata 42
Chipembere, Henry 18
Chiradzulu 11, 15
Chiradzulu Forest Reserve 110–11
Chirwa Orton 19, 22
Chitakali 123
Chitimba **239–41**
Chizumulu Island 219–20
Chombe Bay 239–41
Chongoni Forest Reserve 164–6
cichlids 35–6
climate 23–4
clothing 52–3
Club Makokola 153–4
Cobue 45
communicating with Malawians 76–9
conservation areas 25–7
crime 70–2
Cuamba 45
curios 74
currency declaration forms 48
customs 46–7
cycling 64–5

Dar es Salaam 44
Dedza **161–4**, *162*, *163*
Dedza Mountain Forest Reserve 164
deep vein thrombosis (DVT) 82–3
diarrhoea 87–9
drinks 68–9
Dwangwa 206
Dzalanyama Forest Reserve 181

Elephant Marsh 117–19
electricity 76
email *see* town listings
embassies 176
equipment 53–5
Ethiopianism 114–16
eye problems 94

fish 35–6
foreign exchange 60, 107, 176
forests 26–7
Fort Lister Pass 130
Fort Johnston 150
fuel 62

geography 23
getting around Malawi 61–6
getting to Malawi 37–45
government 3–4

Harare 41
health 81–97
history 4–22
hitching 65–6
horse safaris 232

immigration 46–7, 177
internal flights 61
itinerary 55–7

Johannesburg 41
Johnson, Rev William 13, 215
Johnston, Sir Harry 13–14, 204, 244
Jumbe 8, 11, 204

Kachulu 139–40
Kambiri Point 185–7

Kamwama, Edward 15, 207
Kande Beach Campsite 206–7
Kapichira Falls 115
Karonga **243–6**, *243*
Kasito Dam 201
Kasito Lodge 200
Kasungu **195–6**, *194*, *196*
Kasungu National Park 26, **196–8**
Kaya Mawa 219
Kazuni Safari Camp 235–6
Khondowe 241–3
Kirk, John 11
kwacha 59
Kyela 44

Lake Chilwa 23, 34, **139–41**
Lake Chiuta 23
lake ferry 63, **213–15**
Lake Malawi 10, 23, 34, 35
Lake Malawi National Park 26, **155**, *156*
Lake Malombe 23
Lake Tanganyika 44
language 4, 247
Laws, Dr Robert 12, 14, 155, 207, 241
Lengwe National Park 26, **115–16**
Lenten Letter 21
Lifupa Lodge 198
Likhubula 127
Likoma Island 12, 45, **215–19**, *216*
Lilongwe 3, *168*, **169–81**, *172*
    accommodation 171–4
    climate 170
    getting around 171
    getting there 170
    information 175–9
    orientation 170
    restaurants 174–5
    things to do 179–81
Lilongwe Nature Sanctuary 179
Limbe *see* Blantyre
Livingstone, David **10–13**, 101, 109–10, 117, 204, 241
Livingstone, William 15, 110
Livingstonia 155, *238*, **241**
Livingstonia Mission **12**, 207, 241
Liwonde 45, *132*, **141**, *142*

Liwonde National Park 26, **143–7**, *144*
  accommodation 145–6
  getting there 143–5
  information 143
  things to do 146–7
Lizard Island 186
Luangwa National Park, Zambia 180
luggage 49
Lusaka 41–2
Luwawa Dam 199–200

Mackenzie, Bishop **11**, 110, 113
Magomero 11
Magomero Mission 15
Majete Wildlife Reserve 26, **114–15**
malaria 81, **90–1**
Malawi Congress Party (MCP) 3–4, 18–22
mammals 27–33
Mandimba 45
Mangochi 45, *148*, **150–2**, *151*
Maples, Bishop Chauncey 204, 215
maps 54–55, 107, 177
Maravi 7, 20
matola 65
Mbeya 44
Mchacha James 118
Mchinji 42
media and communications 75–6
medical 108, 177
meningitis 95
Mfecane 9–10
Mganja 166
Michuru Mountain Conservation Area 109–10
Migowi 130
migrant labour 14
Milange 45
Mlozi 13, 244
Mocuba 45
money **47–9**, 59
Monkey Bay 154
Mountain Club of Malawi 129
Mozambique 41, 43–5, 108
Mpatsanjoka Dambo 186–7
Mua Mission 167, **187–8**

Mua-Livulezi Forest Reserve **166–7**
Mulanje 45, **123–5**, *124*
Mulanje Massif 121, **125–9**, *126*
  accommodation 127–8
  getting there 127
  hiking 128–9
  information 125–7
Muluzi, Bakili 4, 22
Muona Mission 119
Mvuu Lodge and Camp 145–7
Mwabvi Wildlife Reserve 26, **117**
Mwanza 45
Mzimba **189–9**, *199*
Mzuzu *194*, **223–6**, *222*, *224*

Namwera 45
Nayuchi 45
Nchalo 116
newspapers 75, 176
Ngoma, Mr 237–9
Ngoni 9,12
Nkhata Bay 18, *194*, **210–12**, *211*
  accommodation 210–12
  getting there 210
  information 210
  restaurants 212
  things to do 212
Nkhoma Mountain 167
Nkhotakota *194*, **203–6**, *202*
Nkhotakota Wildlife Reserve 26, **192–3**
Nkopola 153
Nkopola Lodge 153
Ntchisi *192*, *190*
Ntchisi Forest Reserve 191–2
Nyasaland 5, **13–14**, 17–18
Nyika National Park 25, *222*, **227–34**, *228*

orchids 25
overcharging 69–70

Palm Beach Resort 153
palm trees 24
passport 46
Petauke 42
Phalombe 130

photographic tips 50–1
population 3,14
Portuguese 7–8
post 75–177
prehistory 5–6
prices 60–1
prickly heat 94–5
public holidays 59
public transport 62–5

rabies 96
rail 62–3, 103
restaurants 67–8, *see also* town listings
road conditions 61–2
Rumphi **226–7**, *226*

safe sex 96
Salima *182*, **184**
Satemwa Tea Estate 122–3
Scott, Rev Clement 101
'Scramble for Africa' 13
self-drive 61–2
Senga Bay *182*, **184–7**
Shaka 9–10
Shire River 11, 19, 23, 150
Shire Valley *112*, **113–19**, *132*
skin infections 93
slave trade 8–13
snakes 96–7
South Luangwa National Park 180
Sucoma Sugar Estate 116

Tamanda Kadzamira, Cecelia 19–22
Tanzania 44, 214–15
telephone 75
television 76
Tembo, John 21–2
Tete 45
Tete Corridor 41, 43
Thyolo 122–3
Thyolo Forest Reserve 122

ticks 92
Tonga tribe 10
tour operators 108, 178
tourist information 59
tours 39–40
travel clinics 84–6
travel insurance 86
tropical fish farm 187
Tukuyu 44
Tuma Forest Reserve 179–81
Tumbuka tribe 10

United Democratic Front (UDF) 3, 22
Universities Mission to Central Africa (UMCA) 11

vegetation 24–5
Victoria Falls 42
Viphya Forest Reserve 200
Viphya Plateau 200
visas 46
Vwaza Marsh Wildlife Reserve 26, *222*, **234–6**

water sterilisation 88
websites 252
when to visit 37
wild animals 94–5
wildlife **27–36**
women travellers 72–3

Yachting marathon 154

Zambezi Expedition **10–11**, 113
Zambia 41–44, 180
Zimbabwe 41–3
Zobue 45
Zomba 18, **131–5**, *132*, *135*
Zomba Forestry Lodge 137
Zomba Plateau **135–9**, *136*
Zuwurufu Hanging Bridge 239